Descartes's Method of Doubt

❖

Descartes's
Method of Doubt

❖

JANET BROUGHTON

PRINCETON UNIVERSITY PRESS

PRINCETON AND OXFORD

Library of Congress Cataloging-in-Publication Data

Broughton, Janet, 1948–
Descartes's method of doubt / Janet Broughton.
p. cm.
Includes bibliographical references and index.
ISBN 0-691-08818-7 (alk. paper)
1. Descartes, René, 1596–1650—Contributions in theory of knowledge.
2. Knowledge, Theory of. 3. Belief and doubt. I. Title
B1878.K6 B76 2002
194—dc21   2001027849

British Library Cataloging-in-Publication Data is available

This book has been composed in Dante Typeface

Printed on acid-free paper. ∞

www.pup.princeton.edu

Printed in the United States of America

1   3   5   7   9   10   8   6   4   2

FOR JOHN

❖

❖ *Contents* ❖

❖ *Preface* ❖

THIS IS A BOOK about Descartes's method of doubt, about his rationale for using it and the way he thought it worked. Radical doubts surface in the *Discourse on the Method* and the *Principles of Philosophy*, and the method of doubt guides the fragment of the *Search for Truth* that has come down to us. But Descartes shows us the method of doubt most clearly in the *Meditations on First Philosophy*, and that is the book that will concern me in the chapters ahead.

In the first of his six meditations, Descartes offered the dream argument, which calls into doubt the existence of the things we see and touch, and the deceiving God argument, which in addition calls into doubt the truth of claims like "Two plus three equals five," claims that we grasp "clearly and distinctly." Descartes resolved to carry his meditations forward by affirming only what can withstand these radical skeptical arguments. He affirmed first that he himself exists and has various states of consciousness, or ideas. He argued that his own existence as someone with an idea of God requires that God exist, and then he appealed to God's benevolence for the validation of his clear and distinct ideas. From various of these clear and distinct ideas, he drew out the distinction between mind and body and the existence of a physical world describable in austerely mathematical terms.

When we reflect upon the trajectory of these meditations, we may find ourselves with some disturbing reactions: we may find it difficult to resist the radical skeptical arguments with which Descartes began, and yet impossible to accept his argument that God must exist if we have the idea of God. Then we seem to be left in need of something we cannot have: certainty that all of our most evident judgments are true. For the radical skeptical arguments seem to show that we cannot claim knowledge of anything beyond our own ideas unless we have something like a divine guarantee that our ideas correctly reflect the mind-independent world outside of our thought. The scope of our knowledge, then, appears to be tiny: each of us knows only his own existence and can attribute to himself only his states of consciousness. Those states we know through and through; that is our consolation prize. But everything outside this bubble of perfect illumination is veiled in darkness. To alter the metaphor, each of us is an island and forever lacks any bridge for crossing the gap between self-knowledge and knowledge of the world beyond. And to alter the metaphor again, this time to a favorite of Descartes's, we have torn down our rickety structure of belief, excavated a trench for new foundations, and filled the trench with solid rock, only to find that there are no materials with which we can construct a building.

If this is not really our predicament, then something must be wrong with the trajectory of Descartes's inquiry. But what? In recent decades, philosophers have given several very provocative answers to this question, answers that offer diagnoses of where we go wrong if we see philosophical inquiry as shaped in the way that Descartes shapes it. To some, Descartes's mistake lies in a conception of good cognitive life that misunderstands certainty or overestimates its importance. To others, the mistake comes in thinking that the dream argument or the deceiving God argument offers any reason for doubt, any consideration that ought to make people withdraw their claims to know things. Still others think that the most basic mistake is an underlying conception of the mind as having states that are transparent to itself, or that mirror a world that lies beyond.

These are ideas that are much discussed by contemporary philosophers—rightly so, I believe. But our sense of their importance can distort our understanding of Descartes in subtle and not-so-subtle ways, making us project onto him philosophical assumptions that are ours, not his, and making us miss philosophical ideas he wanted to communicate. I hope to be giving an account of the method of doubt that corrects at least some of these distortions. While in some ways I think Descartes is closer to us than we might have imagined, in many ways he is far more remote.

Several years ago I heard the philosopher David Hills gloomily describe two sorts of people who work on the history of philosophy: those who ask, "Where is he coming from?" and those who ask, "Where does he get off?" Of course, as I know Hills would agree, we cannot understand our philosophical history without understanding *something* about where our predecessors come from—especially what their philosophical, scientific, theological, and literary assumptions, sources, and foes were. And *sometimes* we must engage their claims and arguments directly, as we might critically engage the claims of a contemporary of ours. But I find that my guiding question about Descartes's method of doubt is this: what is he up to? By that I mean that I want to develop a good way to describe Descartes's ambitions for philosophical inquiry, especially as they reveal themselves in distinctive moves that he makes as he carries his inquiry out. I should say right now that I think his ambitions are splendid but doomed, and highly instructive.

In describing what I think Descartes is up to, I do not pretend somehow to be stepping out of my twenty-first-century skin. My general interests in Descartes are those of a post-Cartesian, post-Humean, post-Kantian, post-Moorean, post-Wittgensteinian philosopher. Some of the questions about the method of doubt that I will raise concern aspects of what Descartes was doing that did not interest him very much, or in some cases at all, but I do not think it follows that my reading of Descartes is anachronistic.

There are two main points I want to make about Descartes's use of the method of doubt. The first is that the doubt is artificial; it is strategic in character. The second is that using doubt is supposed to yield knowledge by uncovering its own preconditions.

In the introduction I locate the method of doubt in the more general terrain of "methods," and I describe several ways of seeing Descartes's motivations for using the method of doubt. In Part One I turn to the First Meditation and bring out its strategy, especially in relation to the authority of commonsense belief. In Part Two, chapter 6 introduces the idea that Descartes's use of doubt is supposed to yield knowledge by uncovering its own preconditions. Chapter 7 is about the parts of the Second Meditation in which Descartes argues that he can be certain that he exists and that he thinks. Chapter 8 is about the argument in the Third Meditation that God exists. Finally, in chapter 9 I step back a little and reflect upon several questions: how my reading bears upon the problem of the "Cartesian Circle," how Descartes's arguments are connected with "transcendental" arguments, and what becomes of the authority of common sense once the inquiry of the *Meditations* has reached its end.

I hope it is clear that this is not meant to add up to a commentary on the *Meditations*. I have little to say about Meditations Four, Five, and Six, and I have nothing to say about many important questions raised by the first three Meditations. What falls within my purview is the way in which Descartes thinks using the method of doubt can yield knowledge, and, of course, the *Meditations* offers much more than that.

. . . . .

In working on this book I have accumulated many debts of varied kinds, and it is with real pleasure that I acknowledge them here.

An earlier version of the first section of chapter 9, along with several pages from chapters 6 and 7, appeared in a paper I contributed to *The Rationalists*, an anthology edited by Derk Pereboom. I want to thank Rowman and Littlefield for permission to use that material here.

I finished a draft of this book in 1998–1999, during a year's leave that was supported in part through a Humanities Research Fellowship, and I am grateful to the University of California at Berkeley for that generous award.

Ian Malcolm, of Princeton University Press, has been unfailingly helpful throughout the final stages of my work on the book. I feel fortunate to have worked with such a kind and effective acquisitions editor. Lauren Lepow's work as copyeditor has been thoughtful and meticulous, and I want to thank her for all the improvements her red pencil has produced.

In the spring of 1998, Tony Long and I gave a seminar on ancient and modern skepticism, and I appreciate having had that opportunity to work with him on Pyrrhonian and Academic skepticism. I also want to thank Paolo Mancosu: in the spring of 2000 he and I cotaught a seminar that explored a broad range of methodological issues in Descartes's philosophy, science, and mathematics.

I want to express my gratitude to those who have helped me think through the issues that I take up in this book. My particular thanks go to all the people who generously took the time to give me comments on parts of the book: Randall Amano, Nancy Daukas, Gail Fine, Hannah Ginsborg, Paul Hoffman, Alan Nelson, Derk Pereboom, Casey Perin, Marleen Rozemond, Sam Scheffler, Shoshana Smith, Daniel Warren, and Wai-hung Wong. Tim Crockett was my research assistant during the 1999–2000 academic year, and he made valuable suggestions about every section of every chapter. It was my good fortune to receive detailed, thoughtful, and encouraging comments on the entire book from John Carriero and Ed McCann, who read the typescript for Princeton University Press. They went far beyond the call of duty, and I am very grateful to them for their help.

I am glad to have this chance to acknowledge the large intellectual debts that I owe to Tom Clarke and Barry Stroud, whose work on philosophical skepticism has shaped my sense of what questions to bring to the *Meditations*. Finally I want to record my deep gratitude to my teacher, Margaret Wilson, whose memory I hold dear.

❖ *Abbreviations* ❖

THROUGHOUT the book I will refer to Descartes's works by giving two sets of volume and page numbers. First I will give references to *The Philosophical Writings of Descartes*, the three-volume English translation by John Cottingham, Robert Stoothoff, Dugald Murdoch, and, for the third volume, Anthony Kenny. A reference to page 12 in volume 2, for example, would read, "2:12." Second I will give volume and page references to the standard edition of Descartes's works, edited by Charles Adam and Paul Tannery. A reference to page 17 in volume 7, for example, would read, "AT 7:17." Readers using *The Philosophical Writings of Descartes* will find volume and page references to Adam and Tannery in its margins. Except where I note otherwise, I give the English translations provided by Cottingham, Stoothoff, Murdoch, and Kenny.

Sometimes for ease of exposition I use letters of the alphabet in expressions that signify what someone thinks, believes, doubts, and so on; and I also use them to signify corresponding sentences. I may say, for example, that the meditator believes that *p* even though *p* is false. Strictly speaking this usage is not consistent, but consistency would require clutter and complications that I want to avoid. I hope readers will find that the inconsistency is a reasonable price to pay for smoother exposition.

Descartes's Method of Doubt

❖

❖ Introduction ❖

Descartes's procedure in the *Meditations on First Philosophy* is extraordinary. In order to discover the fundamental principles of philosophy, he puts forward the dream argument and the deceiving God argument as reasons for doubt, and he vows to suspend judgment about everything to which those radical skeptical considerations apply. It is hard to imagine a present-day investigation of basic philosophical principles beginning in this way—say, Derek Parfit's *Reasons and Persons* or John Searle's *Intentionality.* Of course, there are many reasons why this is so. A few present-day philosophers are dissatisfied with all of the available ways of trying to rescue some sort of knowledge from radical skeptical attack. And many philosophers today would not expect that by showing how to answer the skeptic we would uncover fundamental principles of philosophy; they would expect that once the skeptic had been answered, our claims to knowledge would be much as they were before we raised the radical skeptical worries.

Descartes sees the problems and prospects of philosophy very differently from the way we do. In this introduction, I want to sketch a context that will allow us to develop a sympathetic appreciation of Descartes's extraordinary way of proceeding in the *Meditations.*

As a preliminary, I want to remind readers of a sequence of discoveries that Descartes claims to make in the *Meditations.* (I will be examining most of these steps in detail in the chapters to follow.) In the First Meditation, Descartes briefly raises ordinary grounds for doubting beliefs, but he gives his attention mainly to radical grounds for doubt. First he offers the dream argument (and a similar "lunacy" argument), which calls into doubt even the most evident of the beliefs we get from our senses—for example, my present belief that my hand is in front of me. Then he gives us the deceiving God argument (and a similar argument designed for atheists), which calls into doubt not just sense-based beliefs but also beliefs about what we grasp "clearly and distinctly," like the belief that two plus three equals five. Descartes resolves to suspend judgment about all of the beliefs to which these radical arguments apply, and at the beginning

1

of the Second Meditation he worries that he has left himself in the position of suspending judgment about everything. He discovers, however, that "I exist" can somehow be salvaged, and indeed that he can also be certain of claims in which he attributes conscious states to himself. In the Third Meditation, he helps himself both to the causal principle that effects cannot be greater than their causes, and to the subsidiary principle that the cause of an idea must contain at least as much "formal reality" as the idea has of "objective reality." He then argues that given his certainty that he exists and has an idea of God, and his certainty that the causal principles are true, he can be certain that his cause, or creator, is God, a perfect being. This in turn assures him that his mind has been created so that his clear and distinct ideas are true. In the Fifth and Sixth Meditations, he draws upon a number of clear and distinct ideas to show that he can be certain that his beliefs in mathematics are true and that at least some of his beliefs about the world of material things are true too. During the course of these reflections, he recognizes that he cannot clearly understand the nature of his own mind or of material things unless he thinks of them as entirely distinct: mind as a nonextended consciousness, and material things as nonconscious extended things.

THE METHOD OF DOUBT AND OTHER CARTESIAN METHODS

Many of today's students of Descartes will have read only the *Meditations*. While there are good reasons for this focus, it can lead to a lopsided picture of Descartes as a philosopher whose concern with "method" was above all a concern with a method for answering radical skeptical doubts and achieving absolute certainty. Descartes gave many more pages, and much more time, to describing methods of inquiry that did *not* begin with radical skeptical doubt, than to describing one that did.

He was hardly alone in his interest in methods of inquiring. Since ancient times philosophers had been deeply concerned with questions about method, and questions about "method" were hotly debated in the sixteenth and seventeenth centuries.[1] But Descartes shared with many

[1] Neal Gilbert (1963) gives a sense of how disparate the concerns were that clustered around "method." Peter Dear (1998) provides a short and very helpful history of the

of his contemporaries a particular version of this concern. In the seventeenth century, philosophers were increasingly drawn to the belief that nature is fundamentally homogenous and has a simple, underlying order. This led them to suspect that someone was unlikely to achieve an understanding of nature by conducting a series of theoretically uninformed investigations of this phenomenon and that. Successful investigation would require methodic discipline imposed by a general theory of nature.[2]

Descartes's own interest in method rarely led him to concern himself with how to generate and analyze empirical data in answer to a scientific question. Rather, he was nearly always more interested in how to find the correct way to pose, or conceptualize, a problem,[3] and he was convinced that there would always be some way of describing the route to this correct conceptualization that would equally well describe a route to insight into virtually everything else. Thus when he achieved success in one area, he sought to describe his procedure very generally so that he could turn to other areas and go on in the same way there as well.[4] He found his successes in mathematics especially useful: in the *Rules for the Direction of the Mind*, the *Discourse on the Method*, and its appended essays in optics, geometry, and meteorology, Descartes represents himself as watching himself solve problems about quantities and their relationships, and then using his mind in this same distinctive way to solve problems in the physical sciences.

He apparently wanted his descriptions of these methods of discovery to enable his readers to use their minds in this distinctive way, too, though

---

idea of method in the seventeenth century. He argues that "method" is absent from the *Meditations*; while that may be true given the notions of method that concern him, Descartes is happy to describe the *Meditations* as guided by a "method"—the method of doubt.

[2] Although I think that this correctly describes something important about this juncture in the history of human understanding of nature, I agree with Catherine Wilson that seeing this should not blind us to other ways in which that understanding was developing (1995, esp. chap. 1).

[3] See Nelson 1995 and Gaukroger 1989, chap. 4; compare Clarke 1982, chaps. 4 and 5. Gaukroger (1993) reminds us, however, that Descartes was not crudely aprioristic.

[4] "By reflecting on their thoughts, [people] can notice which method they used when they were reasoning well and which was the cause of error when they were mistaken. They can then form rules based on these reflections to avoid being caught off guard in the future" (Arnauld and Nicole 1996, 9).

the general descriptions are *so* general that they often sound like plati-tudes—for example, the advice to "make enumerations so complete, and reviews so comprehensive, that [you can] be sure of leaving nothing out" (1:120; AT 6:19). It is easy to sympathize with Leibniz, who complained that Descartes's rules of method really just said, "Take what is needed; do as you ought; and you will get what you wanted" (1875–1890, 4:329). I imagine that most readers who learned something from Descartes about how to tackle problems in mathematics and physics found his ac-tual explorations of specific problems much more helpful than the very general maxims of method.

When Descartes refers to the "method of universal doubt" (2:270; AT 9A:203), he means a method that begins with consideration of grounds for radical skeptical doubt. This is a distinctive method of inquiry, though in both the *Rules* and the *Discourse*, Descartes says things, as he strains for a high enough level of generality, that sound as though he thinks *any* decent method of discovery will require using the method of doubt. In the *Rules* he says, "We need a method if we are to investigate the truth of things" (1:15; AT 10:371), and most of the book is devoted to describing a general method for investigating many sorts of truths: mathematical, physical, psychological, and metaphysical. In Rule Two he calls upon us "to believe only what is perfectly known and incapable of being doubted" (1:10; AT 10:362), and that may sound as if he is propounding the method of doubt as at least a part of the method for getting at the "truth of things." He isn't, though. Instead of telling us to test our beliefs by raising the radical skeptical doubts, he is exhorting us to reject "merely probable cognition" (1:10; AT 10:362). He notes that by using this rule, we will straightaway *accept* the evident propositions of mathematics, and it may even be that we will accept such obvious nonmathematical claims as "Here is a hand."[5] But the method of doubt requires us to *suspend judg-*

---

[5] Descartes disdains the "fluctuating testimony of the senses" (1:14; AT 10:368), but he is mainly concerned with systematic sciences, as he makes clear in Rule One, and while we are not supposed to base the theoretical claims of a physical science simply on the testimony of the senses, we may nonetheless be allowed by Rule Two to make claims like "Here's a hand." For example, in Rule Eight, where Descartes tells us how to go about finding the anaclastic in optics, one step we are to follow requires us to note how the angles of incidence and refraction change with differences in the media through which light travels (1:29; AT 10:394).

ment about mathematical claims and obvious nonmathematical claims like "Here is a hand." Nowhere in the *Rules* does the general method of discovery involve the procedures dictated by the method of doubt.[6]

In the *Discourse*, Descartes does describe the method of doubt as the special method he used to investigate "the foundations of . . . philosophy" (1:126; AT 6:30), but the *general* method he describes there is not the method of doubt. True, the first of its four rules is "never to accept anything as true if I did not have evident knowledge of its truth: that is, carefully to avoid precipitate conclusions and preconceptions, and to include nothing more in my judgements than what presented itself to my mind so clearly and so distinctly that I had no occasion to doubt it" (1:120; AT 6:18). But Descartes goes on to say that his first applications of this rule (and the three others he gives) concerned problems in mathematics; a little later he adds that by using this general method he was able to solve "many problems" in optics and even meteorology (1:125; AT 6:29). Clearly he did not mean to be saying that he conducted these investigations by starting with, say, the dream argument.[7]

So Descartes envisioned methods for achieving knowledge that did not pose the challenge of radical skepticism, and indeed such methods occupied more of his attention over the years than the special method of doubt did.[8] Of course, once we see this, we are bound to ask exactly

---

[6] This is by now a widely accepted view. See Garber 1992, chap. 2. In any case this claim will gain considerable support from the account I give later of the method of doubt. It will be easy to see that nothing like *that* goes on in the *Rules*.

[7] It is not at all clear how the general rules of method are related in the *Discourse* to the investigation in Part Four that does begin with radical doubt. The call for a general overthrow of opinion comes in Part Two before the enunciation of the four rules of the method, but the general overthrow is postponed for an interlude of progress in mathematics according to the method. When Descartes does begin to carry out the general overthrow, his first strategy is to "roam about in the world" (1:125; AT 6:28)! He then raises radical doubt, but it is not clear whether he means to be overthrowing his results in mathematics, and all of his results in optics and meteorology. If he doesn't, then why does he appear to call into doubt demonstrations in geometry (1:127; AT 6:32)? But if he does, then why is he apparently giving up the distinction he drew in Part Two between mathematical sciences, which do not depend upon soon-to-be-overthrown philosophy, and the other sciences, which do?

[8] Even when Descartes talks about the method of the *Meditations*, he does not always focus upon the fact that its method is a method of doubt. For example, in the Second

when and why he thought we need to use the method of doubt. I will return to this question several times later in this book, and indeed later in this introduction. But for now let me briefly note two points.

The first is that Descartes associates the method of doubt with a special subject matter. It is the method he turns to when he begins "to search for the foundations of any philosophy more certain than the commonly accepted one," as he puts it in the *Discourse* (1:126; AT 6:30), and it is the method he uses for exploring "First Philosophy," as the full title of the *Meditations* tells us. The subtitle of the *Meditations* tells us something about this special subject matter: it concerns *"the existence of God and the distinction between the human soul and the body."* This has a misleadingly bland and pious sound to it. In fact, Descartes aims to establish all of the following substantive principles:

1. God, a perfect being, exists;
2. We ought to assent only to what we understand clearly and distinctly;
3. The essential attribute of material things is extension, the continuous quantity studied in mathematics;
4. The essential attribute of the human mind is thought, and the mind is a different substance from the human body;
5. Human sense experience allows us to know that material things exist and affect our sense organs; it can usually be trusted to indicate what we should pursue and avoid; but although pat- terns of change in our sense experience do reflect patterns of change in the material things that affect us, we should not attribute to material things the qualities with which our sense experience directly acquaints us.

Not only are these substantive claims; as I will explain shortly, many of them were highly controversial in Descartes's time (as in ours). They are also, in an intuitive sense, foundational: they tell us what basic kinds of things there are, and how we can and cannot hope to learn something about them.

Replies (2:110–12; AT 7:155–57), he contrasts the "analytic" method of demonstration (or "discovery" or "writing" or "instruction") that he used in the *Meditations* with a "synthetic" method; and again it is clear that using the analytic method—for example, in mathematics—does not entail using the method of doubt. (What it *does* entail is a good question; see Gaukroger 1989, chap. 3; Curley 1986; and Flage and Bonnen 1999.)

There is a second point I want to make here about the special subject matter that calls for using the method of doubt. Although Descartes seems to think that someone might well use the general methods of inquiry over and over again as he tackles new questions in mathematics or science, he imagines that each of us needs to use the method of doubt just "once in the course of . . . life" (2:12; AT 7:17; also 1:193; AT 8A:5; compare 1:30–31; AT 10:395–98), to restructure our basic picture of the world and of our own faculties for understanding it. This is not to say that he thinks using the method of doubt properly is easy. He thinks readers may need "several months, or at least weeks" to ponder the doubts he raises in the First Meditation, and then "at least a few days" to form distinct conceptions of the mind and the body (2:94; AT 7:130–31). So unlike our use of general methods of inquiry, our use of the method of doubt is supposed to produce a lasting change in the limited set of our fundamental beliefs.

THE METHOD OF DOUBT AND DESCARTES'S CONCEPTION OF KNOWLEDGE

So far I have been locating the method of doubt in relation to Descartes's general interest in methods of inquiry. I have not yet done anything to explain why he thought that a good way to grasp the principles of First Philosophy is to begin by raising radical skeptical doubts. My full account of Descartes's reasons for using the method of doubt will emerge in the chapters that follow, but let me begin here by presenting a common assumption about his reasons.

Many readers have assumed that it is Descartes's preoccupation with knowledge, along with his demanding conception of what knowledge consists in, that motivates and explains his use of the method of doubt. Such readers see Descartes as thinking first that mere reasonable belief, belief that does not amount to knowledge, is to be disdained by people who are using their minds properly. The idea that only knowledge should satisfy us completely is a compelling one, whose ancestry we can trace back at least to Plato; but, of course, what it comes to depends upon what "knowledge" is taken to be. On the assumption that I am spelling out, Descartes would be requiring of knowledge that it be something of which we can be *certain*. Why would he build this requirement into his conception of knowledge? Probably the best answer to this question would invoke Descartes's relation to mathematics. Looking at human beings' successes and failures in coming to understand truths, Descartes thought that in the natural sciences we had in earlier times achieved nothing of lasting worth. One century's theories would be overthrown by the next century's theories, and at any one time distinguished intellectuals would disagree among themselves about how to explain even the simplest phenomena. Only in mathematics could Descartes discern steady accomplishment, progress, and agreement, and he thought that we would succeed in other fields of inquiry only when we could pursue other sciences in much the same way that we pursue mathematics. And here is what impressed him about mathematics: "of all those who have hitherto sought after truth in the sciences, mathematicians alone have been able to find any demonstrations—that is to say, certain and evident reasonings" (1:120; AT 6:19).

So knowledge—really worthwhile cognition—requires certainty. And what is it to be certain? On the assumption I am spelling out, Descartes took it that the concept of certainty required ruling out not just ordinary, everyday grounds for doubt but also, if we stop to think about it, the radical skeptical grounds for doubt as well. That is, on this interpretative assumption, Descartes supposed that if we were really to reflect upon what it is to be certain, we would see that the radical skeptical grounds for doubt are a natural extension of the sorts of doubts we raise in everyday life, and that certainty requires ruling out not just the grounds of doubt that we ordinarily consider, but also some that do not occur to us in the course of everyday life.

So the picture would be this: we ought to pursue knowledge in our inquiries; knowledge requires certainty; and certainty requires ruling out radical skeptical doubts. If this picture were correct, it would provide a very simple way to explain why Descartes uses the method of doubt. He begins his inquiry into the principles of first philosophy by raising radical skeptical doubts so that he can show when and how we can rule them out. That will be the same as showing when and how we can have certainty, and *that* will be the same as showing when and how we can have knowledge, which is what we want to arrive at in our method-guided inquiry.

There is much about this reading of Descartes that I think is right. He was undeniably impressed with the success of mathematics and thought it was instructive. He also, I am sure, thought that a person who knew something was in a better cognitive state than someone who had only a reasonable belief. And there are at least a few places where he seems to be saying that a person who has knowledge must be able to defend his beliefs against radical skeptical attack. Consider this passage from the Second Replies:

> The fact that an atheist can be 'clearly aware that the three angles of a triangle are equal to two right angles' is something I do not dispute. But I maintain that this awareness of his is not true knowledge, since no act of awareness that can be rendered doubtful seems fit to be called knowledge. Now since we are supposing that this individual is an atheist, he cannot be certain that he is not being deceived on matters which seem to him to be very evident. (2:101; AT 7:141)

Because he believes that God does not exist, the atheist will not assent to the claim that God exists and is not a deceiver. Descartes is saying that this leaves the atheist with no way to combat the deceiving God argument, and thus with no "true knowledge" in mathematics. So here Descartes seems plainly to be saying that a belief counts as knowledge only if the person who holds it can defend it against radical skeptical challenges (and, presumably, ordinary challenges too).

Despite all that is right about this reading, though, I think it gives us a mistaken impression of Descartes's concerns and strategies.[9] My main reasons for saying this will come out in Part One of this book, where I take a closer look at the First Meditation and the way in which Descartes raises the radical skeptical doubts. Here I want mainly to draw attention to several points that should make us suspect that this reading is at least

---

[9] In making this general claim, I am in agreement with what Bernard Williams says in "Descartes's Use of Skepticism" (1983), but I do not agree with the claim he seems to make in *Descartes* (1978), that it is helpful to think of the First Meditation doubts as extensions of the norms of rational inquiry that we use in everyday life. I will say more about this in Part One.

not giving us the full story about Descartes's reasons for using the method of doubt.

Let me first point out that this account of the atheist mathematician is in some tension with passages in which Descartes seems happy to allow that more general methodological maxims will safely guide us to knowledge in, say, mathematics or optics. In the *Discourse*, for example, he describes himself as "growing in the knowledge of the truth" (1:126; AT 6:30; trans. altered) *before* learning how to combat radical skeptical doubt.[10] But even if Descartes's use of the method of doubt is closely tied to his conception of knowledge, it is not clear what explains what. Mightn't Descartes's use of the method of doubt be what explains the very demanding account of knowledge that he articulates in the Second Replies? Someone defending the assumption that the conception of knowledge explains the use of the method of doubt might reply that if we reverse the order of explanation, we will have to come up with some other way of explaining the use of the method of doubt. But there *is* another way to explain Descartes's use of the method of doubt; in fact, there are several.

Descartes's Reasons for Deploying the Method of Doubt

Over the past two decades, a number of scholars have focused attention on the relation between Descartes's philosophical writings and his intellectual milieu: the science, theology, philosophy, and mathematics of his day. These scholars have stressed several very important aspects of the context in which Descartes used the method of doubt, aspects that may help us understand why he used it.[11]

First, we know that by the mid-1630s Descartes faced a particular rhetorical challenge. He was committed to a natural philosophy of mechani-

---

[10] He might mean that he has achieved certainty (in mathematics, at any rate) sufficient to withstand everything *but* the radical doubts, though arguably in the *Discourse* he has not yet seen how to craft a skeptical argument radical enough to call simple propositions in mathematics into doubt. Still, I think the general point I will go on to make stands: it isn't clear whether the conception of knowledge explains using the method of doubt, or whether it's the other way around.

[11] See especially Hatfield 1993.

cal corpuscularianism that was deeply opposed to the Aristotelian natural philosophy still entrenched in the Schools. He was shaken to learn, in 1633, that Galileo had been condemned by the Roman Inquisition for claiming that Earth moves around the Sun. He wrote to Mersenne that "if the view is false, so too are the entire foundations of my [natural] philosophy, for it can be demonstrated from them quite clearly" (3:41; AT 1:271). He decided not to publish *Le Monde*, the scientific treatise he had been working on for three years, and he was, understandably enough, very worried about whether and how he could advocate his natural philosophy without alienating a large and powerful segment of the learned world.

Against this background, we can easily see Descartes as intending the *Meditations* to hide and yet strengthen his advocacy of mechanistic corpuscularianism.[12] He would be hiding his advocacy by considering just the general metaphysical underpinnings of his worldview, leaving undiscussed the controversial details of the view itself. He would be strengthening his advocacy by beginning with radical doubt and thus ostentatiously forgoing presuppositions about whether the scholastics or their opponents were right.

There is good support for such an account of his intentions. In 1640, he wrote to Mersenne about a plan to write a commentary on Eustache's *Summa Philosophica Quadripartita*, a compendium of scholasticism, but he asked Mersenne not to tell anyone about this plan until the *Meditations* was published, because it "might . . . hold up the approbation of the Sorbonne, which I want, and which I think may be very useful for my purposes, for I must tell you that the little book on metaphysics which I sent you [the *Meditations*] contains all the principles of my physics" (3:157; AT 3:233). A few months later, again to Mersenne, he wrote:

> I may tell you, between ourselves, that these six Meditations contain all the foundations of my physics. But please do not tell people, for that might make it harder for supporters of Aristotle to approve them. I hope that readers will gradually get used to my principles, and recognize their truth,

---

[12] This is at least part of Gaukroger's view, though he doesn't spell it out in quite the way I do. I strongly disagree with his further contention that the method of doubt is designed in part to work out problems in the doctrine of God's free creation of the eternal truths (1995, 316 ff.). See also Curley 1978, 38.

before they notice that they destroy the principles of Aristotle. (3:173; AT
3:297–98)

Understood in their historical context, passages like these suggest that
Descartes had a strong motive for showing his readers how to use a
method of discovery that not only led to the Cartesian metaphysical principles but did so in a way that did not rest upon offensive presuppositions.

Inquiry conducted according to the method of doubt is ostentatiously
free of presuppositions. Descartes underlines this point in the Second
Replies:

[T]he arguments in respect of which I ask my readers to be attentive and
not argumentative are not of a kind which could possibly divert their attention from any other arguments which have even the slightest chance of
containing more truth than is to be found in mine. Now my exposition
includes the highest level of doubt about everything, and I cannot recom-
mend too strongly that each item should be scrutinized with the utmost
care. . . . [N]o one who restricts his consideration to my propositions can
possibly think he runs a greater risk of error than he would incur by turning
his mind away and directing it to other propositions which are in a sense
opposed to mine. (2:112; AT 7:158)

In the Fifth Replies Descartes happily accepts Gassendi's description of
the *Meditations* as a "project for freeing my mind from preconceived opinions" (2:241; AT 7:348). And the presuppositionless character of the
method of doubt is at least part of the point of Descartes's rotten-apple
metaphor:

[My critic] must have read somewhere in my writings that any true opinions
which we have before we begin to philosophize seriously are mixed up with
many others that are either false or at least doubtful. And hence, in order
to separate out the true ones, it is best to begin by rejecting all our opinions
and renouncing every single one; this will make it easier, afterwards, to
recognize those which were true (or discover new truths). . . . Now this is
just the same as if I had said that if we have a basket or tub full of apples
and want to make sure that there are no rotten ones, we should first tip
them all out, leaving none at all inside. . . . (2:348–49; AT 7:512; see also
2:324; AT 7:481)

So the method of doubt must have appealed to Descartes as a presuppositionless way to insinuate the foundations of his anti-Aristotelian, corpuscularian, worldview.

A second motivation has been stressed recently by scholars who see Descartes as responding to the late Renaissance rediscovery of, and fascination with, ancient skepticism.[13] Both Pyrrhonian and Academic skepticism were understood by sixteenth- and seventeenth-century intellectuals to be sweeping in scope and radical in character, leading to suspense of judgment about very nearly everything. Many of these readers found the considerations put forward by Cicero and by Sextus Empiricus to be persuasive.[14] The times were right for radical skepticism: something very like the skeptical problem of the criterion was already being raised by Reformation and Counter-Reformation theologians arguing about the foundations of religious authority, and the entrenched conception of the world was already being rocked by reflection upon the voyages of discovery and the cosmological theories of Kepler and Copernicus. The learned world was ready for skeptical ideas and took them seriously.

Edwin Curley claims that "sometime around 1628 Descartes came to feel that pyrrhonian skepticism was a more dangerous enemy than scholasticism, and came to feel the force of skeptical arguments which cut against both his own position in the [*Rules for the Direction of the Mind*] and that of the scholastics" (1978, 38). Seen from this perspective, Descartes was indeed trying to "answer the skeptic," but not because he had built into the conception of knowledge a requirement of skeptic-proof certainty. Rather, *other* people were offering skeptical arguments and accepting skeptical conclusions. Descartes thought he could show that they were wrong to do so, and that in the course of correcting their mistakes he could at the same time show the underpinnings of his own worldview to be uniquely defensible.

This perspective helps to make sense of several passages in which Descartes wrote about skeptical ideas. In some of these passages he apolo-

[13] A Latin edition of the *Outlines of Pyrrhonism* of Sextus Empiricus was published in 1562, and a Latin edition of the complete works of Sextus was published in 1569. The Greek texts were printed in 1621. Academic skepticism, especially as Cicero represented it in *Academica*, came in for attention in the sixteenth century.

[14] See Popkin 1968 and Schmitt 1972. The introductory essay in Sanches 1988 is also useful.

gized for beginning the *Meditations* with skeptical arguments: he was not trying to "sell them as novelties" (2:121; AT 7:171); he hesitated to "reheat and serve this stale cabbage" (2:94; AT 7:130; trans. altered). I myself think that the radical skeptical arguments of the First Meditation *are* novelties, and I will return to this point in Part One. For now, what I want to note is that Descartes clearly thinks of skeptical ideas as commonplace. It should not surprise us to find that he wants to show how to refute them.

In fact, there are several passages in which Descartes explicitly recommends the method of doubt on the grounds that by using it he can show what is wrong with the arguments of the skeptics. Frans Burman reports that in his conversation with Descartes of April 16, 1648, Descartes said that people should not dig more deeply into metaphysical questions than he did in the *Meditations*, because he had dug as deeply as anyone needs to: "The author did follow up metaphysical questions fairly thoroughly in the *Meditations*, and established their certainty against the sceptics, and so on; so everyone does not have to tackle the job for himself, or need to spend time and trouble meditating on those things" (3:347; AT 5:165). In a passage in the Seventh Replies, Descartes seems to feel greater urgency in the task of answering the skeptic:

[I]t is wholly false that in laying down our foundations in philosophy there are corresponding limits which fall short of complete certainty, but which we can sensibly and safely accept without taking doubt any further. For since truth is essentially indivisible, it may happen that a claim which we do not recognize as possessing complete certainty may in fact be quite false, however probable it may appear. To make the foundations of all knowledge rest on a claim that we recognize as being possibly false would not be a sensible way to philosophize. If someone proceeds in this way, how can he answer the sceptics who go beyond all the boundaries of doubt? How will he refute them? Will he regard them as desperate lost souls? Fine; but how will they regard him in the meantime? Moreover we should not suppose that sceptical philosophy is extinct. It is vigorously alive today, and almost all those who regard themselves as more intellectually gifted than others, and find nothing to satisfy them in philosophy as it is ordinarily practised, take refuge in scepticism because they cannot see any alternative with greater claims to truth. (2:374; AT 7:548–49)

Radical skeptical arguments were being given and accepted by actual people. Descartes thought he could show what was wrong with the arguments these people were accepting, and what they should be accepting instead.[15]

So far we have seen two reasons why Descartes might have wanted to use the method of doubt, neither of them involving the interpretative assumption I sketched out earlier, the one that has Descartes appealing to conceptual connections among good cognition, knowledge, certainty, and refutation of radical skepticism. There are two more motivations to which I now want to turn.

Descartes begins the Synopsis of the *Meditations* this way:

> In the First Meditation reasons are provided which give us possible grounds for doubt about all things, especially material things, so long as we have no foundations for the sciences other than those which we have had up till now. Although the usefulness of such extensive doubt is not apparent at first sight, its greatest benefit lies in freeing us from all our preconceived opinions, and providing the easiest route by which the mind may be led away from the senses. (2:9; AT 7:12)

On Descartes's own view of human life, our beliefs about ourselves and the world around us are pervasively distorted by a tendency, acquired in our earliest years, to cede too much authority to our senses (1:218–20; AT 8A:35–37). We assume that the things we see and touch are the basic sorts of things that there are, and we assume that they are much as we perceive them to be. Descartes thought these assumptions were false. Conscious things are basic sorts of things, but we cannot possibly see or feel them. Moreover, the basic components of physical things are bodies that are too small to see or feel, and even middle-size physical things do not really have the colors that we see, the warmth that we feel, and so

---

[15] There is thus an irony in the fact that Descartes himself was accused of being a Pyrrhonian skeptic. This charge, along with many others, was leveled against him by the Dutch philosopher Voetius, who succeeded in having Cartesian philosophy condemned by the faculty of the University of Utrecht in 1642. Descartes defended himself vigorously, both by securing political protection from the prince of Orange and by publishing letters that launched counterattacks against Voetius (3:223; AT 8A:169–70; see also 2:393; AT 7:596). Radical skepticism, at least of a sort, was emphatically a living presence in seventeenth-century philosophy.

on. We all make false assumptions about these matters, assumptions that are long held and deeply ingrained. We are capable of overcoming them, but this is very difficult for us to do. We need help, and that is what the method of doubt can provide.

So Descartes thinks that it will help us to inquire into the truth by starting with radical skepticism because this will loosen the grip of the senses upon our minds.[16] If I am suspending judgment about whether anything I sense even exists, then I am, at least temporarily, freeing my thoughts from the distorting assumptions I have grown up with. This may subsequently allow me to discern and embrace principles that can replace the bad assumptions that have taken root in my mind.

Some of these new principles will concern the nature of physical things themselves, and Descartes the scientist is certainly eager to help us grasp that the essence of physical things is to be extended, and that all of their properties are just so many "modes" of extension, or ways of being extended. But he is equally eager for us to understand ourselves better. From the perspective of enlightened dualism, Descartes would describe our prereflective beliefs about ourselves as a jumble. We seem dimly to understand that what is special about us is that we have conscious states, but we mix that up with the further thought that we are corporeal things. We have no coherent way of putting these thoughts together, but we do not recognize our difficulty. Again, what can get us to see the problem, and prepare us for grasping a solution and sticking with it, is an inquiry that begins with radical doubt:

> I wanted to prepare my readers' minds for the study of the things which
> are related to the intellect, and help them to distinguish these things from
> corporeal things; and such [skeptical] arguments seem to be wholly neces-
> sary for this purpose. (2:121; AT 7:171–72)

So Descartes sees a special heuristic value in beginning inquiry into first principles with radical skeptical doubts. (We might wonder why this isn't just an instance of the value of avoiding presuppositions. Reasons for treating this as a distinct motivation will emerge in Part One.)

---

[16] See M. Wilson 1978, 7–11. In Descartes's writings, see 2:9, 94, 121, and 406; AT 7:12, 130–31, 171–72 and 10:507–9.

The passage I have just quoted comes from Descartes's reply to an objection Hobbes made to the First Meditation: what, Hobbes had wondered, is the point of retailing these skeptical arguments? In addition to the heuristic point, Descartes mentions two others. One we have seen already: by giving the skeptical arguments, he can later show just how they can be decisively answered. But he continues with yet another reason for beginning with radical doubt: "partly I wanted to show the firmness of the truths which I propound later on, in the light of the fact that they cannot be shaken by these metaphysical doubts" (2:121; AT 7:172). This echoes the third reason in a slightly different trio of reasons he had given in the Synopsis: this extensive doubt "brings it about that we are not able to doubt further what we subsequently discover to be true" (2:9; AT 7:12; trans. altered). Both here and in the reply to Hobbes, Descartes is claiming a special sort of advantage that this doubt brings with it. The advantage does not lie in the presuppositionless character of the inquiry, nor in the satisfactions of answering irritating skeptical *libertins*, nor in the heuristic benefits of loosening the grip of the senses on our thinking. Rather, it somehow lies in the nature of the basis that we will have provided for the claims that we go on to discover.

Many readers will be inclined to think that this is where Descartes's demanding conception of knowledge comes in. They will take it that he is saying the method of doubt gives us the advantage of establishing truths in such a way that we can claim to have *knowledge* that they are true, where "knowledge" *means*, among other things, what we can defend against radical skeptical attack.

In Part One, I will be arguing that Descartes does indeed think there is a special advantage to establishing truths in such a way that we can defend them against radical skeptical attack. But this is not because he has a prior commitment to a very demanding conception of knowledge. Rather, I will argue, Descartes's use of the method of doubt enables him to execute a simple and coolly calculated strategy for establishing the first principles of philosophy he believes to be true. It is this strategic advantage that Descartes is alluding to in the Synopsis and in the reply to Hobbes, and once we see what it is, I believe, the appeal of the interpretative assumption I have begun questioning here will fully evaporate.

Before turning to the First Meditation, let me draw attention to another puzzle about the method of doubt that the Synopsis passage raises.

Descartes says that using the radical doubts of the First Meditation will "bring it about that" (*efficiat*) our subsequent discoveries are established in an especially valuable way. How exactly will beginning with doubt do this? Descartes does not establish truths by first showing that the radical skeptical arguments are invalid or that they have false premises. But if he does not criticize the arguments in either of these ways, then their breathtaking scope suggests that there will not be *any* way to establish *any* truths if we take radical skepticism seriously at the outset. So why did Descartes think not only that knowledge of the truth could be salvaged from storms of skepticism, but that those very storms somehow brought the salvage about? My aim in Part Two will be to answer this question.

PART ONE

Raising Doubt

❖

❖ 1 ❖

Who Is Doubting?

T HE First Meditation is short but devastating. After some preliminaries, Descartes raises a series of increasingly disturbing reasons for doubting increasingly large collections of our beliefs, until, it seems, there is "not one of [our] former beliefs about which a doubt may not properly be raised" (2:14–15; AT 7:21). He ends the meditation by describing the way in which he will discipline himself into suspending judgment about everything for which he has found a reason for doubt.

His presentation of reasons for doubt begins with the beliefs he has acquired by using his senses: by looking at things, smelling them, tasting them, listening to them, and touching them. At the start he alludes to problems of ordinary sense-deception, but he quickly zeroes in upon the beliefs for which no such problems arise: "for example, that I am here, sitting by the fire, wearing a winter dressing-gown, holding this piece of paper in my hands" (2:13; AT 7:18). He raises two reasons for doubting such beliefs: first, that he is like madmen, who "say they are dressed in purple when they are naked," and second, that he can find "no sure signs by means of which being awake can be distinguished from being asleep" and dreaming (2:13; AT 7:19). Further reflection suggests that these considerations also count as reasons for doubting many quite general beliefs, for example, the belief that eyes, heads, and hands exist (2:13–14; AT 7:20).

Still untouched, however, are "the simplest and most general things" that are dealt with by "arithmetic, geometry and other subjects of this kind" (2:14; AT 7:20). But Descartes finds reasons for doubting these beliefs too. How, he wonders, does he know that his omnipotent Creator has not made him so that he is deceived in these beliefs—even in his belief that two plus three equals five—as well as in all of his sense-based beliefs? Or if God does not exist, how does he know that his original cause—"fate or chance or a continuous chain of events"—has not botched his creation so that he is "deceived all the time" (2:14; AT 7:21)?

There are, then, four radical grounds for doubt: the lunacy argument, the dream argument, the deceiving God argument, and the "fate or chance" argument. The lunacy argument is sketchier than the dream argument, and for ease of exposition I will sometimes refer just to the dream argument when, in fact, what I am saying applies to the lunacy argument as well. Similarly, sometimes I will refer to the deceiving God argument when what I am saying applies equally to the "fate or chance" argument. When I speak of Descartes's "radical" skepticism, or his "radical" grounds for doubt, I will be referring to the considerations he is raising in these four arguments.

In Part One of this book, I will be explaining how and why Descartes begins with these radical skeptical arguments. In chapter 2 I will be taking a detour into the ancient skepticism whose rediscovery was causing such a stir. By bringing out several features of Academic and Pyrrhonian skepticism, I hope to be able to identify some related features of Cartesian doubt, features that are easy for readers like us to miss. In subsequent chapters I will return to the First Meditation, looking for ways to answer these questions: What does Descartes count as a reason for suspending judgment? What does he count as a reason for doubt? And what does he cede to the authority of common sense? But first in this chapter I want to explore the question who is raising the doubts of the First Meditation.

The Meditator as Anyone

The First Meditation is seductive: we find it easy—all too easy—to project ourselves into the position the 'I' seems to occupy. It can seem to us that the meditator's confrontation with the skeptical arguments must be ours as well, that what moves him should move any thoughtful person who examines his beliefs in a disciplined and thoroughgoing fashion.

It is true that we do not ordinarily consider the radical grounds for doubt when we assess our beliefs, or candidates for belief. There is also a sense in which we would be wrong to do so: any judge would declare a mistrial if a juror were to advance the dream argument as providing grounds for reasonable doubt about whether the defendant committed the crime with which he was charged. Some philosophers have concluded from this that the radical grounds for doubt are illegitimate. Thomas

Reid, for one, argued that "what is absurd at the bar, is so in the philosopher's chair. What would be ridiculous, if delivered to a jury of honest, sensible citizens, is no less so when delivered gravely in a philosophical dissertation" (1969, 623).

Still, it is easy to see the meditator as using nothing but a natural extension of the standards that are implicit in our ordinary ways of evaluating our beliefs, and then finding that by those standards, virtually nothing that we believe deserves our assent. Several distinguished philosophers in recent years have interpreted Descartes as intending for us to see the meditator's reflections in this way, and they have explored the question why we find it so easy to see the First Meditation in the way they think Descartes wants us to.[1] (There are large questions here about how philosophical reflection is related to everyday belief; I will take some of them up in chapter 5.)

In the rest of this chapter I will be arguing that in important respects we are wrong to suppose that this is how Descartes thought matters should appear to the meditator in the First Meditation. Of course, *we* may nonetheless still wish to think about radical skeptical arguments in this way. But if I am right about Descartes, we will need to find the precursor of our wish somewhere outside the *Meditations*. So by raising the question who the 'I' is, who the meditator is supposed to be, I hope to be able more clearly to see how Descartes thought someone could raise and take seriously the radical skeptical arguments.

The *Meditations* is not an autobiographical work. Descartes's own intellectual development did not pass through the phases the *Meditations* describes, as his correspondence and other philosophical writings make clear. So the 'I' of the *Meditations* is not Descartes himself. In at least some respects, Descartes suggests, the meditator's position is one that any thoughtful person could occupy.[2] For example, in the Second

[1] See B. Williams 1978 and Stroud 1984 for two rather different ways of explaining what sorts of resources Descartes might have drawn upon if he were challenged to explain why he assumes that the doubts of the First Meditation are natural extensions of our everyday practices. In a less sympathetic vein, Michael Williams argues (1986) that Descartes misrepresents his doubts as ordinary when, in fact, he has already put substantive and controversial philosophical theorizing in place.

[2] Descartes does say that not everyone is suited for reflection on first principles (e.g., 3:139; AT 2:596), but he seems to think anyone who tries hard and who attentively follows out the course of the *Meditations* will arrive at the correct principles.

Replies, he says that the "order" of the *Meditations* is this: "the items which are put forward first must be known entirely without the aid of what comes later; and the remaining items must be arranged in such a way that their demonstration depends solely on what has gone before" (2:110; AT 7:155). The "demonstration" of "the remaining items" proceeds by "analysis":

> Analysis shows the true way by means of which the thing in question was discovered methodically and as it were *a priori*, so that if the reader is willing to follow it and give sufficient attention to all points, he will make the thing his own and understand it just as perfectly as if he had discovered it for himself. But this method contains nothing to compel belief in an argumentative or inattentive reader; for if he fails to attend even to the smallest point, he will not see the necessity of the conclusion. Moreover there are many truths which—although it is vital to be aware of them—this method often scarcely mentions, since they are transparently clear to anyone who gives them his attention. (2:110; AT 7:155–56)

Descartes intends the *Meditations* to instruct the attentive reader by putting ideas in the order in which the reader can come to know them, and by laying out demonstrations that show how the later things can be "discovered methodically" from consideration of the earlier things. "Earlier" and "later" here are not altogether metaphorical, as they might be, say, in reference to the steps of the proof of a theorem in Euclid. Descartes is trying to show how an ideal inquiry might go: a person who first had the thought that A, would then recognize that B, which in turn would show him that C. The order, A–B–C, is partly a matter of various relations among the propositions designated, but it is also partly a matter of the state of the person at the successive moments at which he entertains A, B, and C, and the ways in which the occurrence of the earlier states may help to bring about the later ones. (I will fill out this schematic description more fully in chapter 3.)

So by narrating a first-person-singular inquiry, Descartes is dramatizing a very general sort of "order" and (in one sense of the term) "method" that he is using to instruct the reader. These considerations do not by themselves rule out the use of, say, the second person plural. But once "you," the readers, had done what Descartes urged you to do, and had suspended judgment about all your former beliefs, you would be suspending judgment about the existence of the person addressing you in the second person plural, and about the existence of the other people ostensibly being addressed. The first person singular is ideally suited to the lonely inquiry Descartes narrates.[3]

In the Second Replies, Descartes says that the order of the *Meditations* requires that he start with "items which are . . . known entirely without the aid of what comes later." This suggests that as readers we should try to avoid interpretations that attribute to the meditator at one stage of his inquiry some idea or belief that he acquires at a later stage. When we think about the meditator, we should always ask, "What did he know, and when did he know it?" We may, however, find that there are places where we simply cannot make sense of what the meditator says without reading Descartes as putting words in the meditator's mouth. I will argue presently that the very first sentence of the First Meditation is one such place, and that this complication is philosophically significant.

We can see how the idea of progressive discovery fits later sequences of the meditator's thoughts: for example, the meditator achieves certainty that God exists without relying upon the knowledge of the material world that he acquires later. But we should not be surprised to find that it is harder to see how this idea fits the earliest stages of the *Meditations*. To be sure, once the meditator has suspended judgment about all of his "former beliefs" (2:14; AT 7:21), there is a sense in which he has a clean slate: he does not claim to know anything at all and thus cannot be claiming to know something by relying upon what comes later. But then on what basis does he first come to know something? And what about the *very* beginning, before the meditator has raised the grounds for doubt? What are the former beliefs of the 'I', and what exactly has persuaded him to seek out and take seriously such outré grounds for doubt?

Let me make this last question more specific by bringing it to bear upon the opening of the First Meditation. Descartes begins by having the meditator say, "Some years ago I was struck by the large number of false

---

[3] Descartes himself tries several other modes of presentation: a dialogue, to which I will revert several times in what follows, and the *Principles*, in which he retraces some of the route of the *Meditations* in the first person plural. Both works are less successful than the *Meditations*, I think, and at least part of the reason concerns the way in which Descartes reasons about himself in the Second Meditation. (See chapter 7.) For a stimulating account of the complex structures of the narrative of the *Meditations*, see Kosman 1986.

things that I had accepted as true in my childhood, and by the highly doubtful nature of everything that I had subsequently built on top of them" (2:12; AT 7:17; trans. altered). What are these falsehoods? How did the meditator come to recognize that they *are* falsehoods? How had he built on top of them, and why do they make this superstructure of belief "highly doubtful"? Questions multiply as the meditator is made to continue by saying, "I realized that it was necessary, once in the course of my life, to demolish everything completely and start again right from the foundations if I wanted to establish anything at all in the sciences that was sturdy and lasting" (2:12; AT 7:17; trans. altered). We can understand why lasting results in the sciences are unlikely to flow from beliefs that are "doubtful," but again, why are those beliefs doubtful? And in any case, isn't the meditator overreacting when he says he must "demolish everything"? To answer these questions, we need a better understanding of who this meditator is, and how he sees his situation.

The Meditator as Scholastic Philosopher or Person of Common Sense

John Carriero has argued that in the First Meditation Descartes is engaging someone who holds a specific set of philosophical tenets, those of the Thomistic metaphysics derived from Aristotle. This scholastic meditator would bring to his inquiry several assumptions that Descartes wants him to drop. One is that our knowledge begins in our senses, when the *species*, or forms, that are in sensible things also lodge in our souls. Another is that what we do with our intellects in acquiring knowledge, even of God and mathematical truths, is basically to engage in abstraction from these sensible *species*. Carriero argues that Descartes poses the dream argument to the scholastic meditator in order to get him "to suspend faith in the epistemic linkage with the world provided by the senses" (1997, 11). The role of the deceiving God argument is different: Carriero sees it as Descartes's way of setting an agenda for defending the innatism he wishes to put in place of the scholastic assumptions. Roughly, if Descartes wants to claim that ideas innate to our intellects, rather than sensible *species*, are the source of our capacity to grasp the nature of reality, then he had better be able to explain why he thinks that ideas that originate from us will properly reflect truths that are independent of us.

But it is hard to see the 'I' of the First Meditation primarily as a scholastic philosopher. Think again about the opening of the First Meditation: the scholastic philosopher wouldn't fret the way the meditator does. He thinks he *has* established the framework for results in the sciences that are "sturdy and lasting." From his point of view, there is no particular reason to undertake an inquiry that begins with the resolve to "demolish everything completely." I think what we *can* imagine is the scholastic philosopher, smug in his invincibility, eavesdropping on someone *else's* worries about the doubtfulness of the superstructure, and then sitting up and getting worried when the meditator begins to construct reasons for doubting what his senses tell him.[4] We can also imagine a scholastic philosopher who, for reasons we would need to articulate, had already grown uneasy with his assumptions about the role of the senses in human knowledge. So I think that Carriero may be right in saying that Descartes, as author of the *Meditations*, is crafting the book so that early episodes would present the scholastic philosopher with just the challenge and question Carriero articulates. But what is salient about the 'I' is not his scholasticism.

Harry Frankfurt has argued that the perspective of the meditator in the First Meditation is "the perspective of common sense" (1970, 15). The meditator is meant to be a "philosophical novice" (32) whose "philosophically naïve position" will be "undermined" (15) as the *Meditations* progresses. The position this person holds, Frankfurt says, is that "he has no knowledge except what the senses provide" (32). Frankfurt draws particular attention to Burman's report of his 1648 conversation with Descartes, in which Burman quotes Descartes as saying, "[T]he author is considering at this point the man who is only just beginning to philosophize, and who is paying attention only to what he knows he is aware of" (3:332; AT 5:146).

I agree with Frankfurt that Descartes wants the *Meditations* to show how a person of common sense may arrive at the truth. But I do not think that saying this much is saying enough. In his conversation with Burman, Descartes is silent about something we need to know: how or

[4] See Garber 1986, 85–88, and Rozemond 1998, 69 ff.

27

why a person of common sense would describe himself as "struck by the large number of falsehoods that I had accepted as true in my childhood." Of course, the plain man Descartes describes might recall having believed in his youth that toadstools shelter elves, and that all that glitters is gold. But that does not help us with our interpretative task, because retrospectively recognizing these sorts of mistakes would not lead someone to despair of establishing lasting results in the sciences, and would not explain his wish to "demolish everything."

Either the scholastic philosopher or the naive person of common sense might have a general sense of the doubtfulness of his beliefs, and a general motivation for demolishing them, in one sense of "demolish." For either of them might simply be impressed by the debates raging between the Aristotelians and the new scientists, or by the voyages to the New World, or the discovery of the moons of Jupiter and the phases of Venus, or the flourishing of Protestantism, or even by the skepticism of the new Pyrrhonists. In such an age, any well-informed and thoughtful person might be astonished to see what turns out to be false or debatable, and might think that any inquiry that aims at achieving sturdy and lasting results had better take nothing for granted—had better be ostentatiously free of presuppositions. In this spirit a person might propose to "demolish" his opinions in the sense that he would not rely upon their truth in the inquiry he is going to conduct.[5]

But this appeal to the general culture still does not help us to understand the meditator's specific claim, which is that he recognizes that he had accepted a lot of basic claims *in his childhood* that he now knows to be *false*. What might those be? And if he now recognizes that they are false, what exactly is their bearing on all his other beliefs: why should he now regard the recognized falsehood of some beliefs as generating suspicion about everything else?

THE MEDITATOR'S PROBLEMATIC PERSONA

I think that at the beginning of the First Meditation the meditator does not have an identity altogether his own: this is a place where Descartes

---

[5] In chapter 3, I will return to this sense of "demolish" and argue that it does not capture all of Descartes's intentions.

is putting words into his meditator's mouth. As I said in the introduction, it is Descartes himself who thinks that we—ordinary people and scholastic philosophers alike—have beliefs that are systematically distorted by falsehoods accepted as true in childhood.[6] He explains in the *Principles* how our embodiment and infancy conspire to mislead us:

> In our early childhood . . . the mind had various sensations corresponding to the different areas where, and ways in which, the body was being stimulated, namely what we call the sensations of tastes, smells, sounds, heat, cold, light, colours, and so on—sensations which do not represent anything located outside our thought. At the same time the mind perceived sizes, shapes, motions and so on, which were presented to it not as sensations but as things, or modes of things, existing . . . outside thought, although it was not yet aware of the difference between things and sensations. The next stage arose when the mechanism of the body . . . twisted around aimlessly . . . in its random attempts to pursue the beneficial and avoid the harmful; at this point the mind that was attached to the body began to notice that the objects of this pursuit or avoidance had an existence outside itself. And it attributed to them not only sizes, shapes, motions and the like, . . . but also tastes, smells and so on, the sensations of which were, it realized, produced by the objects in question. (1:218–19; AT 8A:35–36)

Descartes goes on to draw out further consequences from this basic account of our cognitive development. He explains how in infancy we come by more specific beliefs, for example, the beliefs that air is nothing, that stars are tiny, and that the earth is still and flat. He adds that "in later childhood [our mind] regarded [these preconceived opinions] as known by the senses or implanted by nature, and accepted them as utterly true and evident" (1:219; AT 8A:36). And even when we are adults, and capable of reflecting critically upon our beliefs, our general preconceived opinions linger: "it is not easy for the mind to erase these false judgements from its memory; and as long as they stick there, they can cause a variety of errors" (1:219–20; AT 8A:36).

Someone who shared with Descartes this account of human cognitive development would inevitably be "struck by the large number of falsehoods" he had "accepted as true in [his] childhood," and would have rea-

---

[6] Garber reads this sentence in the same way (1986, 81–91), although he does not focus upon the same questions of motivation that I am raising here.

29

son to mistrust "everything [he] had subsequently built on top of them."
The pervasiveness and obstinacy of our beliefs that things have the colors
we see, the warmth we feel, and that in general our sensations "represent
[things] located outside our thought" (1:219; AT 8A:35) mean that we
cannot easily assure ourselves that we have rid ourselves of all such beliefs,
and of their false presuppositions and consequences. We can see why
someone recognizing this difficulty would want to attempt a "general
demolition" (2:12; AT 7:17) of all his opinions. That would be the only
sure way to root out the insidious false beliefs of infancy; to use Descartes's own metaphor, we must dump all the apples out of the barrel to
find the rotten ones and prevent the rot from spreading (2:324; AT 7:481).

By attributing this appraisal to the meditator, we can connect his interest in sturdy and lasting results in the sciences not just to his wish to
demolish all his opinions but also to the overarching aim that the title of
the book announces: grasping the principles of "First Philosophy." That is,
the meditator sees that he will need to be able to replace the demolished
opinions with some general basis for belief other than the one his cognitive development has given him. (Of course, this is at this point a highly
schematic goal, with no content as yet. We will see later how the meditator arrives at the substantive principles about God, mind, and nature that
I listed in the introduction.)

I think the surviving fragment of the dialogue *The Search for Truth*
bolsters the attribution to the meditator of Descartes's own beliefs about
our cognitive development. Descartes has *three* characters conversing:
Epistemon, the scholastic philosopher; Polyander, the thoughtful person
of common sense; *and* Eudoxus, the enlightened Cartesian who nudges
the other two into methodic doubt. Eudoxus urges Epistemon to stay on
the sidelines during the exchanges corresponding to the First and Second
Meditations, but Eudoxus's prodding is essential to the development of
Polyander's conviction that seeking the demolition of his opinions is a
good thing.[7] And this, it seems to me, gets the personae of the First
Meditation just about right: the person of common sense is center stage;
Descartes is engineering the course of reflection so that the scholastic

---

[7] I don't want to make too much of this: in the *Search*, Polyander's initial motivations
for seeking the overthrow of his former opinions merge into the lunatic and dream arguments themselves.

philosopher will recognize a threat to his basic philosophical tenets; and he is motivating the inquiry by drawing, as he must, upon his own enlightened account of human cognitive development.

This might suggest that we have found a complex but coherent persona to attribute to the meditator. But there is something wrong with Descartes's putting his account of human cognition into the mouth of the meditator. The meditator does not himself arrive at anything like such a view until he has reached the *end* of the inquiry upon which he is embarking. The Sixth Meditation is the point at which the meditator discovers how poor his grounds are for attributing the colors he sees, and so on, to physical objects (2:55 ff.; AT 7:80 ff.). It might be thought that the meditator could simply pick up the Cartesian view of human cognitive development from a conversation, or from a textbook or a lecture. But it is a consequence of the Cartesian view that correcting our mistakes is not that easy. They are deeply ingrained, and it takes a special procedure to root them out. As I will go on to stress in chapter 3, the method of doubt is supposed to constitute just such a procedure.

So the motivations Descartes describes for undertaking an inquiry guided by the method of doubt are not the motivations that might persuade any actual meditator to begin as the fictional meditator begins. I believe that this is not just a flaw in the rhetorical structure of the *Meditations*: I think the 'I' of the *Meditations* does not have a set of epistemological beliefs and goals that we can see as fully rational.[8] Descartes represents the retrojected account of human cognitive development as what gives the meditator his reason for thinking that achieving success in the sciences requires him to overthrow his beliefs: the retrojected account is what the meditator cites as his reason for giving a negative assessment of his edifice of belief, and it is also what gives the meditator his reason

---

[8] I suspect that because Descartes thought of the First Meditation doubt as artificial, he was not inclined to probe the question how to provide it with a rationale. I also suspect that he simply did not think enough about the significance of several differences between the *Discourse* and the *Meditations*: he has replaced the educated and reflective person who accepted "principles"—*philosophical* principles—in his youth (1:117; AT 6:14) with the Polyander figure and his commonsense reliance upon his senses. This figure's dissatisfaction cannot be attributed to reservations that he has about his scholastic education; he is instead uncomfortably equipped with Cartesian theories about human cognitive development.

to think that nothing short of overthrow of the entire edifice will help. But as I will argue in chapter 3, Descartes *also* represents the meditator as requiring a reason to overthrow his beliefs if he is to have any rational ground for suspending judgment about all of his "opinions which are not completely certain and indubitable" (2:12; AT 7:18). Without a reason for undertaking a general overthrow of belief, the meditator will have much more reason to believe than not to believe that, for example, he has a piece of paper before him, or that two plus three equals five, even if he considers the radical grounds for doubt. If I am right about this, then no ordinary person, untutored in Cartesian metaphysics, would ever have a good reason for suspending judgment about something simply by considering the radical grounds for doubt. This is a serious internal flaw in Descartes's representation of the method of doubt, one that I think he did not recognize.[9]

My account of the 'I' of the First Meditation does not itself settle the question with which I began this chapter, the question whether Descartes will ask us to see radical skepticism as arising from a natural extension of the standards implicit in our ordinary evaluations of belief. I will return to this question in chapters 3 and 4. But my account of the meditator's persona should already make us suspect that we will find no simple correlation between how the 'I' of the *Meditations* thinks about radical skepticism, and how we do.[10]

[9] Here I think I am in agreement with Garber (1992, esp. 57). I should add that I am not claiming that the ordinary person would somehow be unable to recognize the radical skeptical scenarios as grounds for doubt. Rather, he would simply dismiss them. (I say more about this in chapter 5.) But there are limits to how deep my criticism of Descartes will cut: even the theoryless ordinary person might see the point of the high strategy that I describe in the second section of chapter 3. (I am grateful to Ed McCann for pressing me to clarify the limits of this criticism.)

[10] I am in agreement to that extent with M. Wilson (1984), though she does not discuss the possibility that accepting the Cartesian account of human cognition would turn out to be part of the rational motivation for being moved by radical skeptical considerations to suspend judgment.

❖ 2 ❖

Ancient Skepticism

Hᴀᴠɪɴɢ ᴘʀᴏᴘᴏꜱᴇᴅ to himself the aim of demolishing all of his opinions, the meditator accepts a maxim for belief:

> Reason now leads me to think that I should hold back my assent from opinions which are not completely certain and indubitable just as carefully as I do from those which are patently false. So for the purpose of rejecting all my opinions, it will be enough if I find in each of them at least some reason for doubt. (2:12; AT 7:18)

This is a puzzling maxim for assent, but before I consider it, I want to sketch out some features of the Academic and Pyrrhonian skepticism with which Descartes must have been familiar.[1] I will then return in chapter 3 to the meditator and his maxim.

There are three features of ancient skepticism that I want to bring out. The first is that ancient skeptics were not directly concerned with knowledge or certainty or with the grounds for doubt that would make us withdraw claims to knowledge or certainty. Rather, they were directly

---

[1] See 1:181–82 (AT 9B:6–7); 1:309 (AT 8B:367); 2:121 and 243 (AT 7:171–72 and 351); 2:413 (AT 10:519–20); and esp. 2:94 (AT 7:130), where Descartes says, "I have seen many ancient writings by the Academics and Sceptics on this subject [of reasons for doubting corporeal things]." But it is not clear whether he himself read Cicero's *Academica* or any of the works of Sextus Empiricus. Certainly he read other works of Cicero (Gouhier 1958, 93), and he seems to have regarded Cicero's prose as a model of clarity (3:166; AT 3:274). Too, there are Stoic strains in his thought and outlook, as Gouhier for one points out, which might have made *Academica* of special interest to him. But not even Charles Schmitt (1972) can say whether Descartes read *Academica*. Nor, as far as I know, is there any decisive evidence that Descartes read anything by Sextus. Still, Descartes rarely has much to say about what he has read, and I do not think he would refer to the arguments of the Pyrrhonists and Academic skeptics without being fairly well acquainted with them, whether through reading the primary texts or through reading secondhand accounts of them.

concerned with assent, or judgment, and how we may be led to withhold it. Second, when they lay out the ways in which we may be led to withhold assent, they do not themselves advocate normative rules about belief. They do not advocate maxims of the form "A reasonable person ought to withhold assent in such-and-such circumstances." Third, to the extent that they engage with ordinary or commonsense belief, they do not treat it as exerting any special authority.

I want to sketch two rather different dialectical situations in which these features emerge. One is the Academic skeptics' reactions to the Stoic doctrines of assent to "cognitive impressions." The other is the presentation, to a broader range of interlocutors, of the "Ten Modes" by which suspense of judgment may be induced. Let me take these up in turn.

ACADEMIC SKEPTICISM AS A CRITICISM OF STOIC EPISTEMOLOGY

The Stoics claimed that each of us has many "cognitive impressions," typically sense impressions of a particular sort, and that these cognitive impressions are in one way or another the basis for everything that we can know. A cognitive impression is one that "[1] arises from what is and [2] is stamped and impressed exactly in accordance with what is, [3] of such a kind as could not arise from what is not."[2] What these clauses mean is the subject of considerable dispute. One way or another, the first two add up to the requirement that the impression be true. Before I turn to the third clause, I need to explain how the Stoics thought cognitive impressions should figure in our lives.

The Stoics held up as the ideal human being a person who would always think and feel in accordance with things as they are. Such a person would assent only to impressions that are true; he would withhold assent from all other impressions. The wise person thus needs a criterion of truth by which to regulate his assent, and the Stoics held that the cognitive impression serves as such a criterion. That is why they included the

---

[2] Sextus Empiricus, *Against the Logicians* 7.248 (1997, 132–33). Here I use the translation provided by Long and Sedley (1987, 243). See also Cicero, *Academica* 2.6.18 and 2.24.77 (1951, 490–91, 564–65).

third clause in their definition of the kind of impression that allows genuine cognition of objects. For if my impression of, say, Socrates, is of exactly the same kind as my impression of his twin brother, then there could be circumstances in which I would have an impression indistinguishable from my impression of Socrates even though "Here is Socrates" would be false.[3] In such a case, my criterion would be telling me to assent to a proposition that is false. So without the feature described in the third clause, the Stoics agreed, the cognitive impression could not serve as the criterion of truth that the wise man needs.

The Stoics thus held, first, that there *are* cognitive impressions, that is, impressions that meet all three clauses of the definition, and second, that the wise person withholds assent unless he is presented with a cognitive impression, or a proposition suitably related to a cognitive impression. So if a Stoic could be persuaded that *no* impression meets all three clauses of the definition, then he would hold that the wise person will withhold assent from every proposition. The Academic skeptics could thus lead Stoics to withhold assent from every proposition simply by leading them to agree that there are no impressions that meet all three clauses of the definition of "cognitive impression."

(Of course, someone who is not a Stoic might agree with the Academic skeptics that there are no cognitive impressions but disagree with the Stoics about when a wise person will give his assent to a proposition. For example, someone might hold that many impressions, while not cognitive in the Stoic sense, are nonetheless all we need in order to form judgments worthy of our assent.)

What the Academic skeptics said to the Stoics, over and over, was that no putative cognitive impression actually satisfies the third clause: no impression is "of such a kind as could not arise from what is not." The Academics had two strategies for persuading a Stoic philosopher of this. One was to argue that for any impression derived from a particular existent object, we can imagine an impression that is just like it in every *sensible* detail but that is nonetheless derived from some other object.[4]

---

[3] I am glossing over some important and difficult questions here, about how exactly the third clause is motivated and what exactly it means. See Frede 1983.

[4] Cicero, *Academica* 2.26.84–87 (1951, 572–77); Sextus Empiricus, *Against the Logicians* 7.409–10 (1997, 218–19).

And so for the impression of Socrates, we can imagine an impression of his twin brother; for the impression of this egg, we can imagine an impression of an exactly similar egg. ("Nothing so like as eggs," as Hume remarked centuries later.)[5]

The other Academic strategy concerned a *general* feature of impressions that the Stoic philosopher might point up. Here, the Academics seem to have had in mind a Stoic who would say that cognitive impressions are "of such a kind" as to be uniquely convincing, intense, and apt to provoke emotions, action, and assent.[6] The Stoic philosopher would be claiming, then, that all cognitive impressions have a sort of real-like character that a noncognitive impression could not have. In reply, the Academics pointed to the impressions people have while drunk, dreaming, or mad:

> For as in waking life the thirsty man feels pleasure in indulging in drink, and the man who flees from a wild beast or any other object of terror shouts and cries aloud, so also in dreams delight is felt by the thirsty when they think they are drinking from a spring, and similarly fear is felt by those in terror:
>
> > Achilles up-leapt in amazement,
> > Smiting together his hands, and a doleful word did he utter.
>
> And just as in a normal state we believe and assent to very lucid appearances, behaving, for instance, towards Dion as Dion, and towards Theon as Theon, so also in a state of madness some are similarly affected. Thus Heracles, when he was mad and had received a presentation of his own children as though they were those of Eurystheus, followed up this presentation with corresponding action. And the corresponding action was to destroy his enemy's children, which he did.[7]

---

[5] Hume, *Enquiry*, sec. 4, pt. 2 (1975, 36). I am sure he is alluding to the Academics in this little bit of drollery.

[6] Cicero, *Academica* 2.15.47–54 (1951, 526–35); Sextus Empiricus, *Against the Logicians* 7.403–8 (1997, 214–19). It is not clear to me how exactly these two Academic strategies were supposed to be related to one another, or for that matter how the corresponding Stoic claims were supposed to be related.

[7] Sextus Empiricus, *Against the Logicians* 7.403–5 (1997, 214–17). The quotation is from the *Iliad* 23.101.

The impressions of drunkards, dreamers, and madmen can be as convincing and real-like as those of the sober, wide-awake, sane person: delight, fear, assent, and action can attend false impressions as well as true ones with the same general character. So putative cognitive impressions do not have some real-like quality in virtue of which they are "of such a kind as could not arise from what is not."

The Stoic who is persuaded by these observations will reluctantly agree that no impressions are cognitive. If he also sticks to his maxim that the wise man will withhold assent whenever his judgment does not rest on a cognitive impression, then to be consistent he must suspend judgment about everything, becoming a skeptic *malgré lui*. In the encounter between the Stoic and the Academic skeptic, the Academic plays the part of the judo fighter, using the strength of the Stoic's own maxim to flip him into suspense of judgment.

Should we care whether or not there are cognitive impressions if we do not endorse the Stoic maxim for assent? The answer depends upon whether we think the Stoic doctrine of the cognitive impression also correctly describes the character that any normal person takes much of his sense experience to have. And even if we do not hold ourselves to the Stoic maxim for assent, perhaps on reflection we would be reluctant to say that any of our beliefs are reasonable unless we could also say that at least some of them rest upon experiences that can be described in roughly the same terms as those the Stoics used for cognitive impressions.[8] These are important and delicate issues, I think, and I see no signs that the Academics or Stoics themselves worried about them very much. I will argue in chapter 5 that one of Descartes's innovations was to take more seriously, and consider more directly, the claims of common sense.

PYRRHONIAN REFLECTION

Let me now sketch out a different skeptical strategy, one used by the Pyrrhonian skeptic in engagement with a range of interlocutors wider than just the Stoic philosophers. This is the strategy presented by Sextus

---

[8] See C. I. Lewis (1971, 186): "If anything is to be probable, then something must be certain."

Empiricus in the "Ten Modes," which are ten fairly similar ways of inducing suspense of judgment. In each mode the Pyrrhonist begins by asking
us to consider two conflicting impressions, and then he leads us into
conceding that we have no grounds for deciding that one rather than the
other is correct. The result of this concession is that we suspend judgment
about how things are, and give credence only to propositions that state
how things appear to us to be. The Pyrrhonist welcomes this result, for
it brings with it the tranquillity of mind that he had originally assumed
would come to him only if he reached settled judgments about how
things are.

Sextus emphasizes different points in different modes; for our purposes
a sort of composite will be useful. I will lay out five steps, though in none
of the modes are all five steps explicit.[9]

1. Various considerations are brought forward to get me to agree that
the same object produces conflicting impressions (in different animals, in
different people, in different sense organs, and so on). For example, I agree
that the same wine tastes sweet to me and sour (not sweet) to you.

2. My impression makes it evident to me that this wine is sweet, and
your impression makes it evident to you that this wine is sour. If I were
to judge that the wine is as it appears to me, I would judge that it is
sweet; and if I were to judge that the wine is as it appears to you, I would
judge that it is sour. So I cannot trust both my own impression and yours;
that would be "attempting the impossible and accepting contradictories."[10]
So if I judge that the wine is sweet, I am preferring my impression over
yours.

3. If I attempt to offer a reason for preferring my impression over yours,
I fail, for my attempt will lead me into absurdity,[11] circularity, or an infinite

---

[9] Nor is every detail of each step fully compatible with each of the modes. I don't think
this matters here, given the fairly broad features of Pyrrhonism I am trying to bring out.

[10] Sextus, *Outlines of Pyrrhonism* 1.88 (1993, 52–53). In Modes Six through Ten, Sextus
moves rapidly from this point to suspense of judgment. It may be that he is taking the
intervening steps for granted, having rehearsed them often enough in the earlier modes.

[11] I mean here to be alluding not to the Agrippan trilemma in *Outlines* 1.169–74 (1993,
96–99) but to a variety of argumentative moves sketched in the Ten Modes. For example,
in the Second Mode, at 1.88–89 (1993, 52–55), the interlocutor is to find absurd the options
of believing all men and accepting the views of the majority; in the Fourth, at 1.112, the

regress. (The arguments here are highly abstract and schematic; their details will not concern us.)

4. If I prefer my impression over yours for no reason, then I am discredited. So either I am discredited, or I do not prefer my own impression.

5. But I am not discredited. So I do not prefer my own impression, and I do not judge that the wine is sweet.

The first two steps set up conflicting impressions; the third brings me to see that the impressions are "equipollent"; and in the last two I take the only available alternative to being discredited, and suspend judgment.[12]

Notice that the Pyrrhonist does not himself endorse any norms for assent, and that he shapes this line of thought so that his interlocutor seems able to reach suspense of judgment even if he is sensitive to only very weak norms of belief. The interlocutor does not have to have high standards; he certainly does not have to hold himself to anything like a Stoic ideal of assent. It seems that he simply needs to think (a) that an absurdity, circular argument, or infinite regress does not constitute a reason for assent, and (b) that when faced with conflicting impressions, he ought to have some sort of reason for going with one rather than the other.[13]

These modes for suspending judgment seem aimed, then, at anyone who judges how things are on the basis of how they appear to him to be, and who is sensitive to the two weak norms for belief that I have just described. That is, they seem to be aimed at the beliefs of ordinary people as well as at those of philosophers.[14] Well, suppose an ordinary person

---

option of claiming that he is in no disposition (1993, 66–67); and in the Fifth, at 1.122, the option according to which he would confute himself (1993, 72–73).

[12] In *Against the Logicians*, Sextus sometimes writes about Stoic philosophers as if this pattern of thought, rather than the judo-like pattern, were what would induce them to suspend judgment. The conflict would be between the Stoics' and Academics' accounts of impressions; the arguments of the Stoics would be counterpoised by those of the Academics; and in the face of the resulting equipollence of considerations pro and contra, one would suspend judgment to avoid being discredited.

[13] There are also considerations by which he must be moved in the third step. I think it is a good question just how weak the demands are on him there, though the Pyrrhonist seems to think they are very weak indeed.

[14] Michael Frede (1997) has argued vigorously that the Pyrrhonist is concerned with ordinary-sounding claims like "The wine is sweet" only to the extent that they are taken

says, looking at his hand, "Here is a hand. I'm looking at it up close, in broad daylight, wide awake, sane, and sober. Nothing can move me to suspend judgment about this." The Pyrrhonist will reply by first getting this person to agree that there is a conflicting impression, and then asking him to say why he prefers his impression over the conflicting one. No matter what the interlocutor says—for example, that we ought always to judge that things are as the sane, wide-awake person can plainly see them to be—the Pyrrhonist will trot out schematic arguments to show that the effort to rationalize the preference leads to absurdity, circularity, or an infinite regress. And then the interlocutor will be moved to suspend judgment.

I want to bring out the Pyrrhonist's refusal to grant authority to common sense by looking at how Sextus uses dreams to generate conflicting impressions. I want also to bring out the way the role of dreaming in the Ten Modes differs from its role in the Academic arguments against the Stoics; I will argue in chapter 4 that Descartes's use of dreaming is different from both the Pyrrhonist and Academic uses.

The Fourth Mode is based upon "conditions or dispositions": it deals with "states that are natural or unnatural, with waking or sleeping, with conditions due to age, motion or rest, hatred or love, emptiness or fullness, drunkenness or soberness, predispositions, confidence or fear, grief or joy."[15] Sextus brings up dreams in parallel to the observation, say, that "the same honey seems to me sweet, but bitter to men with jaundice."[16] He says:

> Different appearances come about depending on sleeping or waking. When we are awake, we view things differently from the way we do when asleep, and when asleep differently from the way we do when awake; so the exis-

---

in a special, philosophical way, as expressing claims about things insofar as they are objects for reason. I find it hard to square this interpretative claim with the considerations Sextus offers us in the Ten Modes; it seems to me that it fits other arguments in the *Outlines* better, though even then there are difficulties. See, for example, 3.65, where "Motion exists" is something "assumed by ordinary people and by some philosophers" (1993, 373). I am thus inclined to agree with Myles Burnyeat (1997) about the range of interlocutors and beliefs at which the Pyrrhonist takes aim.

[15] *Outlines* 1.100 (1993, 60–61).
[16] *Outlines* 1.101 (1993, 60–61).

tence or non-existence of the objects becomes not absolute but relative—relative to being asleep or awake. It is likely, then, that when asleep we will see things which are unreal in waking life, not unreal once and for all. For they exist in sleep, just as the contents of waking life exist even though they do not exist in sleep.[17]

Sextus is mining the realms of sleeping and waking life for conflicting impressions. In my sleep last night it appeared to me that my scarf is striped; it appears to me now that it is flowered. Once I concede that these conflicting impressions exist, the Pyrrhonist will lead me through the rest of the steps toward suspense of judgment. Any commonsense preference I may have for my waking impression will be discredited by the schematic argumentation in the third of the five steps I described earlier. In fact, Sextus gives a more detailed argument for the discredit of such a preference: if I am awake, I will be prejudiced in favor of the waking impression, and if I am asleep, I will be prejudiced in favor of the sleeping impression; but since I am always either awake or asleep, my preference for an impression will always be prejudiced and therefore discredited.[18]

So the Pyrrhonist does not appeal to dreaming because there is some real-like quality to the experiences we have in dreams; his use of dreams is in this respect quite different from the Academic skeptic's use. The Pyrrhonist adverts to sleeping impressions simply to set them in conflict with waking impressions.

There is a great deal to puzzle us in what the Academic and Pyrrhonian skeptics do, and I do not aim here to clarify their philosophical endeavors any further. I do, however, want to bring out some striking differences between what they were doing and what Descartes did. Let us now return to the First Meditation.

---

[17] *Outlines* 1.104. Here I use the translation of Annas and Barnes (1985, 79); cf. Sextus Empiricus 1993, 62–63.

[18] *Outlines* 1.112–13; (1993, 66–67).

41

CHAPTER

❖ 3 ❖

Reasons for Suspending Judgment

MORE THAN ONCE Descartes suggests that he is doing nothing new in the First Meditation. Apropos Mersenne's suggestion that methodic suspense of judgment is "merely a fiction of the mind" (2:87; AT 7:122), he says in the Second Replies, "Although I had seen many ancient writings by the Academics and Sceptics on this subject [of doubting all things, especially corporeal things], and was reluctant to reheat and serve this stale cabbage, I could not avoid devoting one whole Meditation to it" (2:94; AT 7:130, trans. altered). Hobbes scathingly remarked that "since Plato and other ancient philosophers discussed this uncertainty in the objects of the senses, and since the difficulty of distinguishing the waking state from dreams is commonly pointed out, I am sorry that the author, who is so outstanding in the field of original speculations, should be publishing this ancient material" (2:121; AT 7:171). Descartes meekly replied:

> I was not trying to sell [the arguments for doubting] as novelties, but had a threefold aim in mind when I used them. Partly I wanted to prepare my readers' minds for the study of the things which are related to the intellect, and help them to distinguish these things from corporeal things; and such arguments seem to be wholly necessary for this purpose. Partly I introduced the arguments so that I could reply to them in subsequent Meditations. And partly I wanted to show the firmness of the truths which I propound later on, in the light of the fact that they cannot be shaken by these metaphysical doubts. Thus I was not looking for praise when I set out these arguments. (2:121; AT 7:171–72)

And Burman reports that while Descartes may have regarded the deceiving God argument (actually its cousin, a "malicious demon" argument) as an innovation, he described much of the First Meditation as taken up with "the customary difficulties of the sceptics" (3:333; AT 5:147).

If Descartes really does think[1] he is simply rehashing Academic or Pyrrhonian skepticism in the First Meditation, he is wrong. It is true that Descartes is like his predecessors in some respects. He makes use of reflection on madness and dreaming,[2] and in his own way he is concerned with suspending judgment and not just with impugning claims of knowledge or certainty. But I think in many important ways what Descartes is doing in the First Meditation is radically different from what the ancient skeptics did.[3] In this chapter, I will explain Descartes's innovation concerning suspense of judgment, and in the next, his innovation in using reflections on madness and dreaming. In chapter 5, I will articulate what I think is the most important difference between ancient and Cartesian skepticism, a difference in the relation between skeptical reflection and common sense.[4]

THE MAXIM FOR ASSENT

Let us look again at Descartes's maxim about suspending judgment. The meditator says:

> Reason now leads me to think that I should hold back my assent from opinions which are not completely certain and indubitable just as carefully

[1] I find it hard to say whether he is sincere or not. He is sometimes outright arrogant in his dismissal of the idea that he has been influenced by someone else's work: for example, concerning Galileo he says, "I have never met him, and have had no communication with him, and consequently I could not have borrowed anything from him" (3:127–28; AT 2:388). This might suggest that when he brings himself to concede he is doing nothing new, he means it. But he also sometimes gratefully seizes upon possible precedents for controversial parts of his work: for example, he begins the Fourth Replies by thanking Arnauld "for bringing in the authority of St. Augustine to support me" (2:154; AT 7:219). This tendency might make us wonder whether he is sincere in saying that his skepticism is not innovative.

[2] In *Academica* 2.15.47, Cicero even invokes the power of the deity to give humans misleading experiences (1951, 526–27).

[3] So do other readers, though they have focused upon different contrasts from the ones I will be stressing. See especially Burnyeat 1982 and M. Williams 1986.

[4] Gail Fine (2000) argues that in many ways Descartes did not himself see the First Meditation as a very radical departure from ancient skepticism. Most of her particular conclusions are, I think, compatible with what I am going to be arguing.

as I do from those which are patently false. So, for the purpose of rejecting all my opinions, it will be enough if I find in each of them at least some reason for doubt. (2:12; AT 7:18)

The maxim he is resolving to follow is this:

Strong maxim: I should withhold my assent from opinions that are not completely certain and indubitable, that is, those in which I find some reason for doubt.

This maxim is much, much stronger than the very weak norms of assent that the Pyrrhonist expected from his interlocutor. The Pyrrhonist expected just that we would agree that we ought to have *some* reason for preferring one impression over a conflicting impression, and that we would not count absurdities, infinite regresses, and circles as rationalizing our preference. By contrast, the meditator's strong maxim is not structured around cases where there are conflicting impressions, and it demands that there be *nothing* to be said *against* what we assent to, not simply that *more* be said *for* it than against.

In fact, the meditator's maxim sounds something like the demanding Stoic maxim for assent. Is the meditator then one of nature's Stoics? Does Descartes mean to imply that we all are, or ought to be? I don't think so: there are at least two respects in which the meditator is unlike a Stoic philosopher.[5] First, as we will soon see, the meditator is ready to concede that it is much more reasonable to assert than to deny claims like "Here is a hand" or "Two plus three equals five," even though he has adduced reasons for doubting them. Second, he *aims* at rejecting all his opinions, though not, like the Pyrrhonist, because he finds it brings him tranquillity, but because he aims at establishing something sturdy and lasting in the sciences.

I think he is invoking this aim as he introduces the strong maxim. The meditator says that reason *"now"* (*jam*) persuades him to regulate assent according to this maxim,[6] and I take that to mean "now that I am eager

---

[5] Thus I disagree with Michael Ayers, who says that the broadly Stoic features of Descartes's epistemology help to explain why "he chose to expound his theory in the context of an internalized dispute with a sceptic" (1991, 83).

[6] The 1647 translation of the *Meditations* has *"des-ja"* for *"jam"* (AT 9:14), which is perhaps why both Haldane and Ross (Descartes 1972, 1:145) and Anscombe and Geach

to find ways to achieve a general demolition of my opinions." So the point is not that conscientious believing requires me to withhold judgment about anything for which I can find some reason for doubt. Rather, the point is that *if* I want to demolish all my beliefs, then sticking to the strong maxim will help me to do what I want to do.

Of course, it might turn out that for many of my beliefs there is not even the least reason to doubt them. In that case, using the strong maxim will not have moved me much closer to my goal of demolishing all my beliefs. But presumably whatever grounds I have for suspecting that the whole body of my beliefs is riddled with error will also be grounds for suspecting that by using the strong maxim I will achieve my goal of general demolition.[7]

Notice that the meditator's motivation for using this maxim arises out of his initial characterization of his epistemic situation: he embraced a number of falsehoods in his childhood, and now that leaves him regarding the body of his beliefs as suspect. In chapter 1 I argued that to make sense of this initial characterization, we must see Descartes as putting words into the meditator's mouth, which means that the meditator is not consistently the figure of common sense that Descartes represents him as being. We can now add that it follows from this that a person of common sense would not have a reason to regulate his judgment in accordance with the strong maxim, as Descartes is presenting it.

Leaving that difficulty aside, let me raise another question about the meditator's maxim. If he is moved to accept it because he wants to demolish his former opinions, then we might wonder whether his maxim, and the doubts he goes on to raise, are really *necessary* for a meditator who is sufficiently strong-willed. After all, Descartes thinks it is always in our

---

(Descartes 1971, 61) translate *"jam"* by "already." Of course, "already" is a possibility for *"jam,"* but I agree with Cottingham et al. that "now" is preferable. My reasons are simply that prior commitment to such a demanding maxim for assent makes no sense for the meditator in his guise as the man of common sense, and that "now" brings out the connection the meditator draws between his strong maxim and his wish to demolish all his opinions.

[7] This does not, however, mean that my prior reason for regarding the body of my beliefs as suspect will *itself* be a reason for doubting my beliefs as I go on to consider them.

power to suspend judgment.[8] So why doesn't he have the meditator just do it? That was one of Gassendi's questions. He agreed with Descartes that it was a good idea to begin by suspending judgment in order to avoid having preconceived opinions, but he thought Descartes should simply announce that that is what he is doing. Fussing with the dream argument and the deceiving God argument and the rest is just a waste of words. In reply, Descartes says that it is not so easy to "free ourselves from all the errors which we have soaked up since our infancy" (2:242; AT 7:348; see also 2:270; AT 9A:204). Rehearsing reasons for doubt helps us to suspend judgment. It is instrumentally related to the goal of suspense.[9]

But could that be Descartes's only reason for having the meditator use the strong maxim? Surely this maxim and the radical grounds for doubt are not just crutches for the weak-willed thinker. I will return to this point after I have addressed yet another question about the meditator's maxim.

The meditator says his "reason" (*ratio*) delivers up his maxim. Almost everyone[10] takes this to mean that Descartes thinks it is a rule that any meditator should recognize as constitutive of conscientious believing. It would be a maxim like "Don't believe something when your only basis for belief is the word of an unreliable informant" or "Don't believe something when you have equally good reasons to believe something incompatible with it." As I have already said, I disagree: I think that Descartes does *not* represent the strong maxim as an ordinary rule for conscientious belief. Let me now lay out some more evidence for my reading.

---

[8] See the Fourth Meditation. He need not be read as saying that for any proposition *p*, I can believe that *p* by deciding to believe that *p*. Rather, he need only be saying that believing that *p* is deciding that *p* is true, and that deciding is an operation of the will. (See B. Williams 1978, 177.) But I do think he must be read as saying that for any *p*, I can suspend judgment whether *p* by deciding to suspend judgment whether *p*, though there are complications when my grasp of *p* is very simple and very clear and distinct. I will say a bit more about will and judgment presently.

[9] Frankfurt gives a complex and interesting account of the instrumental value of the reasons for doubt (1970, chap. 2).

[10] Gaukroger sees Descartes as engaged dialectically with an *opponent* who endorses a "definition" of knowledge (1995, 312); the First Meditation would then be aimed at showing this opponent that various sorts of claims fail to meet the preferred definition. The dialectic would thus be something like that between the Stoics and the Academics. For reasons I will go on to give, I don't think this is the best way to read the First Meditation.

First, if Descartes *did* think that the strong maxim is straightforwardly like ordinary ones, then surely he would be wrong. As I sit here in my campus office, I can think of *a* reason for doubting whether my house is at this moment standing: perhaps the tall eucalyptus trees in back have finally toppled, as eucalyptus trees sometimes do, and where would the ones in back fall if not right onto the roof? So I cannot say I am *absolutely certain* that my house is at this moment standing. But it would be crazy of me to suspend judgment about whether my house is standing. It is far more probable that it is standing than that it is not, and I would be a lot more reasonable to believe that it is standing than not to believe it.

It is a seldom noticed but very important point that at this early stage of his inquiry, Descartes is ready to agree.[11] After giving all of his radical reasons for doubt, he notes that he is having trouble doing as the strong maxim dictates because he keeps thinking of beliefs like "Here's a hand" as

> *what in fact they are*, namely, highly probable opinions—opinions which, despite the fact that they are in a sense doubtful, as has just been shown, it is still much more agreeable to reason [*multo magis rationi consentaneum*] to believe than to deny. (2:15; AT 7:22; trans. altered; emphasis added)

So he is not representing the strong maxim as one that is constitutive of what anyone would count as reasonable, responsible believing.[12]

Of course, sometimes we treat "doubt" as incompatible with belief. I once lived next door to a woman who tried hard to keep up the basic civilities, but whose life lurched from one disaster to the next: she spent her tiny paycheck mainly on beer and bad boyfriends. One morning she borrowed five dollars from me and promised to pay it back that night. Had I said to myself, "I doubt whether I'll see that five bucks again," I would have meant that I was in no position to guess, one way or the

---

[11] David MacArthur (1999) also stresses this point, though by fitting it into a very different interpretative scheme. Peter Markie (1986, esp. chap. 2) stresses this point in a way I find broadly congenial.

[12] Of course, I am not denying that Descartes thinks it is reasonable to use the strong maxim. I have already said that Descartes represents the meditator as seeing an instrumental value in using this maxim. I will go on to explain a strategic value he thinks the strong maxim has, though how this might lead the meditator to adopt it is, I think, a difficult question.

other, whether I'd be repaid, or perhaps even that it was somewhat more likely that I wouldn't than that I would. My "doubt" would be incompatible with my holding a belief about repayment. (For the record, she came through.)

I believe Descartes is saying that the First Meditation doubts are instead like the eucalyptus-falling-on-my-house worry. They are opposed to *certainty*, but not to reasonable belief. This is why he calls them slight, exaggerated, metaphysical, and hyperbolical,[13] and why he thinks he can cleanly sever his meditations from questions about acting reasonably.[14]

Of course, by the end of his inquiry, the meditator will be obliged to reject, or at any rate to revise, many of the beliefs he initially regards as reasonable. For example, the meditator will in the end replace "My dressing gown is purple" with something more like "My dressing gown has surface features, characterizable simply in terms of extension and motion, that cause me to see it as colored purple." But this outcome does not mean that he was unreasonable at the outset when he regarded "Here is my dressing gown" as an opinion it is "much more agreeable to reason to believe than to deny." (I will say more about this at the end of chapter 9.)

Descartes makes just this sort of point in the preface to the French edition of the *Principles*. He says that until he undertook his own philosophical work, people had attained only four "levels of wisdom," the first containing "notions so clear in themselves that they can be acquired without meditation," the second, what we learn from sense experience, and the third and fourth, what we learn from conversing and reading (1:181; AT 9B:5). In previous ages, he says, people had sought in vain a "fifth way of reaching wisdom," one that is more "elevated" and "sure" (1:181; AT 9B:5). In their frustration, these pre-Cartesian philosophers erred in two directions: on one side by doubting everything, even in the "actions of life"; on the other, by embracing as certain every deliverance of the senses (1:182; AT 9B:6). He explains what they *ought* to have done: "so long as we possess only the kind of knowledge that is acquired by

[13] E.g., 2:25 (AT 7:36), 2:121 (AT 7:172), 2:159 (AT 7:226), 2:308 (AT 7:460), 2:373 (AT 7:546) and 2:408–9 (AT 10:513).

[14] E.g., 2:15 (AT 7:22), 2:106 (AT 7:149), 2:243 (AT 7:350–51), 2:308–9 (AT 7:460), 2:320 (AT 7:475).

48

the first four degrees of wisdom we should not doubt what seems true in what concerns the conduct of life, while at the same time we should not consider these things to be so certain that we are incapable of changing our views when we are obliged to do so by some evident reason" (1:182; 9B:7; trans. altered). So long as we have no fifth and more elevated level of wisdom to guide us, we ought to find many of our beliefs worthy of our assent, even while acknowledging that some "evident reason" may oblige us in the end to change our views.

In the First Meditation Descartes's meditator does not yet have any obligation to change his views. Shouldn't he then continue to give his assent to claims it is much more reasonable to assert than to deny? Why should he suspend judgment just because he has found some slight reason for doubt? Why wouldn't that be as ridiculous as it would be for me to suspend judgment about whether my house is still standing?

High Strategy

Many readers assume that Descartes gives the meditator this extreme reaction to "slight" reasons for doubt because he is obsessed with knowledge and certainty.[15] I disagree. I believe that high strategy lies behind the strong maxim, and that when we have appreciated this, we will see the maxim in a new light. I think it is helpful to compare the method of doubt to a game, a game whose rules demand that players do things it would be ridiculous to do if they weren't playing the game. Suppose a girl is playing Statues. When her friend says, "Statues," she immobilizes herself midstride. This would be ridiculous behavior if she weren't playing the game. But because she *is* playing the game, what she does makes sense. The method of doubt is something like a game that requires a player to suspend judgment about any propositions that have a certain characteristic. This characteristic is *not* unreasonableness. The player winds up suspending judgment about things it would be quite reasonable

---

[15] As I read him, his discovery of reasons for doubting even "Here is a hand" does show that we would be wrong, here in the First Meditation, to claim to be absolutely certain that a hand is here. But getting us to withdraw our ordinary claims to *certainty* is not what interests Descartes about the radical reasons for doubt, as I will argue.

to believe. This would be ridiculous behavior if she weren't playing the game. But because she is playing the game, her suspense of judgment makes sense, or so I will argue.

If I am playing the meditator's game, the characteristic that signals me to suspend judgment about a reasonable belief is this: I have a reason for not being completely certain that my belief is true. *For someone using the method of doubt,* a reason for being less than completely certain that *p* is a reason for suspending judgment about *p*.

Now, ordinarily a reasonable person will, and should, strive to assent to what he recognizes would be reasonable for him to believe, and to withhold assent from what he recognizes would be unreasonable for him to believe. So why does the meditator obey a rule for judgment that requires him to do an unreasonable thing, for example, to suspend judgment about whether a hand is here? The answer must be that the meditator wants what he thinks the method of doubt can give him: a way to achieve sturdy and lasting results in the sciences. More specifically, he aims to discover, establish, and embrace the fundamental truths that should replace the basic errors that took root in his mind during his early cognitive development. That is his intellectual motivation for treating the radical grounds for doubt as grounds for suspending judgment.

I am comparing the method of doubt to a game in order to bring out the idea that for Descartes the meditator is supposed to be conducting himself according to a special set of rules that people do not impose upon themselves in ordinary life. But now I must stress a disanalogy between using the method of doubt and playing Statues. If we came across a group of children who all immobilized themselves when one of them called out, "Freeze," or, for that matter, "Yoo-hoo," we would think they were playing a game just like Statues. It doesn't matter much, if at all, what sign it is that triggers their immobility, so long as everyone playing the game knows what it is. The players will have fun in much the same way whichever sign they choose to use. The sign is in that sense arbitrary.

What triggers my suspense of judgment about a reasonable belief is my having a reason for not being completely certain that my belief is true, and that is not an arbitrarily chosen trigger, or even a trigger valuable merely for its usefulness in helping me to suspend judgment. It is nonarbitrarily linked to my aim in playing by the rules of the method of doubt, that is, to my aim of discovering, establishing, and embracing the principles of First Philosophy.

The linkage is simple, but crucial to recognize. Suppose I reflect upon two beliefs, my belief that p and my belief that q. I find upon reflection that both are reasonable for me to hold, and indeed that both are completely free from the everyday worries we may have about our beliefs. Suppose that upon further reflection I can find no grounds whatsoever for being less than entirely certain about p, but that I discover *some* slight grounds for being less than certain about q. (Call my belief that p "absolutely certain," and my belief that q "morally certain.")[16] Now suppose that p and q conflict. Where should I give and withhold my assent? If my reflection upon p and q has been careful—thorough, thoughtful, clear—then I ought to believe that p: I am in the best possible epistemic relation to p. But if I ought to assent to p, and p and q cannot both be true, then I ought to disbelieve that q. I ought to assent to the negation of q. So here are two principles—that in these circumstances I ought to believe that p, and that in these circumstances I ought to disbelieve that q—that are essential to making the method of doubt productive. I ought to believe what I am absolutely certain about, and I ought to disbelieve whatever conflicts with these absolute certainties, even if that means disbelieving something about which I am morally certain. Further, Descartes never entertains the thought that two absolute certainties might conflict with one another. So by enabling me to discover absolute certainties, not only does the method of doubt show me where to give my assent when my investigations lead to propositions incompatible with my ordinary, morally certain beliefs; but also in doing this the method of doubt leads me to the discovery of *incontrovertible* beliefs, beliefs that will be absolutely sturdy and lasting.[17]

[16] I owe this use of the term to Peter Markie (1986, esp. chap. 2).

[17] Bernard Williams says that for Descartes, "absolute knowledge" is impossible without certainty because, in his "historical situation," he took it that "if a claim to . . . the most basic and general kinds of knowledge . . . was not certain, then it must be *relative*, the product, to an undetermined degree, of one's peculiar circumstances" (1983, 344). I do not think we need to see Descartes as making this assumption. His point is simply that, other things being equal and good, we should assent to what is absolutely certain when it conflicts with what is morally certain. The only two contenders, really, will be

51

As I am seeing it, the strategy of the method of doubt is not just a general strategy of forgoing presuppositions and assumptions. Descartes means it to be a strategy uniquely well equipped to work against the authority of common sense, as he conceives that authority. In chapter 5 I will say more about Descartes's engagement with common sense; here I want simply to underline the idea that he sees the method of doubt as uniquely capable of dislodging beliefs that a person of common sense has good reason to believe. In fact, the method of doubt has no strategic role to play unless there is an incompatibility between very well entrenched beliefs of ours and other claims that somehow emerge as absolutely certain.[18] As an epistemological strategy, its point is to show us what to do if we suspect that our commonsense beliefs are in conflict with true propositions. I think this is at least part of what Descartes means in a passage in the Second Replies about the method of the *Meditations*: he says that the primary notions in metaphysics "conflict with many preconceived opinions derived from the senses which we have got into the habit of holding from our earliest years. . . . Indeed, if they were put forward in isolation, they could easily be denied by those who like to contradict just for the sake of it" (2:111; AT 7:157).

If I am right about the simple strategy of the method of doubt, then we must see Descartes's interest in certainty as cool and calculating. He thinks that being absolutely certain has the advantage over being morally certain, and that this advantage is what will permit the overthrow of the dogmas of everyday life (and of scholastic philosophy too). By attending to radical grounds for doubt, we will ultimately be able to discover new, fundamental, and highly consequential truths, and we will have to change our minds about many things. We will not just be buffing a sheen of certainty onto selected beliefs that we had had all along.

So as readers of the *Meditations*, if we see the strong maxim as driven by the strategy of the method of doubt, we are seeing it as highly artificial.

---

the fundamental set of beliefs delivered by common sense and the fundamental set, partly incompatible with these, delivered by the power of clear and distinct understanding.

[18] This is one of the ways in which Descartes's use of the method of doubt differs from his use of the first general rule of the "method," which enjoins us to include in our judgments only what is so clear and distinct that we have "no occasion to doubt it" (1:120; AT 6:18; see also 1:10; AT 10:362). I will bring out further differences in subsequent chapters.

It is a maxim useful to someone with a special aim, not a rule meant to be naturally expressive of the norms of conscientious belief.[19]

Of course, there is nothing about the strategy of this method that guarantees it will do what we want it to do. Perhaps we will find that all claims can be impugned by a reason for doubt. Perhaps we will find some that cannot, but then discover that they are very general or have few interesting implications. But Descartes thinks that, in fact, this method does what we want it to do, that it allows us to establish claims about the existence and character of the self, God, and nature. These claims conflict with competing claims actually made by prereflective people and by many philosophers, for example, the claim that what I am fundamentally is a living organism, or the claim that physical objects are colored. However reasonable those claims may be, they must be rejected in favor of the competing claims that are established by the method of doubt.

Now, Descartes was *wrong* about where the method of doubt would lead: crucial steps of his argument are mistaken. But we must distinguish that criticism from the charge that he assumed certainty was the only epistemic state worth being in and that without it we could never have any good reasons for believing anything. Descartes did think that a *consequence* of the argumentation of the *Meditations* is that we can be certain about fundamental matters, and in Part Two I will argue that he also thought that we would not otherwise be able to believe reasonably, or even to think at all. But that is an *outcome* of his argumentation, not its presupposition.

Notice that once again we are obliged to read Descartes as retrojecting later developments into the motivations for the meditator's conduct in the First Meditation. When the meditator enunciates the strong maxim, he really has no particular reason to think he will benefit from a strategy like the one I have described, because for all he knows so far, it may turn out that *nothing* will emerge as absolutely certain. Now, the meditator need not anticipate strategic developments in order to appreciate the *instrumental* value of his maxim in helping him to demolish his opinions.

---

[19] In a very different way, Bernard Williams makes roughly the same sort of general point, arguing that we might be led to endorse the meditator's maxim by wishing to tailor ordinary strategies of inquiry to a setting free of practical considerations (1978, 37–48).

That part of his motivation for using this strong maxim does not require him to foresee that he will be absolutely certain of propositions that are incompatible with his most reasonable everyday beliefs. But even there the meditator's motivations are not entirely coherent: remember that we cannot make complete sense of his wish to demolish his opinions without seeing him as somehow equipped with Descartes's own view of human cognitive development, a view he cannot adopt as his own until he has actually carried out the strategy of the method of doubt.

One last comment about the strong maxim. Earlier I said that it is a very strong principle by comparison with the ones to which the Pyrrhonist's interlocutor is sensitive. But by seeing it as artificial, we can also see it as in one way quite weak. The meditator conforms his assent to the strong maxim, not because it expresses his norms for belief, but because he thinks this is a good means to his ends. He thinks it will help him achieve the goal of demolishing his beliefs, a goal he has set for himself for other reasons, and he thinks (or Descartes thinks for him) that by using it he will be able to discover and establish the principles of First Philosophy that he wants to erect on the rubble of his demolished beliefs. And in order for the strong maxim to effect this strategy, the meditator needs to make only the weak normative claim that if two propositions conflict, and one is absolutely certain, then he should assent to it and to the negation of the other.

WITHHOLDING ASSENT AND BRACKETING BELIEFS

I turn now to the question whether suspending judgment isn't overkill. Here is what I mean. The comparison between method-driven meditation and a rule-driven game may suggest that Descartes's meditator needn't really suspend judgment, any more than I need really to go to jail playing Monopoly. During a Monopoly game, I go to jail in the sense that something happens inside the game that is like going to jail in real life. (For example, I become unable to participate in certain transactions.) Similarly, one might think that Descartes's method-driven suspense of judgment needn't really be *suspense of judgment*; it need only be something I do inside the meditation that is *like* really suspending judgment. Perhaps inside the meditation I could regard propositions of such-and-such type as having been taken out of play and see which, if any, would then be left in play. My situation would then be comparable to that of jurors who deliberate only after conscientiously following the judge's instructions and putting aside disallowed testimony even though they may believe it to be true.

We could finish this line of thought in two ways. One is by saying that Descartes made a mistake in insisting on suspending judgment. The other is by saying that what Descartes *means* by "suspense of judgment" really just *is* this "bracketing" of propositions: that it is simply a refusal, within the stepwise progress of meditation, to rely upon the various propositions revealed to be not absolutely certain by the radical grounds for doubt.[20]

This second option may seem tempting, because for all I have said so far, bracketing is the aspect of suspense of judgment that matters the most to Descartes's project. He wants to discover and establish fundamental truths, and careful bracketing should enable him to do just that.

Yet I do not think that the notion of bracketing captures everything about method-driven suspense of judgment that is important to Descartes. It is compatible with my bracketing a proposition that I should flat-out continue to believe that it is true: think of the conscientious juror. But I do not believe Descartes would be happy to compare the meditator to the juror. After he lays out the grounds for doubt, he says, "I must withhold my assent from these former beliefs," and he goes on to complain that his "habitual opinions"—those "highly probable" ones "it is much more agreeable to reason to believe than to deny"—"*keep coming back*" (2:15; AT 7:22; trans. altered; emphasis added). What could he mean by saying they "keep coming back"? If the meditator were like the juror, Descartes's complaint would be that these beliefs keep inserting themselves into his deliberations as a basis for subsequent conclusions. But the meditator has not yet tried to deliberate about any conclusions: his complaint cannot at this stage be that his habitual opinions are coloring his deliberations. Rather, his complaint is that he keeps finding himself in the state of believing that these things are true—that a hand is before

---

[20] My description of bracketing is in some ways like Frankfurt's description of the "general overthrow" of belief (1970, chap. 2). I disagree, however, with his claim that Descartes takes up this attitude toward his beliefs prior to considering the skeptical scenarios. Frankfurt acknowledges some of the textual problems for his interpretation.

him, that two plus three equals five, and so on. When he aims at suspending judgment, he is in *some* sense aiming at *not being in the state of believing* that these things are true.

Why is this important to him? In this chapter I have been treating the method of doubt mainly as a method for discovering and establishing truths. But as I mentioned in the introduction, Descartes thought that using the method of doubt had another, very important, function to play in our thinking. It would dispose us to assent to different fundamental (and not-so-fundamental) propositions from those to which we have been accustomed to assent. We systematically distort our beliefs and ideas, attributing sensed qualities to bodies, mixing together ideas of corporeal and thinking natures in our ideas of ourselves, and failing to have any clear idea of the nature of mind or the nature of body. This systematic distortion arises from the domination of our thinking by our senses, and Descartes thinks the method of doubt will help us to notice our mistakes and to correct them by cultivating a habit of detachment from the senses.[21]

What exactly is the habit of mind Descartes wants us to acquire, and how exactly would using the method of doubt help us achieve it? To answer those questions, let me consider secondary qualities and my idea of myself. Descartes does not, of course, expect that at the end of his reflections the meditator would stop perceiving (say) a red color when looking at a tomato, any more than an astronomer would fail to see twinkling bright dots when looking at stars. But I think he *does* expect the meditator to stop judging that what he is looking at is red, just as he thinks the astronomer will have learned to stop judging that what he is looking at is a field of pulsing dots. And I think he may also expect the meditator to stop assuming that he is having a sense perception of a tomato as being red.[22] That is, Descartes thinks that a successful application of the method of doubt would change the meditator's most pervasive habits of judgment about objects, and perhaps his habits of judgment about the nature of his sense experiences, too.

---

[21] Hatfield (1986) gives a sensitive account of the transformative or revelatory character of the meditator's inquiry, especially in its relation to the role his senses play in his system of concepts and beliefs.

[22] This sounds odd, I know. What Descartes perhaps thought we should stop assuming is this: that our sense perceptions represent as a possible state of affairs a physical object—a tomato—with the quality of being red.

In the *Meditations*, Descartes does not unequivocally say that the thought "This tomato is red" or "I am seeing a tomato as being red" is obscure and confused, nor does he unequivocally say that the meditator should deny the truth of these propositions. But he does leave the meditator in a position to see that he has no adequate reason for assenting to them.[23] The meditator is supposed to stop making these judgments, and he is supposed to have gotten out of the habit of making them by using the method of doubt.

Much the same can be said about the cluster of beliefs I hold concerning myself. Here Descartes does unequivocally say that propositions in which I run together mental and physical characteristics—that is to say, most of my "habitual opinions" about myself—are obscure and confused, and that by successfully using the method of doubt, I will stop making those judgments, and will get out of the habit of making them.

These two kinds of examples strongly suggest that the suspense of judgment enjoined by the method of doubt is more than bracketing. After all, I can bracket a proposition while still believing it is true, and if I believe that tomatoes are red throughout my meditations, then I am not going to find that my meditations have prepared me to stop believing that tomatoes are red. (Of course, if my application of the method of doubt led me away from the judgment that physical objects are colored, then at that point I would be rationally obliged to stop believing that tomatoes are red. But my use of the method would not have prepared me for actually making such radical revisions in the system of my beliefs.)

If the suspense of judgment enjoined by the method of doubt is more than bracketing, then what *is* the something more? I have given textual reasons for thinking that Descartes's answer will be that the meditator who suspends judgment about *p* stops believing that *p* is true. Yet in what sense is he not to believe these things to be true? Not in a *completely* ordinary sense, for as Descartes goes on to say, "[T]he task now in hand does not involve action but merely the acquisition of knowledge" (2:15; AT 7:22). So he is "suspending judgment" in some sense relative to "the task now in hand." But what could this special sense be, if not merely the notion of bracketing?

---

[23] Though not, I think, because they fail to be rescued from the scope of First Meditation doubt, as perhaps Rozemond is saying (1998, 72).

I think that Descartes's own answer to this question is unsatisfying, but that he says some things that provide materials for a more satisfying answer. Let us recall that for Descartes, affirming, denying, and withholding assent are all acts, and acts that are operations of the will.[24] There are several familiar questions about exactly what Descartes means by this, but I will mention them only to put them aside. One is the question whether Descartes means to say that I have the power, here and now, to believe just anything, for example, that I am twenty feet tall, or to deny just anything, for example, that I am more than one inch tall. Another is the question whether Descartes means to say that when I am grasping clearly and distinctly some simple truth like "Two plus three equals five" I then and there have the power to deny it or to suspend judgment about it.

About suspending judgment in the First Meditation I think Descartes is clear: it is here and now within my power to suspend judgment about the truth of anything I have believed. At the end of the Fourth Meditation, he resolves to suspend judgment about everything he fails to grasp clearly and distinctly, and he describes the obstacle to this course of action as being the difficulty of remembering this resolution, not some inability to carry it out while trying (2:43; AT 7:61–62). And at this midway stage of his meditations, he would have to be suspending judgment about whether a hand is before him, or indeed whether any material world exists at all,[25] for he does not yet understand these matters clearly and distinctly. Now, the fact that my power of suspending judgment is an operation of my will would not *imply* that in all these First Meditation suspendings of judgment I withhold assent by willing not to assent. It might be, for example, that I withhold assent by considering the evidence in favor of doing so. But I believe that Descartes *does* think that in the First Meditation I withhold assent by willing not to assent, and that he must think this precisely because the evidence—the radical grounds for doubt—does not as it were all by itself demand that I withhold assent. The evidence is relevant to what I do, but it is not enough by itself fully to explain what I do. (I will elaborate this point in chapter 4.)

[24] For a good discussion of this doctrine, and of its relation to the First Meditation, see Rosenthal 1986.

[25] But not, perhaps, about whether two plus three equals five.

I must say I think that Descartes's picture of method-driven suspense of judgment is false to the psychology of human intellectual activity and at odds with the concepts with which that psychology is to be described. People cannot simply will to stop believing the things they find it most reasonable to believe. They can do related things: deliberately seek out new evidence unfavorable to the things they now find it reasonable to believe; or, like the conscientious juror, refuse to allow a belief to play any role in some set deliberation. The meditator, we may agree, does both of those sorts of things. But he can no more suspend judgment by willing to do so than he can believe by willing to do so.

There is, however, another thing that people *can* do, and I think that Descartes usefully emphasizes this related activity. We can imagine what it would be like to believe false the things we actually believe to be true. To take an ordinary kind of case, that is one thing we can do to understand better the perspective of people with whom we disagree: for example, I can imagine being someone who believes that infants are sinful. And sometimes in doing this imaginative work we may find it useful to imagine that the things we believe to be true actually are false. For example, I can imagine that infants are sinful.

When he finds his habitual opinions creeping back in, Descartes decides to imagine that the things he keeps believing to be true actually are false: "I think it will be a good plan to turn my will in completely the opposite direction and deceive myself, by pretending [*fingam*] for a time that these former opinions are utterly false and imaginary. I shall do this until the weight of preconceived opinion is counter-balanced and the distorting influence of habit no longer prevents my judgement from perceiving things correctly" (2:15; AT 7:22). In his reply to Gassendi he uses a different metaphor: "in order to straighten out a curved stick, we [bend] it round in the opposite direction" (2:242; AT 7:349). Of course, Descartes describes this imaginative work as aimed toward rectifying his judgment, here, presumably, by inducing its suspense. But the imaginative project itself is important for Descartes, I think, whether or not he insists on the link to suspending judgment at will. It is important because it gives content to the schematic idea that using the method of doubt will help the meditator become detached from his senses and will prepare him for accepting fundamental beliefs at odds with those his senses seem to teach him. By imagining that "the sky, the air, the earth, colours, shapes, sounds and all external things" (2:15; AT 7:22) are not real, Descartes prepares a place in his mental economy for the eventual conclusion that colors and sounds should not be attributed to objects, and that the extent, shape, and externality of objects are not to be grasped through purely sensuous representation. By imagining "myself as not having hands or eyes, or flesh, or blood or senses" (2:15; AT 7:22–23), I get used to conceiving of myself as something whose nature is not exhausted by those bodily attributes, and even as something that can be thought of apart from such attributes. In fact, these imaginative projects sometimes constitute thought experiments that I must carry out if I am to make my ideas clear and distinct. So not only do they prepare me for new beliefs; in some cases they will be indispensable in helping me form the thoughts—the clear and distinct ideas—that I will come to believe true.

So, when Descartes speaks of "suspending judgment" as the outcome of the First Meditation, he has in mind a complex set of intellectual and imaginative activities, dispositions, and states. Of special importance to the method's goal of establishing fundamental truths is what I have called bracketing. The imaginative work I have just described is of special importance to the goal of detachment from the senses, and ultimately the replacement of one set of fundamental beliefs with a quite different set. To these Descartes conjoins willful ceasing to believe true. This is the least satisfying component of "suspending judgment," but it is also the least crucial to the method of doubt, whose main goals do not require it.[26]

Let me step back a little and compare Descartes's handling of suspense of judgment with that of the Academic and Pyrrhonian skeptics. First, Descartes is like his Hellenistic predecessors in concerning himself with suspending judgment, rather than, say, simply adducing grounds for doubt or hesitation about beliefs he had taken to be certain.[27] Second, he

[26] Of course, Descartes has other interests in the doctrine that we can suspend judgment at will. For him it is part of a theory of human nature, judgment, and error, and part of a theodicy. Is it a *crucial* component of those theories? I am not sure.

[27] Of course, Descartes sometimes uses the *word* "doubt" when the more precise term for what he is interested in would be "suspense of judgment." I think this is because often he wants to draw attention to the radical grounds for doubt that precipitate suspense of judgment in the meditator who is using the method of doubt. It may also be that his choice of words is influenced by the ambiguity in the meaning of "doubt" to which I

is like them in concerning himself with achievement of a state in which the inquirer genuinely does not judge, one way or the other, about a very wide range of matters, rather than with achievement of a state in which the inquirer finds only that he cannot say what the grounds are for a great many of his beliefs. Third, he is like them in considering suspense of judgment about a very wide range of matters to be a form of success, rather than a measure of failure.

But there, I think, the similarities end. For Descartes, the goal of inquiry is knowledge, and suspense of judgment is a preliminary step toward that end. For the Pyrrhonists, and perhaps the Academic skeptics, the goal is a tranquil state, and although they begin inquiring because they are convinced that their inquiry will end in knowledge and knowledge will bring tranquillity of mind, they find that their inquiry ends in suspense of judgment, and that it is suspense of judgment that brings them tranquillity.[28]

There is a more important difference. What I am calling the artificial or method-driven character of Descartes's suspense of judgment means that he does not think of it as fully natural. And I think that for the Pyrrhonist, at any rate, suspense of judgment *is* supposed to be natural. The least that this means is that the Pyrrhonist, but not Descartes, expects that a person who is attentive and who is sensitive to weak norms for belief will find that by attending to the skeptical considerations, he is led to suspend judgment. That is, for the Pyrrhonist, but not for Descartes, considering aspects of dreaming and waking experience will lead to suspense of judgment in as fully natural a way as would considering equally balanced pros and cons. I will say more about this contrast between ancient and Cartesian skepticism in the next two chapters.

---

drew attention earlier. But despite these complications, he is very clear in the *Meditations* that suspense of judgment is what he is after.

[28] It is not clear to me whether the Pyrrhonist who has suspended judgment and achieved tranquillity nonetheless has an independent, truth-seeking motive to continue inquiring. I think this is an important question.

CHAPTER

❖ 4 ❖

Reasons for Doubt

THE MEDITATOR begins his search for reasons for doubting his former opinions by considering his former opinion that what his senses tell him is true. Even a little reflection shows him that what his senses tell him is not always true: sometimes they deceive him, for example, when he is looking at things that are small or far away. So he revises his approving opinion about the reliability of his senses: he holds in effect that what his senses tell him in favorable circumstances is true. His examples are these: "that I am here, sitting by the fire, wearing a winter dressing-gown, holding this piece of paper in my hands, and so on" and "that these hands [and] this whole body are mine" (2:13; AT 7:18). It is not clear exactly what leads him to say that he has formed these opinions in favorable circumstances. They don't involve looking at things that are small or distant; they don't involve situations that create sensory illusions, like the differing media that make a half-submerged oar look bent; they don't involve expert identifications or discriminations, as when a gardener judges that what he holds in his hands is an Icelandic poppy.[1] But it is hard to tell whether one or another of these features is supposed to define this class of opinions.

The meditator at first says that "doubt is quite impossible" (2:13; AT 7:18) when he considers what his senses tell him in favorable circumstances. But he goes on nonetheless to offer two reasons for doubting these opinions, first by comparing himself to a lunatic, and then by reflecting upon dreaming. After he raises the lunacy and dream considerations, the meditator asks himself whether any of his former opinions

[1] Though one culture's generic objects may be another culture's exotica. If shown a seventeenth-century winter dressing gown, I don't think I would know what sort of garment I was looking at, and few seventeenth-century inhabitants of the Americas would have been able to identify the flat thing in the meditator's hand.

remain untouched by doubt. He says that simple truths of arithmetic and geometry survive, for example, "Two plus three equals five" and "A square has no more than four sides." He may also be saying that the lunacy and dream arguments leave untouched his very general belief that corporeal things exist, though this is not clear. He does not offer any account of how he knows these things; he seems at this point to have let go of the idea that what he has accepted as "most true" is what he has acquired from the senses (2:12; AT 7:18). But, he goes on to say, there are reasons for doubt that impugn even these surviving opinions, along with all the other beliefs that were impugned by the lunacy and dream arguments. These reasons for doubt concern God or whatever it is that causes the meditator to be as he is—fate or chance, perhaps.

Of course, the radical grounds for doubt impugn beliefs that the meditator can also doubt for other reasons. ("That distant tower is round.") But what is important about the radical grounds for doubt is that they also give him reasons for doubting beliefs like "Here is a hand" and "Two plus three equals five," beliefs that are otherwise impeccable. While it is not clear how Descartes would want to characterize the norms that these beliefs meet, it is clear that he thinks the *only* way anyone could doubt such beliefs is by invoking the radical doubts. So these are beliefs that a prereflective person of common sense would rightly regard as beliefs that meet the norms we respect in our everyday lives. In the previous chapter, I called these "moral certainties"; I will continue to call them that, though I want to stress that the reservation the term suggests ("*merely* morally certain") is not one that Descartes would attribute to anyone who hadn't already launched himself into an inquiry guided by the method of doubt.[2]

I think that all four of the radical grounds for doubt—lunacy, dreaming, God, and "fate or chance"—have a similar structure, and their structure is what I want to focus upon in the rest of this chapter. This will be useful in two ways. First, it will help me clarify how Descartes saw what I have been calling the artificial character of the radical doubt. And second, it will help me explain in Part Two of this book how Descartes thought he could *use* his doubt to discover and establish principles of First Philosophy.

---

[2] Markie (1986, chap. 2) gives a very clear account of several aspects of this notion of moral certainty; as I mentioned in a note to the previous chapter, I have borrowed from him this use of the term.

Skeptical Scenarios as Explanations for False Beliefs

The structure of radical grounds for doubt is clearest in the lunacy and deceiving God arguments, but I think once we see it in those arguments, we can discern it in the dream and "fate or chance" arguments as well. In all four cases, Descartes constructs a *skeptical scenario*. A skeptical scenario is a story about how I have come to have the beliefs that I have, a story according to which those beliefs are false. Take my current belief that I have shoes on my feet. I ordinarily assume that I believe this because I see and feel the shoes on my feet. But consider this story: I falsely believe that I have shoes on my feet because my brain is damaged by "persistent black bile vapors" (2:13; AT 7:19; trans. altered), so that when I look at and wiggle my bare toes, they look and feel shod to me. Now, of course, I don't think that this story gives a correct account of my belief: I think I have shoes on and that my brain is normal. But on reflection, I do not see how to rule this story out. To rule it out, it seems, I would need somehow to appeal to the fact that I, unlike a lunatic, am currently seeing and feeling the shoes on my feet. But the brain-damaged lunatic would take himself to be able to make just such an appeal, and so it seems that my appeal will not do the work I need it to do. A skeptical scenario, then, is a story about how I have come to have the beliefs I have, a story according to which the beliefs are false; and it is a story that I see no way to rule out as the correct story about my beliefs.[3]

The lunacy scenario is robustly causal: the story is one that features an explicitly causal hypothesis about how I have come to have my beliefs. While Descartes himself did not fully subscribe to the theory of humors that he alludes to here, he did believe that madness was a state in which people acquire false beliefs because their brains are diseased.[4] Here is how he describes madness in the *Optics*:

> [I]t is the soul which sees, and not the eye; and it does not see directly, but only by means of the brain. That is why madmen and those who are asleep often see, or think they see, [*voyent . . . ou pensent voir*] various objects which are nevertheless not before their eyes: namely, certain vapours disturb their

---

[3] Curley also argues that for Descartes the skeptical scenarios must be causal or explanatory in character (1978, 86–91), and MacArthur makes a similar claim (1999, 34 ff.).

[4] See also 3:262 (AT 4:281–82) and 2:160 (AT 7:228).

brain and arrange those of its parts normally engaged in vision exactly as they would be if these objects were present. (1:172; AT 6:141)

So the state of the lunatic is one in which the causal mechanism of sense perception malfunctions, leaving him seeing, or thinking he sees, what is not there. The way he is seeing, or thinking he sees, explains why he has the false beliefs that he has.[5] In the *Meditations*, Descartes describes the causal glitch in terms that the ordinary person or the scholastic inquirer might use; his own theory, though rigorously mechanistic, also postulates a disturbance of the normal cerebral mechanisms of sensation.

As the passage I have just quoted suggests, Descartes himself sees the occurrence of dreams as having the same basic kind of explanation as the occurrence of deranged waking sensation.[6] In sleep, the "animal spirits" that course through our nerves continue to move even though they are not being moved by the usual impingements of objects upon our sense organs. These continued motions themselves move the pineal gland this way and that, and the motions of the pineal gland cause us to have various sorts of experiences, just as they do in waking life.[7] Descartes[8] would

---

[5] Descartes has close to nothing to say about the way in which these delusions must be fairly systematic, if the person convinced his head is made of glass, for example, is to see no incompatibility with the fact that rapping it smartly does not cause it to shatter. I should mention here that many acute readers think that he is not really offering a skeptical scenario in the passage about lunatics. (See, for example, B. Williams 1983, 340, and Frankfurt 1970, 37 ff.) They read him as sketching such an idea only to dismiss it; Frankfurt, for one, thinks that his reason for doing this is to stress that the meditator assumes, at least provisionally, his own rationality. This is incompatible with a passage in the Seventh Replies (2:310; AT 7:461) and more generally with Descartes's account of madness, and I argue (in Broughton forthcoming) that this is to miss the heuristic and argumentative force of the lunacy and dream arguments.

[6] He also links them in a letter to Princess Elizabeth (3:262; AT 4:281–82).

[7] See the *Traité de l'Homme*, AT 11:197 ff., and *Passions of the Soul*, pt. 1, art. 26 (1:338; AT 11:348–49). As the latter suggests, Descartes is sometimes drawn to the view that dreaming involves a contribution from the faculty of imagination (see also 2:248; AT 7:358–59), and in at least one place, he tries out the same idea concerning madness (2:407; AT 10:511). I can see why his efforts at theodicy would make this attractive to him, but I think this view is incompatible with the actual character of dreams, as most people experience them, and with the character of lunacy as Descartes describes it.

[8] He was not the only one. Malebranche, for example, lumps together "a madman" and "someone asleep or in a high fever" as people who have ideas of things that do not exist (1997, 217).

expect his readers to be unsurprised by his structuring a dream argument in the same way he had structured a lunacy argument: for the ancient skeptics, the two phenomena also provided similarly structured skeptical considerations (though if I am right, the ancient structure differs from the Cartesian structure).[9]

Now, the meditator does not explicitly state his worries about dreaming in causal terms. He does not say that for all he can tell, his present visual experience is caused in the same way that his dreams are caused. Nor does Descartes give the meditator a theory about how dreams are caused, analogous to the theory he gives him about madness. But the skeptical scenario in the dream argument is like the lunacy scenario in *explaining how the meditator could have acquired this belief if it were false.* And that is really all I am saying when I say that the scenario is causal. (In Part Two I will explain why this matters.)

It is pretty clear that the deceiving God argument sketches out a causal scenario. Descartes works out the following story: "omnipotent God" who "made me the kind of creature that I am," has "brought it about that there is no earth, no sky, no extended thing, no shape, no size, no place, while at the same time ensuring that all these things appear to me to exist just as they do now," and that "I go wrong every time I add two and three" (2:14; AT 7:21). So I have been made to be the kind of creature to whom it seems evident that things with shapes and sizes exist and that two added to three equals five; yet these things are false. This scenario is unlike the lunatic scenario in offering no specific account of the mechanism by which I acquire the false beliefs, and it is unlike the dream scenario in offering no common experience to which I can refer in order to gesture at the relevant cause ("whatever it is that causes dreams"). But it does have some bite to it, for it does not *hypothesize* the existence of "omnipotent God" who "made me the kind of creature that I am." The meditator says that the existence of such a being, and his relation to me, is a "long-standing opinion" that is "firmly rooted in my mind" (2:14; AT 7:21). What the skeptical scenario hypothesizes is that this being has made me so that I err systematically, in the most basic and obvious matters. I may try to rule this hypothesis out by saying that God, being good, would

---

[9] This is true not just of Cicero and Sextus, but also of Plato (1992, 22; *Theaetetus* 157e–58b) and Galen (Annas and Barnes 1985, 86).

not create me so that I am deceived. But I actually *am* deceived at least some of the time, and so that effort to rule out the deceiving God hypothesis fails.

The last skeptical scenario is a sort of deceiving God hypothesis for agnostics[10] or atheists. Even though they would not explain themselves by reference to God, they must have *some* account of how they have been made to be the kind of creature that they are. "According to their supposition . . . I have arrived at my present state by fate or chance or a continuous chain of events, or by some other means" (2:14; AT 7:21). But if that is how I have been made to be the kind of creature that I am, then not only is there a story about how I have come to be the kind of creature who is deceived even about basic and evident matters; it is a story that is if anything more plausible than the deceiving God story. "[S]ince deception and error seem to be imperfections, the less powerful they make my original cause, the more likely it is that I am so imperfect as to be deceived all the time" (2:14; AT 7:21). It seems odd to some readers for the meditator to attribute to anyone the view that fate or chance is a kind of cause, but I think Descartes is giving the meditator a natural enough thought. Certainly many people do try to use such notions in explanations: ". . . because it was meant to be"; ". . . because my number was up."

RADICAL GROUNDS AND THE METHOD OF DOUBT

If we step back and look at the four skeptical arguments, then, we can see them as sharing a very general structure. Each of them presents a skeptical scenario—a causal or explanatory story about how I got my beliefs, one according to which they are false—and in each case, Descartes claims, I cannot rule out the scenario's being correct. Of course, there is a great deal more to be said about each of these arguments, and there are many ways in which they are unlike one another. But I want to focus on this common structure, and to see what it tells us about the method of doubt.

---

[10] Of course, the agnostic could construct a skeptical scenario according to which (a) God exists and (b) he is a deceiver. Depending on the form his atheism took, so could the atheist.

Notice first that this is a different structure from that of the skeptical considerations put forward by the ancient skeptics.[11] We certainly do not see here the Pyrrhonian production of conflicting impressions: there are no pairings of the wine seeming sweet and the wine seeming sour, or of my scarf's appearing in my dream to be striped and appearing now to be flowered.[12] Nor are we under pressure to agree that we have no reason to prefer one impression over the other. Descartes's reasons for doubt are also unlike those adduced by the Academic skeptics to defeat their Stoic opponents. The Academic skeptics did claim that the impressions of dreamers and madmen can be as convincing, intense, and apt to provoke feeling, action, and assent as those of people who are awake and sane. But they did not imagine that *that by itself* was a skeptical consideration. They did not use this claim to argue that no one can rule out the possibility that his present experience arises in the same way that lunatics' or dreamers' experiences arise. Rather, they used this claim to show the Stoics that none of their experiences are cognitive impressions. (I will say more in chapter 5 about these contrasts between Cartesian and ancient skepticism.)

The Cartesian scenarios have two striking aspects: the causal or explanatory component, and the seeming impossibility of ruling them out as correct. In later chapters I will argue that the causal component reflects a deep metaphysical commitment that Descartes thinks we must all make, and that seeing this is crucial to understanding how he thinks the meditator can lever himself out of doubt. For now, I want just to note several points about this causal component. First, it is what saves the skeptical scenarios from being like neurotic worries or sophomoric gainsaying.[13] The meditator does not simply say to himself, "Although I be-

[11] So I disagree with Popkin's claim (1968, 181) that Descartes's dream argument is a standard Pyrrhonian argument, and with Curley's general claim (1978) that Descartes is giving arguments meant to be like those of the ancient skeptics. Gaukroger (1995, 309 ff.) thinks Descartes and the ancient skeptics are unlike, but not quite in the ways I am articulating in this chapter and the next.

[12] Annas and Barnes (1985, 86) clearly describe this contrast between Cartesian and Pyrrhonian appeals to dreaming.

[13] I speculate that in the Second Replies, Descartes is contrasting the robustly explanatory skeptical scenario of the First Meditation with the pallid possibility that the things

lieve I have shoes on, perhaps I don't. And if I don't, I cannot tell that I don't, for I am looking and touching, and I keep seeing and feeling shoes." Second, the deviance of the causal account may actually be more important than the falsity of the belief caused when it comes to making the scenario one worth taking seriously. Barbara Winters (1981) has argued that this is so. Consider this skeptical scenario: my current belief that I have shoes on is true, but it has been caused in the way that dreams are caused (that is, it is a dream). Winters claims that we must regard this as a reason for doubt if we count the false-belief version as a reason for doubt, and she claims further that the skeptical punch comes from the presentation of a causal history for the belief that is incompatible with its constituting knowledge. If this is right, we would have to see the causal component as not just important but indispensable.

In saying that each skeptical scenario has a causal or explanatory component, I am in agreement with Edwin Curley, who says that "a reasonable ground for doubting a proposition must offer some explanation of how it is that we might erroneously believe the proposition even if the explanation is only conjectural" (1978, 86). But I disagree with him about why this is so. The reason for this requirement, according to Curley, is that we have a tendency to believe true such propositions as "Here is a hand" and "Two plus three equals five," and so without an explanation of error, the skeptical hypothesis will not be "persuasive" (88). Curley does not mean that a skeptical hypothesis is a reasonable ground for doubt only if we find ourselves persuaded that it is correct. But he does seem to think that the role of the skeptical hypotheses is to *counterbalance*, or "overcome," the tendency toward belief that we have (89). This would fit with a general claim he makes, that Descartes is trying to show that he could play by the Pyrrhonist's rules and yet end up with knowledge.

If this is what Curley means, then I disagree. I do not think that for Descartes the problem posed by the skeptical arguments has the structure

---

we perceive clearly and distinctly "appear false to God or to an angel" (2:104; AT 7:146)— pallid, because the possibility has no explanatory element. This is the only sort of potentially skeptical possibility that we could raise after we find that it is "impossible for us ever to have any reason for doubting what we are convinced of" (2:103; AT 7:144), and Descartes would be saying that it isn't a ground for doubt; it is just a "kind of story" (2:104; AT 7:146).

of the Pyrrhonian modes.[14] "I see that I have shoes on" is not supposed to be counterbalanced by "I am dreaming that I have shoes on," not even after I see that I cannot rule the latter out. For one thing, the conflicting impressions would have to conflict in their that-clauses to fit the Pyrrhonian schema. For another, the modes balance the conflicting impressions by depriving the interlocutor of any way to offer a reason for preferring the one over the other, but Descartes allows that we have reason to prefer the impressions of waking life; in fact, he insists on it. I will say more about this in chapter 5.

But there may be something else behind Curley's way of seeing the meditator's reasons for doubt, something having to do with the second of the two features I have just mentioned. This is the meditator's inability to rule the skeptical scenarios out as correct. It may seem that this inability means that once the meditator accepts the skeptical scenarios as reasons for doubt, he must also accept them as reasons for suspending judgment. And we might then see the meditator's position in something like the way Curley describes it: he has no basis for choosing between the skeptical scenarios and the beliefs of common sense. I will say more about this, too, in the next chapter, where I will argue that this is not how Descartes sees the meditator's position.

I want to close this chapter by returning to a claim I made earlier about the method of doubt. I said that Descartes thought of it as a way of discovering, as well as establishing and embracing, the principles of First Philosophy. I can now say something more about why he would have thought this. If we consider just the meditator's strong maxim ("Withhold assent from opinions when you find any ground for doubting

---

[14] In order to squeeze Descartes's reasons for doubt into the Pyrrhonian mold, Curley develops an elaborate account of Cartesian reasons for doubt. He thinks Descartes needs to show that the skeptical hypotheses provide an "equally compelling counterargument" (1978, 117) against whatever is to be said in favor of "Here is a hand" or "Two plus three equals five." As Curley is aware, he faces a problem in trying to represent the skeptical hypotheses as being as apparently compelling as "Here is a hand" or "Two plus three equals five." So he represents the particular beliefs as resting upon *principles* that are not themselves terribly credible and can therefore be counterbalanced by the not terribly credible skeptical hypotheses (1978, 120–22). But the only reason to adopt this interpretative strategy is to save the Descartes-as-Pyrrhonist reading, and as I am arguing here in Part One, that is a reading we should not try to save.

them"), we will find little to encourage the hope that by using it we will discover fundamental truths. Descartes's methodic insistence on complete certainty does not by itself explain why he thought the method of doubt would help him discover whether God exists, or what the natures of body and the human soul are.

What is helpful, though, is to consider the meditator's maxim together with the character of the skeptical considerations he actually goes on to offer. The scope of the skeptical scenarios is so wide that when we consider them, we may wonder how it is possible that someone using the strong maxim will ever be in a position to assent to *anything*. This suggests that if someone did somehow manage to assent to something, he would not find himself assenting, say, to "Here is a hand" *and not* to "Here is a piece of paper." He would instead somehow find that he can assent to something underlying, or including, or implying, a very broad class of relatively specific propositions, and we might guess that what would get him into that position would be the discovery of relatively fundamental, or inclusive, or fruitful propositions. And if we consider not just the scope of the skeptical scenarios but also their structure, we can make even more sense of the meditator's confidence that the method of doubt would reveal fundamental truths. Each scenario is skeptical because I cannot see how to rule out the possibility that a very general aspect of my experience is causally connected to reality in a deviant way. To have defeated these doubts, I will need to have established how my sensory experiences are connected to the states of my body and, through my body, to the world around me, and how my experiences as of grasping transparent truths are related to the creator of my intellectual constitution. If defeating the First Meditation doubts somehow involves establishing truths about these very general connections between me and the world and between God and me, then it would be natural to expect that successful use of the method of doubt would involve discoveries about God, mind, and body—about the principles of First Philosophy.

❖ 5 ❖

Common Sense and Skeptical Reflection

I~N THE LAST TWO CHAPTERS~, I have described Descartes as structuring reasons for suspense of judgment and reasons for doubt in ways that mark significant departures from the ancient skeptics. I want now to consider how Descartes puts philosophical reflection into relation to prephilosophical common sense. I will again argue that he departs in significant ways from the ancient skeptics, but I will also argue that his way of conceiving this relation is equally remote from our own, and that in at least one important respect he is more like the ancients than he is like us.

Recall that there are two rather different dialectical situations in which relations between common sense and skeptical reflection might have emerged in ancient skepticism. One is the Academic skeptics' reactions to the Stoic doctrine of assent to "cognitive impressions." The Stoics claimed that each of us has many cognitive impressions, typically sense impressions of a particular sort, and that these cognitive impressions are in one way or another the basis for everything that we can know. A cognitive impression is one that "[1] arises from what is and [2] is stamped and impressed exactly in accordance with what is, [3] of such a kind as could not arise from what is not."[1] The Stoics held that the wise person withholds assent unless he is presented with a proposition suitably related to a cognitive impression. So if a Stoic could be persuaded that *no* impressions meet all three clauses of the definition, then he would hold that the wise person will withhold assent from every proposition. What the Academic skeptics argued was that no putative cognitive impression is "of such a kind as could not arise from what is not." The Academics had

---

[1] Sextus Empiricus, *Against the Logicians* 7.248 (1997, 132–33). Here I use the translation provided by Long and Sedley (1987, 243). See also Cicero, *Academica* 2.6.18 and 2.24.77 (1951, 490–91, 564–65).

two strategies for persuading the Stoic of this. One was to argue that for any impression derived from an existent object, we can imagine an impression that is just like it in every *sensible* detail but that is nonetheless not derived from that object. The other was directed against the Stoic who insisted that cognitive impressions are "of such a kind" as to be uniquely convincing, intense, and apt to provoke emotions, action, and assent. To this the Academics replied by saying that the impressions people have while drunk, dreaming, or mad can be as convincing and real-like as those of the sober, wide-awake, and sane person.

Recall now a different skeptical strategy, the one presented by Sextus Empiricus in the Ten Modes. In each mode the Pyrrhonist begins by asking us to consider two conflicting impressions, and then leads us into conceding that we have no grounds for deciding that one is to be preferred over the other. The result of this concession is that we suspend judgment about how things are, and give credence only to propositions that state how things appear to us to be. So suppose I say, looking at my scarf, "Here is a flowered scarf. I'm looking at it up close, in broad daylight, wide awake, sane, and sober. Nothing can move me to suspend judgment about this." The Pyrrhonist will reply by first getting me to agree that there is a conflicting impression—for example, a dream impression that my scarf is striped—and then asking me to say why I prefer my present impression over the conflicting one. No matter what I say—for example, that one ought always to judge that things are as the sane, wide-awake person can plainly see them to be—the Pyrrhonist will trot out schematic arguments to show that the effort to rationalize the preference leads to absurdity, circularity, or an infinite regress. Considering these arguments will then move me to suspend judgment.

Now I want to go further into the question how Descartes departs from these Academic and Pyrrhonian reflections, paying special attention to how he brings common sense and skeptical reflection into relation to one another. I think there is no question that this relation was important to Descartes; as I have said, he took care to underline the commonsense character of the 'I' of the *Meditations*. (I should add that I think that the growing importance of this relation is one of the most conspicuous and interesting changes in Descartes's work between 1618 and 1640.)[2]

---

[2] See Garber 1992, chap. 2, esp. 48 ff., and Hatfield 1986.

I will say something about the notion of "common sense" presently, but I want to begin by contrasting my view with one that Michael Williams has articulated. Like me, Williams sees Descartes and the ancient skeptics as differing in the way they structure the relation between skeptical considerations and ordinary life, but I disagree with him about exactly how to describe this difference.

Michael Williams's Reading

Williams says that "classical [Hellenistic] suspension of judgment is . . . reached by means that involve an extension of ordinary, nonphilosophical doubting, the sort of doubting that comes as a result of exposure to conflicting opinions, each plausible in its way" (1986, 120). He stresses that the Ten Modes "are not presented as theoretical arguments for the impossibility of knowledge"; "[t]he marshaling of conflicting opinions, therefore, remains the basis of classical skepticism" (121). Pyrrhonian skepticism remains open-ended, since it never pretends to show the impossibility of finding an appearance for which a conflicting appearance cannot be discovered (124). By contrast, Williams says, Descartes aims to raise a "definitive doubt" so that "he will be able subsequently to claim that whatever principles survive his skeptical scrutiny have been established with metaphysical finality" (124). Thus "Descartes must represent the credibility of his former opinions as resting ultimately on certain highly general epistemological principles that can be exhaustively examined for possible sources of error" (124). Descartes says that he will examine such principles for practical reasons, because examining his beliefs one by one would take more time than he has. But, Williams claims, what Descartes is really doing is "projecting into common sense a theoretical conception of justification disguised as a matter of practical convenience" (125).

Williams argues that Descartes implicitly represents common sense as assuming that in sense experience, what we are directly aware of are just our own thoughts, and that in coming to have knowledge of the things around us, we must draw inferences from the existence and character of these thoughts to the existence and character of the things around us. But this, Williams says, is not an assumption of common sense, which holds only "that the (physical) senses are what put us (embodied persons) in touch with external objects (i.e., objects outside our bodies)" (131). The assumption that Descartes attributes to common sense is itself a piece of Cartesian metaphysics, for it draws upon "the Cartesian analysis of sensation into mental and physical components" and thus also upon "the Cartesian conception of the mental" (131). But this spoils Descartes's use of the method of doubt, for he needs to begin his inquiry without presupposing any of the principles that he aims to establish by using the method of doubt.

Williams believes that without the metaphysical assumptions, the First Meditation doubts would not even appear to generate their broad skeptical conclusions; indeed, this is his main reason for saying that Descartes must be retrojecting Cartesian metaphysics into the First Meditation. Williams claims that the principle about the senses that Descartes attributes to the meditator could be undermined by reflection on dreaming only if the principle were understood in Cartesian metaphysical terms. He is not arguing that reflection on dreaming can *never* lead to *any* sort of skepticism without the Cartesian assumptions. Both the Pyrrhonian and Academic skeptics employed reflection on dreaming in skeptical lines of thought. But their conclusions, Williams says, are not equivalent to Descartes's, for they do not conclude with suspense of judgment about the existence and nature of every possible physical object.

Focusing on the Academic use of dreaming, Williams says that the differing Academic and Cartesian conclusions can be traced to a difference in the details of how they actually use dreaming. The Academics use dreaming to show that the convincing and real-like quality of putative cognitive impressions is also characteristic of at least some of the false impressions of dreamers. They do not argue that in addition the *content* of some dreams is indistinguishable from the specific *content* of waking impressions. They employ arguments about indistinguishability of content only in talking about pairs of putative cognitive impressions, like the twin brothers or the eggs; and in those pairs, each impression is true: each "arises from what is and is stamped and impressed exactly in accordance with what is." Descartes, however, *combines* these two sorts of indistinguishability (of real-like quality and of content) in his reflection on dreaming, detaching the indistinguishability of content from the Academic assumption that the impressions are true. And this, Williams claims, Descartes could not do without relying upon Cartesian metaphysical assumptions: "To effect this union [of considerations that the Academics keep distinct], Descartes must dissociate indistinguishability of perceptions with respect to content from causation by near-identical objects. His new conception of the mental, which allows him to think of 'sensations' in abstraction from the senses, makes this possible" (134). I understand Williams to be claiming here that consideration of dreaming will lead to Descartes's skeptical conclusions only if we import a conception of sensation according to which the fact that I am having sensations of S as P (say, of myself as robed in a dressing gown) entails that it seems to me that S is P but does *not* entail that my sense organs are being affected.

I do not think Descartes intends to be attributing this metaphysically loaded conception of sense experience to the meditator here at the outset, nor do I think it is clear that he must. Consider a version of the meditator's claim that is not metaphysically loaded:

> *Ordinary principle about perception*: We come to know of the existence, location, properties, and relations of many things by looking at them, touching them, hearing them, and tasting and smelling them.[3]

This, I think, really is part of our ordinary conception of knowledge and perception, and it does not imply or presuppose any Cartesian metaphysics of sensation.[4] Now consider another claim:

---

[3] This is less loaded than the principle Williams himself supplies: "the (physical) senses are what put us (embodied persons) in touch with external objects (i.e., objects outside our bodies)" (131). It is no more a part of common sense to regard what puts us in touch with objects as simply *physical* than it is to regard our sensations as a species of Cartesian ideas, and while some people surely do think of us as embodied—that is, as having some aspect of ourselves that is *in* a body—others just as surely do not. There are also some cavils to be raised about "objects outside our bodies," I think; for example, surely we think that our senses sometimes "put us in touch with" our own bodies.

[4] And so I disagree with another line of thought that seems to surface in Williams's paper, which is that a "regimentation" of knowledge is reflected in general claims about the bases of our knowledge, and that such regimentation is also an illegitimate effort to disguise philosophy as common sense. This claim would be in some tension with his own readiness to articulate a general, commonsense claim about one basis of our knowledge (see previous note), so perhaps I am wrong to attribute this line of thought to him.

Ordinary claim about dreaming: When I have sense perceptions—that is, when I look at things, or touch, hear, taste, or smell them—I am having experience that is indistinguishable by me at the time from some dreams, which are experiences that I have had when I was not having sense perceptions.

The truth of this claim is just a fact of life, and again the claim does not invoke the special Cartesian conception of sensation.

In the First Meditation, it is surely these *ordinary* claims to which the meditator is helping himself as he describes his former beliefs and then constructs the dream argument. In having the meditator draw upon these ordinary claims, Descartes is right about this much: the ordinary claims are enough to justify the claim that dreams are indistinguishable from sense perception both in content and in convincingness. And *if* that double indistinguishability is all that Descartes needs to generate a doubt about the ordinary principle about perception, then he will have generated a doubt about a very great deal of what we believe without retrojecting Cartesian metaphysics into the meditator's initial way of understanding himself.

I am ready to concede, however, that this leaves unanswered two very important questions. The first is the question whether Descartes departs from the ordinary conceptualization of knowledge and perception in some *other* way. Perhaps this double indistinguishability is *not* all that Descartes needs in order to generate a doubt about the ordinary principle about perception, and perhaps the additional materials he needs are tainted by elements foreign to common sense, either because they are fragments of Cartesian metaphysics or because they represent some departure from the ordinary that is broader in its philosophical appeal.[5] The second question is why the ancient skeptics did not avail themselves of the double indistinguishability of dreams and sense perception. One real advantage of Williams's way of contrasting Descartes and the ancient skeptics is that it helps to explain why the ancient philosophers never gave a Cartesian dream argument. (The explanation would be that they

[5] In chapter 1, I argued that Descartes retrojects his own account of human cognitive development, and in chapter 3 I argued that we must attribute this account to the meditator if we are to make complete sense of his intellectual motivations. But I don't think that the retrojected account of cognitive development would be required to explain why the appeal to dreaming is a reason for doubt.

did not endorse the crucial piece of Cartesian metaphysics.) But if I am right that double indistinguishability does not require acceptance of a Cartesian metaphysics of sense perception, then we need some other way to explain why the ancient skeptics did not try to exploit it.

CONTRASTS BETWEEN ANCIENT SKEPTICS AND DESCARTES'S MEDITATOR

Williams stresses the idea that Descartes and the ancient skeptics have different ways of bringing skeptical reflection into relation to common sense. While I disagree with him about what the difference is, I agree that there is one, and that it is something worth trying to pin down. I explained in chapter 2 why I think we cannot see the Pyrrhonian and Academic skeptics as ceding any special authority to commonsense belief. I think that Descartes does cede authority to commonsense belief, and I think this marks an important departure from the ancient skeptics' way of bringing ordinary belief into relation with skeptical reflection. Ironically, this nearly reverses Williams's sense of the contrast: where he saw the ancient philosophers as preserving something essential to the perspective of common sense and Descartes as distorting it, I see Descartes as attending to something that we think characterizes commonsense belief and the ancient philosophers as ignoring it. Let me explain my view.

I will begin by drawing some contrasts between Descartes and the Pyrrhonist. Descartes has the meditator begin his examination of his sense-based beliefs by putting aside those that are dubitable because they may involve deception by the senses. The only example he gives is that of "objects which are very small or in the distance" (2:12; AT 7:18), and so as I have said before, it is hard to know exactly what class of opinions he has in mind.[6] In any case, the meditator says that the opinions he does *not* put aside are ones about which "doubt is quite impossible" (2:13; AT 7:18). These beliefs—about the fire, the dressing gown, the paper, his

---

[6] I think the question how to characterize this class is difficult. I suspect that a good answer will not line up very tidily with classes of opinion that have been of contemporary concern, for example, opinions about "generic objects," as Cavell describes them (1979, chap. 3).

hands—are the ones I have been calling "moral certainties."[7] Concerning *this* class of beliefs, Descartes does *not* go on to find either conflicting impressions or twins-and-eggs cases, and at this juncture, he is granting something that the Pyrrhonist would not grant: the rationality of the meditator's preference for the impressions had by "us"—sane, sober, wide-awake people—when we are looking at middle-size, nearby things. What I am saying Descartes grants is closely related to the ordinary principle about perception that I articulated earlier. ("We come to know of the existence, etc., of many things by looking at them, etc.") The main difference is that the ordinary principle about perception carries with it the assumption that we often do look at things (etc.) and that we know when we are doing this.

Of course, Descartes immediately goes on to offer reasons for doubting the moral certainties. But even then he does not have the meditator give up his preference for the beliefs that we form when we are sane, sober, wide awake, and looking at middle-size, nearby things. What the meditator gives up is his confidence that (say) here and now he is looking at his hand, and not just dreaming that he is looking at it. By allowing the meditator to retain his preference for sane, waking experience, Descartes takes seriously an idea about the authority of sense experience that is central to the perspective of common sense. He is in this respect very different from the Pyrrhonist.

My reason for saying that Descartes does not have the meditator give up his commonsense attitude toward sense experience is that I believe the meditator *cannot* coherently give this attitude up and still offer the dream argument. It is crucial to Descartes's dream argument that the meditator should find it obvious that if he dreams that p, and believes p on that basis, then he has no reason for believing that p. It is also crucial that the meditator should find it obvious that, at least in the best circumstances, perceiving something provides him with knowledge about it. The meditator's problem is that he can find no way to rule out the possibility that he is in the epistemically bad position (dreaming); this, he thinks, gives him a reason for doubting whether he is in the good episte-

---

[7] The class of moral certainties also includes belief in such propositions as "Two plus three equals five." In this chapter I am focusing upon the sense-based moral certainties; I will say something about the full range of examples in chapter 9.

mic situation he took himself to be in. If he did not take it that perceiving something can give him knowledge, and that dreaming cannot, then the *way* in which he uses dreaming to generate a reason for doubt would not work.[8]

So Descartes's meditator cannot do what the Pyrrhonian inquirer does, and regard himself as having equipollent considerations for and against both *p* and *q* when he dreams that *p* and has a conflicting waking impression that *q*. Descartes does not put the meditator in the position of owing himself an answer to the question what rationale he has for preferring the waking perception over the dream. If asked whether the waking perception is preferable, the meditator answers, "Of course. We become aware of the way things around us actually are when we are sane, wide awake, looking at things close up enough, and so on."

What I am claiming does not, by itself, show that *after* the First Meditation doubts are in place, the meditator continues to find it reasonable to think that his sane, waking experiences are preferable. In fact, I believe, once he uses the method of doubt as he does in the Second Meditation, to peel off a notion of sense perceptions as "thoughts," he is ready to raise the question whether *those* ever yield knowledge. Indeed, that is just what he does at the beginning of the Third Meditation:

> [W]hat was it about [the things I apprehended with the senses] that I perceived clearly? Just that the ideas, or thoughts, of such things appeared before my mind. Yet even now I am not denying that these ideas occur within me. But there was something else which I used to assert . . . [:] that there were things outside me which were the sources of my ideas and which resembled them in all respects. Here was my mistake; or at any rate, if my judgement was true, it was not on the strength of [*ex vi*] my perception. (2:24–25; AT 7:35; trans. altered)

So the meditator's commitment to the commonsense attitude toward perception is not unshakable. But the fact that it is not unshakable should not blind us to its strength and centrality in the thinking of the meditator, as Descartes depicts him. (At the end of chapter 9, I will say something about what becomes of this commonsense attitude later in the *Meditations*.)

[8] Margaret Wilson's reading of the dream argument attributes a different set of assumptions to the meditator (1978, 19–31). I think her reading does not square with the text of

The Pyrrhonian offhandedness about the presumptive strength of the commonsense preference for the perceptions of waking, sane people is in large part responsible, I think, for how weird the Ten Modes seem to modern readers. Sextus gives so much space to reasons for saying that there are conflicting impressions, and so little to what happens after that. On this score, Descartes is a far more accessible builder of skeptical considerations—for us, at any rate.

The contrast between Descartes and the Academic skeptic is not quite the same as the one between Descartes and the Pyrrhonist. The Academic skeptic expects his interlocutor to regard a person who is dreaming that p as being at least sometimes in no position to claim knowledge that p. The Academic skeptic, after all, is using examples where dreams are false and yet real-like and convincing: recall the thirsty person who thinks delightedly in a dream that he is drinking from a spring.

But bear in mind two points about the Academic skeptic. First, he is in direct dialectical engagement not with the person of prereflective common sense but with the Stoic philosopher. Like the Pyrrhonist, the Academic skeptic shows no signs of special interest in characterizing or engaging with the person of common sense. Second, nothing about the Academic use of dreams turns upon the general thought that dreaming that p is no reason for believing that p. The point is just that some dreams combine falsity with a real-like character. The Academic treats the impressions of dreamers in close parallel with the impressions of drunkards, and he does not move from the fact that some drunken experiences combine a real-like character with falsehood to the claim that a drunken impression that p is no reason for believing that p. In the case of drunkenness, I think we would be unwilling to make that move ourselves: while we wouldn't give any credence to a witness who said he dreamed the defendant was playing cards with him at the time of the murder, we would give some credence, in some circumstances, to a witness who said that although he was drunk at the time, he remembers playing cards with the defendant on the crucial evening. My point is not that the Academic skeptic thinks sometimes dreaming that p is a pretty good reason for believing that p: the Academic is not in the business of endorsing episte-

---

the First Meditation, but I agree that it does capture something important about the way the meditator conceptualizes sense perception *later*.

mic principles. Nor am I saying that the Stoic, of all figures, thought such a thing. Rather, my point is that the dialectic between the Academic skeptic and the Stoic makes use of dreams without drawing upon the commonsense idea that dreaming that p gives a person no reason for believing that p.

So again the presumptive correctness of the perspective of common sense plays a crucial role in the First Meditation that it does not play in the work of Descartes's Hellenistic predecessors. But I want to qualify the idea that the perspective of common sense was important to Descartes, for it is important to him in a different way from the way it is important to us. So let me say more about the idea of prephilosophical common sense and how it is treated by contemporary philosophers who are interested in skepticism.

CONTRASTS BETWEEN CONTEMPORARY PHILOSOPHERS AND DESCARTES

I think it would be very difficult to describe correctly and usefully the perspective of prephilosophical common sense, or ordinary life. But it is not hard to indicate in a general way what these phrases are calling attention to. Think of how compelling many beginning students find the dream argument to be, and contrast that classroom perspective, or the perspective "in the study," with the perspective those same students occupy after class, or "outside the study." There they are ready to defend, say, the claim that they know they are wearing a shirt, or are walking on the sidewalk. Many of our ordinary claims to knowledge are highly resilient, and this is a datum of our cognitive life that has attracted philosophical attention in recent decades.

The resilience of these epistemic claims is not the only datum that has interested philosophers. To raise the dream argument outside the study—say, in the jury room—seems to us wrongheaded. Outside the study we seem to grant these claims of ordinary life a kind of authority. Somehow these claims seem to rule out of court the apparently opposing considerations that can strike us, from a different perspective, as worth our serious attention, or even as completely compelling. These ordinary epistemic claims seem, from the ordinary perspective, to enjoy a special authority.

Many philosophers have tried to take these two data into account by treating the skeptical challenge as one calling for a philosophical response that shows how or why our ordinary epistemic claims *ought* to be resilient and *do* have authority. That is, the success of a response to skepticism would consist in some way of showing how or why I am after all *right* to keep claiming, for example, that I know there is a piece of paper here in my hand, and right to dismiss the skeptic's worries. In addition, many philosophers think that to defend the perspective of ordinary life in this way, we need only show that the skeptic's worries miss the mark.

A good way to show that the skeptical worries miss the mark would be to show that the skeptical conclusion does not contradict any of our ordinary epistemic claims. We could show that the skeptic had missed the mark in this way if we could show that when he speaks of "knowing," or "reasonable doubt," or "good reason to believe," he is not evaluating claims according to the same standards that we use in everyday life.

One obvious place to start if this is your antiskeptical strategy is to point out that in ordinary life we don't, for example, require people to rule out the possibility that they are dreaming before they have the right to say they know something. But that is not enough. For the skeptic's demand that we rule out the possibility that we are dreaming may arise in some *subtle* way from evaluative standards to which we really do hold ourselves in everyday life. And indeed we might suspect that we would not ever have found the skeptical considerations compelling if they did not somehow arise from evaluative standards that either are the ones we ordinarily hold ourselves to, or are very hard to distinguish from our ordinary standards.

Earlier in this chapter, I argued that Descartes is more interested in the perspective of common sense than the ancient philosophers were, and that to that extent he is more recognizable a figure to present-day philosophers who are working on the issues I have just sketched. Now I want to argue that we would nonetheless be wrong to assume that Descartes's concern with the perspective of common sense arises from engagement with the very same issues that engage us.

Descartes is interested in accurately and sympathetically depicting the perspective of common sense because the person of common sense is someone he aims to convert by means of rational reflection. That makes it important to him to do a careful job of attributing beliefs and assumptions to the meditator, for if he gets this wrong, then his ordinary readers will be drawing upon resources that he has not taken into account, and may be led by rational reflection to conclusions Descartes would regard as incorrect. The importance of getting common sense right in the First Meditation lies in sending the meditator down the right path to the right metaphysical conclusions. And recall that these conclusions will subvert at least some important aspects of the commonsense starting position. So it is all the more crucial that the meditator, when he faces the prospect of *rejecting* some of his prereflective beliefs, should be able to see how he has been rationally compelled into adopting this new position, and just what it is that he is giving up.

In these respects Descartes's interest in getting common sense right is very different from the interest generated by the set of contemporary ideas that I just sketched. Descartes is *not* interested in the authority of common sense because he thinks that to secure our claim to knowledge would be to defend that authority. He is *not* starting with the person who occupies the perspective of common sense because he himself thinks there is a presumption in favor of its correctness, or that we ought to be able to defend such a presumption if we are to defend knowledge claims against skeptical conclusions.[9] Rather, he is starting there because the person of common sense is the person, or one of the main sorts of people, that he is interested in converting to a philosophical perspective that is in many ways deeply at odds with the perspective of common sense. He does not care about the ordinary person for what he is, but only for what he might become.[10]

This raises a question, one that I will be addressing in Part Two. If Descartes does not accord the ordinary perspective a unique authority, then what, independent of that ordinary perspective, could he think *would* allow us to make correct claims to knowledge? If as prereflective people

[9] Descartes does think that *some* beliefs constitutive of the commonsense perspective are correct, but their *authority* does not lie in the fact that they *are* constitutive of that perspective. It lies in our relation to God, and in the complex relations among our natural endowments and our clear and distinct ideas. I say more about this at the end of chapter 9.

[10] So in this respect Descartes is like the Pyrrhonist, whose interest (such as it is) in the person of common sense lies in the prospect of helping him change.

we join the meditator in taking the radical skeptical scenarios to be grounds for doubt, then how can we possibly hope to vindicate any claims to knowledge? Descartes thought he had answers to these questions, and this fact about him must have shaped his attitude toward the perspective of common sense, even apart from his belief that it is a perspective riddled with confusion and error. It is important that he thought there *was* another option, as well as that he thought this other option is preferable. And for better or for worse, little of this sense of the possibilities remains with us today.

So far, I have not questioned whether Descartes saw, say, the dream scenario in much the same way a contemporary philosopher would. I want now to argue that he did not, and that here Descartes is more like his ancient predecessors than he is like us.

To explain the difference I have in mind between Descartes and contemporary philosophers, let me first lay out some points of similarity. If I consider, sitting in my campus office, that a eucalyptus tree may have just crushed my house, then I have a (slight) reason for doubting whether my house is standing here and now. But, of course, I can rule out this ordinary ground for doubt if I want to; all I have to do is go home and look. Descartes and contemporary philosophers would agree that in this respect, the radical grounds for doubt are supposed to be different from the ordinary ones. Consider the dream argument. If someone takes it as providing him with a reason for doubt, then it is a reason for him to doubt not just his present experience but any of the experiences, like pinching himself, to which he might appeal in trying to settle the question whether he is (say) seeing his hand. The meditator tries shaking his head and holding out his hand to rule out the possibility that he is dreaming, but exclaims, "As if I did not remember other occasions when I have been tricked by similar thoughts while asleep!" (2:13; AT 7:19; trans. altered). The global character of the scenario—its applicability to any putative means of ruling it out—accounts for our inability to rule it out. On this much I think Descartes and contemporary philosophers agree.

What I think Descartes *doesn't* agree with is a point that I think seems completely uncontroversial to contemporary philosophers. That is the point that if the meditator cannot rule a skeptical possibility out because the scenario has a global character, then he really has no grounds at all for judging, one way or the other, whether (say) his hand is before him.

This contemporary idea is nicely reflected in Barry Stroud's examination of Descartes's dream argument. Stroud begins by considering the dream argument as a challenge to such a claim as this: "I know that there's a piece of paper before me." He seeks especially to determine whether Descartes's considerations issue in a denial of what we ordinarily assert in making such a claim; he asks, "How closely does [Descartes's negative assessment] parallel the familiar kind of review of our knowledge that we all know how to conduct in everyday life?" (1984, 4). He identifies as crucial the question whether Descartes is right that I must know I am not dreaming to know there is a piece of paper here. Stroud says that if that requirement emerges naturally from our everyday ways of assessing knowledge claims, then we would have to concede that "[o]ur sensory experience gives us *no basis for believing* one thing about the world around us rather than its opposite" (32, emphasis added). Notice that he says the outcome of the dream argument would be not just that we do not know what we thought we knew, but rather that we have no more basis for believing what we believed than for believing its negation. That is, Stroud thinks that if the dream argument passes muster as a skeptical argument, then it does not just contradict a knowledge claim; it also contradicts a claim to have any reasonable grounds for belief.

In some of the straightforwardly ordinary cases of doubt that Stroud considers, our retraction of a claim to knowledge might be compatible with our *not* retracting a claim to have good reasons for belief. "As a member of a jury I might find that I have been ruling out one suspect in my mind because he was a thousand miles away, in Cleveland, at the time of the crime. But I might then begin to ask myself whether that is really something that I know" (3). Of course, my assessment of the evidence I have for saying the suspect was in Cleveland *might* leave me thinking that I have no more reason to believe he was in Cleveland than to believe he wasn't. In that case, I ought to suspend judgment about his whereabouts. But it might also leave me thinking that (as I might put it) he was probably in Cleveland, though possibly not. In this case, although I ought to withdraw my claim to knowledge, I ought not to suspend judgment about the suspect's whereabouts. It is a good question where exactly that leaves me; for my purposes, it is enough to say that I have more reason to believe he was in Cleveland than not. Stroud takes it that this sort of position would not be available if the dream argument succeeded in offering a reason for doubting whether there is a piece of paper in front of me. The argument would require me to retract not just my claim to knowledge but also any claim to have a good reason to believe that I am awake and not dreaming.

Notice that if we take the radical skeptical arguments in this way, they would render moot the question what motivation Descartes supplies for the meditator's maxim about suspense of judgment. If the skeptical scenarios succeeded as reasons for doubting the things we thought we knew, they would also serve as reasons for suspending judgment about those very things, because they would show that we had no more reason to believe those things than to believe their opposite.

I do not think this is how Descartes sees the situation of the meditator. It is true that as he is considering his inability to rule out the dream scenario, he finds that he feels "dazed" and says that "this very feeling almost confirms the opinion that I am asleep" (2:13; AT 7:19). And looking back at the First Meditation, he says, at the beginning of the Second, "It feels as if I have fallen unexpectedly into a deep whirlpool which tumbles me around so that I can neither stand on the bottom nor swim up to the top" (2:16; AT 7:23–24). But he also calls the radical grounds for doubt slight, exaggerated, hyperbolical, and metaphysical, which should make us suspect that he does not see these grounds for doubt in quite the way that we do.

I think that Descartes sees the skeptical scenarios as unlikely to be true, and thus as scenarios it is reasonable to suppose are not true.[11] That is why, even after giving all the radical grounds for doubt, he can say that opinions like "Here is a piece of paper" are "highly probable opinions— opinions which, despite the fact that they are in a sense doubtful, as has just been shown, it is still much more agreeable to reason to believe

---

[11] Michael Williams thinks that if we were to take up such an attitude toward the skeptical alternatives, then we would make skepticism uninteresting. He also thinks one could not coherently take up such an attitude toward the skeptical alternatives (1996, 48–50). I find it much harder than he does to assess the interest and coherence of this attitude; for one thing, in arriving at an assessment I think we need to take into account the fact that Descartes, who gives us the supposed paradigm of traditional skepticism, himself has this attitude.

than to deny" (2:15; AT 7:22; trans. altered). He sees no incompatibility between treating the radical scenarios as grounds for doubt and regarding them as improbable. They are "powerful and well thought-out," he explains in the Seventh Replies, because in the First Meditation we cannot rule them out (2:319; AT 7:474). That obliges us to see them as genuine grounds for doubt, but by itself it does not oblige us to suspend judgment about whether the scenarios are true or not.

Many of us would find it natural to object that before he rules the scenarios out, Descartes is not entitled to occupy the commonsense perspective from which they can be judged improbable. Perhaps in the end this is correct, though I think it is very hard to say whether it is or not. But I think what *Descartes* would say is that once he has spelled out the First Meditation grounds for doubt, he must acknowledge that he cannot be *certain* whether the perspective of ordinary life is correct. And *if* he is obeying the rules of the method of doubt, he will suspend judgment about whether the perspective of ordinary life is correct. But he needn't always be using the method of doubt; people are to use it only when they want to discover and decisively establish various fundamental truths. Good cognitive life goes on outside the practice of methodic doubt. (I will return to this claim at the end of chapter 9.)

Oddly enough, on this point there is a kind of continuity between Descartes and the ancient skeptics. I have been stressing the differences between Descartes and his predecessors as they explain how suspense of judgment comes about and how skeptical considerations are structured. But here there is one piece of common ground among them. None of them was moved to suspense of judgment by what for us seems to be a paradigm structure of philosophical skepticism. That is a set of considerations that shows, or seems to show, that we cannot rule out a counterpossibility that is incompatible with the situation we ordinarily take ourselves to be in. Of course, *we* are not, or are not always, moved to suspense of judgment by such considerations ourselves. But either we think we ought to be, or we take the fact that we aren't as indicative of some discontinuity between the perspective of ordinary life and philosophical reflection on it.

It is important to realize that this is a fairly recent development. Our inability to rule out the possibility that our present experience is a dream did not always strike philosophers as generating a reason for suspending judgment. It's not that they thought they *could* rule the possibility out: Theaetetus, for example, was stumped by the question "whether in the present instance, at this moment, we are asleep and dreaming . . . or awake."[12] But the Pyrrhonists and Academic skeptics did not treat that fact as one whose recognition would launch anyone into suspending judgment. True, the Academic skeptics constructed an argument that turns on the point that "the [convincing] nature of the visual perception of men mad or dreaming at the moment when their experience was taking place"[13] is indistinguishable from the convincing character of visual perceptions we have when sane, awake, looking carefully at things in a good light, and so on. But the Academic skeptics show no sign of thinking that this *by itself* gives anyone a reason to suspend judgment about anything. Rather, it gives a reason for suspense of judgment *to the dogmatic, Stoic philosopher*, who also believes that the wise person suspends judgment except when he has impressions of such a nature that impressions of that nature could not fail to be true.

I think it is tempting to conclude that the ancient skeptics and Descartes are blind to something about the radical scenarios that we can see. But before we make this judgment, I think we ought to ask *exactly* what it is we think we see. *Why* do we think that if the dream argument contradicts our knowledge claims, then it leaves us with no reason at all for our beliefs about the world around us? Is it just because the global character of the dream scenario means that none of our experiences can serve to rule the scenario out?[14] But why should that matter? I may realize that we will never be able to get decisive evidence about the suspect's whereabouts, and yet still have more reason to think he was in Cincinnati than not. Or is it that we use the scenario on claims that we treat as representa-

---

[12] Plato, *Theaetetus* 158b (1992, 22).

[13] Cicero, *Academica* 2.28.90 (1951, 582–83).

[14] This has been thought by some philosophers to explain, or at least be symptomatic of, the failure of the radical doubts to criticize our ordinary knowledge claims. (See Fogelin 1994, 90 ff.) Confronted with skeptics like Sextus, Cicero, and Descartes, we must press harder to understand why *this* sort of inability to rule out a counterpossibility deprives the counterpossibility of its apparent doubt-generating power. I should say that I see no signs in Descartes that he attaches any significance to the difference between being unable "in principle" to rule out a counterpossibility and just being unable, period.

tive of our best position for knowing things about the world by using our senses?[15] Perhaps this supposed representative character is responsible for the total devastation the radical scenarios seem to wreak. But again, why should this character have this consequence? It would explain why I move from retracting my claim to *know* that a piece of paper is here, to retracting any of my claims to *knowledge* about the world that have their basis in my sense experience. But why in addition would I retract my claim to have *good reason* to believe a piece of paper is here, much less my claim that my sense experience often gives me *good reason* for my claims about the world around me?

In finding it obvious that we would have to make this additional retraction, we are taking a step that I think we don't fully understand. And one good way to try to identify that step would be to look for what we think the ancients and Descartes got wrong. Perhaps one clue to our difference from them is that we think they are too credulous, that they don't understand how mundane ordinary life actually is. We take it that nothing that happens in everyday life will prove to be deeply astonishing. These are not the days of miracles and wonders; no days ever were. Perhaps part of the reason it seems wrong to us to say it is *unlikely* I am here and now dreaming, or the plaything of a deceiving creator, is that this grants these scenarios *too much*.[16]

I want to close this chapter by considering an important claim made by Myles Burnyeat, who sees significant common ground between Descartes and the ancient skeptics. As I have just done, he argues that they agree with one another about something that is alien to contemporary investigations of skepticism. But the common ground that concerns him is not the failure to regard global scenarios as reasons for suspending

[15] It is not clear to me that Descartes means to be structuring his inquiry around the idea that some claims to knowledge are representative in this way. I think it is a good question whether he thinks that if I know anything on the basis of my senses, then I know there is a piece of paper before me. To answer this question in a fully satisfactory way would require a close examination of the "painter paragraph" that follows the dream argument.

[16] If I am right in thinking that Descartes's meditator does *not* find it ridiculous to say these scenarios are unlikely to be correct, then it is ironic that Descartes's own work in philosophy should have contributed so significantly—as I am sure it did—to the development of our contemporary convictions to the contrary.

judgment, but rather the idea that skepticism about such claims as "Here is a piece of paper" is not (to use Burnyeat's term) *insulated* from our ordinary beliefs that such claims are true. We insulate a skeptical argument from an ordinary belief that *p* when the argument does not lead us "actually" to think that *p* is "in doubt," or when we think that the doubt is merely "theoretical or philosophical" and doesn't need to be "reckoned with in the ordinary business of life."[17] Burnyeat contends that the insulated skeptic is "a construction of the modern philosophical imagination" dating from the eighteenth century and deriving mainly from Kant.[18]

I agree with Burnyeat that there is no "insulation" between skepticism and ordinary judgment in the *Meditations*, but I disagree with Burnyeat's suggestion that we see its noninsulation primarily in the relation between skepticism and belief. I think we should see it primarily in the relation between skepticism and certainty. Burnyeat says, "Descartes has to insist that his doubt is strictly theoretical and methodological, not practical, precisely because he believes that the judgements of ordinary life really are put in doubt by the sceptical arguments. They are rendered so completely and utterly doubtful that Descartes feels he must construct a provisional code of conduct to keep his practical life going while he is conducting the inquiry into truth" (1997, 119–20). But as I argued in chapter 3, for Descartes, the radical scenarios are "slight" reasons for doubt in

[17] Burnyeat 1997, 92. This account of insulation would need further elaboration to rule out cleanly the case of Hume, who was *serially* ready to make judgments in ordinary life and to suspend judgment about those very matters.

[18] Burnyeat 1997, 122. I am, as he is, putting to one side what he calls the "country gentleman's interpretation" of insulation (99). I want here to register my disagreement with Burnyeat over the question whether Kant was the first to insulate philosophical skepticism from ordinary belief. Kant did argue that "one can be, simultaneously and without contradiction, an empirical realist and a transcendental idealist" (Burnyeat 1997, 121). But Kant did not just aim to show that a claim like "I know there is a piece of paper here" is *compatible with* the claim that I do not know how things are considered apart from the conditions that make possible my experience of them. He thought that the truth of "I know there is a piece of paper here" *depends upon the truth of* transcendental idealism, which is the doctrine that space and time are nothing but conditions that make possible our experience of sensible objects. That is, for Kant our claims to empirical knowledge depend for their truth upon the truth of claims made at the "transcendental level" (122). And this form of connection between "levels" means that they are not insulated from one another in the sense Burnyeat intends.

much the same way in which the worry that a eucalyptus has fallen on my house is a slight reason for doubt. That is why it would be "foolish" to act on the basis of such slight reasons for doubt; if the ancient skeptics did, they "deserved to be laughed at": "no sane person *seriously* doubts such things" (2:243; AT 7:351; emphasis added);[19] that is, no sane person would, for example, hire a roofer just because it has occurred to her that there is a remote possibility that a tree has fallen on her house. What I have added in this chapter is that not even the global character of the skeptical scenarios changes Descartes's assessment of the radical doubts as "slight."[20]

But I agree with Burnyeat about what I think is crucial: for Descartes there is no insulation between the skeptical scenarios and our ordinary judgments. The skeptical scenarios, Descartes thinks, really are *reasons for doubting* our ordinary beliefs—or they would be if we could not somehow rebut them. So if from the ordinary perspective we make claims about the *certainty* of such propositions as "Here is a hand," then, Descartes thinks, the radical skeptical scenarios show we are wrong to do so. Of course, I do not mean to be suggesting that Descartes considered and rejected the idea of insulating skepticism from ordinary life. Rather, I am claiming that he thought about the relation between skepticism and ordinary life in a way that is different from the way in which we generally

---

[19] In this passage, Descartes actually is writing about the general principle that the senses are trustworthy, and it is not clear what sort of considerations he thinks led the ancient skeptics to suspend judgment about the truth of this principle. I think here, and perhaps everywhere, he assumes that the considerations that moved the ancient skeptics were just as "slight" as those that moved the meditator. Surely a Pyrrhonist would quarrel with this representation of the considerations he offers.

[20] But what about the code of conduct that Descartes lays out in Part Three of the *Discourse*? First, I am not denying that Descartes does suspend judgment about the matters he calls into doubt. Perhaps he needs a code of conduct to help him lead his practical life while he is in suspense about the existence of the world around him. But of the four maxims Descartes gives himself, only the second is a candidate for the role Burnyeat envisions, and it does not tell Descartes how to act if he finds that virtually all the beliefs he had assumed were reasonable are revealed as unreasonable. Its main point is to tell him how to act if he discovers that his supporting beliefs are not *certain*. (See 1:123; AT 6:24–25; see also 3:97; AT 2:34–35.) In any case, the main work the code of conduct does is to help Descartes through the nine years of critical and independent reflection that *preceded* his raising the radical doubts (1:125–26; AT 6:28–31).

think about it. We may decide that Descartes was wrong to think about the radical scenarios in this way. Even if this is what we do, there would remain at least two points of philosophical significance in seeing the difference between his way of thinking and ours. First, we would be reminded that there is nothing necessary about our way of setting up these problems. And second, we would be moved to seek the roots of our way of thinking, an inquiry that would surely help us understand our philosophical predicaments better than we do.

PART TWO

Using Doubt

❖

CHAPTER

❖ 6 ❖

Using Doubt

IN THE First Meditation, Descartes spelled out radical grounds for doubt, grounds that are attenuated but whose scope seems universal. For complex motives, the meditator resolved to suspend judgment about everything that falls within the scope of these reasons for doubt, even though the reasons are slight and exaggerated. He took this bold step both because he thought that to establish something lasting in the sciences, he must first demolish all his opinions, and because he thought that using this maxim would enable him to execute a strategy with the power to go up against the authority of common sense.

We could imagine that for Descartes, the "method of universal doubt" concerns nothing more than this. Such a method would greatly widen the scope of doubt from its everyday limits, and it would require us to suspend judgment about everything that falls within that widened scope. It would not, however, be constructive: it would not point us toward propositions to which we could assent, nor would it help us to answer the question how there *could* be any propositions to which we could assent, or the question how we could hope to discover them. These are urgent questions if the point of the First Meditation is to guide our assent so that we can reach lasting results in the sciences. For how can any propositions lie beyond the scope of the First Meditation doubts? The first two radical grounds for doubt seem to have within their scope each member of the class of beliefs Descartes has acquired by using his five senses, and the second two seem also to have within their scope each member of the class of simple and evident matters. And wouldn't any proposition eligible for inclusion in a lasting science be a member of one of these two classes or rest upon propositions that are members of one of these classes? In fact, it looks as though if Descartes is to assent to *anything*, he must find some way of discovering absolute certainties other than by simply looking for propositions that fall outside the scope of radical doubt.

In the rest of this book I will be arguing that for Descartes, using the method of doubt includes a constructive phase, one that is supposed to help us identify and establish what we can know with absolute certainty. In the *Search for Truth*, Eudoxus says, "[I]f you simply know *how to make proper use of your own doubt*, you can use it to deduce facts which are known with complete certainty" (2:415–16; AT 10:522; emphasis added). In a letter of 1638 Descartes writes: "Although the Pyrrhonists reached no certain conclusion from their doubts, it does not follow that no one can. I would try now to show *how one can make use of such doubts* to prove God's existence and to clear up the difficulties which remain in what I wrote [in the *Discourse*], were it not that someone has promised to send me soon a summary of all that can be doubted on this topic, which will perhaps enable me to do it better" (3:99; AT 2:38–39; trans. altered; emphasis added). He is saying that we are somehow to *use* our doubts constructively to identify and establish what we can know with absolute certainty. In the rest of this book I will be arguing that he has in mind a very specific way to use doubt.

Conditions of Using Doubt

What I believe Descartes aimed to do was to establish the absolute certainty of some of his beliefs *by showing that their truth is a condition of his using the method of doubt*. Among these are the beliefs that he exists and that he has an idea of God. Now, Descartes thought he could show that those absolutely certain beliefs together entail that he is created by a nondeceiving God, and from that, he claimed, it follows that all of his clear and distinct ideas are true. So ultimately the existence of God and the truth of clear and distinct ideas are conditions of his use of the method of doubt. Now, some of his clear and distinct ideas concern mathematics, and from others he draws the further conclusion that some of his sense-based beliefs are true, including the general belief that material things exist. Overall, then, by uncovering the conditions of his doubt, he thinks he can establish truths about his own existence and the existence of God, the truth of his clear and distinct ideas, and then also the truth of his mathematical judgments and of his judgment that the material world exists.[1]

By saying that Descartes is uncovering the conditions that make his doubt possible, I may seem to be saying that his arguments have a transcendental character.[2] At the end of chapter 9, I will take up the question how the Cartesian arguments are related to transcendental arguments; for now let me just say that I think the dissimilarities are philosophically important. So instead of calling Descartes's arguments transcendental, I will label them "dependence arguments."

Let me introduce these dependence arguments by explaining the strategy to which they are crucial. (In what follows I will be using "(B)" and "(A)" to indicate propositions that play special strategic roles.) Suppose I am considering a class of beliefs about which I can have at most only one sort of reason for doubt. Now suppose I somehow managed to show that I could have such a reason for doubting a particular belief—the belief that (B)—only if that very belief were true. By recognizing this, I would be able to see that I cannot rationally doubt whether (B) is true: I would be able to be absolutely certain about (B).

When I succeed in using this strategy, I show that some claim is indubitable. "Indubitable" can have several meanings, and I want to be clear about the one I have in mind. I do not mean to be saying anything, one way or the other, about the power of the human mind to enter into a state of doubtfulness about a proposition. Rather, I mean to be saying

---

[1] Something like this general interpretative idea surfaces in places in Röd 1987, though it appears to be in tension with other things he says. I am grateful to Paolo Mancosu for drawing my attention to that essay. Robert Delahunty remarks in passing that the cosmological argument in the Third Meditation is "transcendental" (1997, 88), though I am not sure exactly what he means by this. Amy Schmitter (2000) argues that there is a sort of transcendental argument nested within the piece-of-wax passage, though, of course, not one that engages with issues of doubt and certainty. Gueroult invokes the idea that Descartes uses a method that uncovers conditions of doubt (e.g., 1968, 42), though I think his interpretation of the first four Meditations works this idea out in a way different from mine. A fair number of readers have thought that some sort of transcendental argument is at work in the famous *cogito* passage of the Second Meditation. Of these, the one whose reading is most congenial to my line of thought is Curley (1978). I acknowledge my debt to Curley more fully in the next chapter.

[2] I have made this comparison myself in various colloquium talks and in Broughton 1999, 7.

first that for some propositions it is impossible *both* that the proposition be false *and* that I be doubting whether it is true. (Of course, it will matter what exactly is to count as "doubting" here.) Second, I mean to be saying that if I recognize that a proposition has this feature, then I can see that I cannot rationally doubt whether the proposition is true. That is why my recognizing this about a proposition allows me to achieve absolute certainty about the proposition: I can see that it is impossible for me rationally to doubt whether the proposition is true.

If I want to achieve certainty about a proposition in this way, then the hard work will lie in showing that raising a doubt about the proposition is dependent upon its truth. I would have to identify an aspect of raising doubt about (B) that entailed (B), and, of course, I would have to make out the entailment relation. The schema for my strategy would look like this:

1. If I raise a doubt whether (B), I must grant that (A) is true.
2. But if (A), then (B).
3. So if I raise a doubt whether (B), I must grant that (B) is true.

I would need to show that granting (A) is essential to raising a doubt about (B), and that the truth of (B) is a necessary condition of (A). Let me call this the dependence strategy: by using it we uncover something that doubt depends on. "Dependence arguments" are what fill in this schema.

In the rest of this chapter, I want to lay out some of the textual evidence in favor of this general way of understanding what Descartes means by "using" the First Meditation doubt, though I will not yet try to show in any detail how these texts are related to the dependence strategy that I have just sketched. After looking at these texts, I will distinguish among several senses in which the truth of a proposition might constitute a condition of someone's using the method of doubt. These distinctions will be useful when, in chapters 7 and 8, I go on to give detailed readings of key claims and arguments. In the final chapter of the book, I will step back a bit and reflect upon the significance of this reading of Descartes. The questions I will take up there are how, if at all, my interpretation bears upon the problem of the "Cartesian Circle," how Descartes's arguments are like and unlike arguments we now classify as transcendental, and what in the end we are to say about commonsense belief and the authority of common sense.

SUGGESTIVE TEXTS

Even in the early *Rules for the Direction of the Mind*, Descartes was playing with the idea of conditions of doubt. In Rule XII, probably written in 1628, he distinguishes between necessary and contingent connections between "simple things" (1:45; AT 10:421). If I say that a body is animate, I mark a contingent connection between being a body and being animate, but "if I say that 4 and 3 make 7, the composition is a necessary one" (1:46; AT 10:421). Then Descartes goes on to give two further examples of necessary connection:

> If, for example, Socrates says that he doubts everything, it necessarily follows that he understands at least that he is doubting, and hence that he knows that something can be true or false. . . . Again, there are many instances of things which are necessarily conjoined, even though most people count them as contingent, failing to notice the relation between them: for example the proposition, 'I am, therefore God exists.' (1:46; AT 10:421)

Of course, Descartes had not yet seen how to use these connections in following a method of doubt, as he does in the *Meditations*, but clearly they were on his mind.

Several retrospective passages in the *Meditations* themselves are a rich source for understanding how Descartes sees what he is up to at one stage or another of his reflections. In the Fourth Meditation there are two passages in which he connects the doubts of the First Meditation with his subsequent discoveries. The first of them is this:

> [I]nsofar as I consider the fact that I have doubts, or that I am a thing that is incomplete and dependent, there arises in me a clear and distinct idea of a being who is independent and complete, that is, an idea of God. And from the mere fact that there is such an idea within me, or that I who possess this idea exist, I clearly infer that God also exists. (2:37; AT 7:53; trans. altered)

This harks back to two passages in the Third Meditation:

> [M]y perception of . . . God, is in some way prior to my perception of the finite, that is, myself. For how could I understand that I doubted or desired—that is, lacked something— . . . unless there were in me some idea of a more perfect being which enabled me to recognize my own defects by comparison? (2:31; AT 7:45–46)

> I understand that I am a thing which is incomplete and dependent on another and which aspires without limit to ever greater and better things; but I also understand at the same time that he on whom I depend has within him all those greater things . . . and hence that he is God. The whole force of the argument lies in this: I recognize that it would be impossible for me to exist with the kind of nature I have—that is, having within me the idea of God—were it not the case that God really existed. (2:35; AT 7:51–52)

In these Third and Fourth Meditation passages, Descartes is describing an argument that somehow moves simply from my understanding of myself as one who doubts—lacks knowledge, or is incomplete—to the claim that someone capable of such self-understanding must be created by God. By starting with the claim that he understands himself as one who doubts or who desires something he doesn't have, Descartes suggests that the First Meditation doubts serve somehow as the starting point of a constructive argument that will show what this starting point depends upon.

The second of the retrospective passages in the Fourth Meditation that I want to look at is this:

> [D]uring these past few days I have been considering whether anything in the world exists, and I have realized that *from the very fact of my considering this* it follows quite evidently that I exist. (2:41; AT 7:58; trans. altered; emphasis added)

This, of course, harks back to the Second Meditation, to the famous passage in which Descartes argues that he cannot doubt whether he himself exists:

> I have convinced myself that there is absolutely nothing in the world, no sky, no earth, no minds, no bodies. Does it now follow that I too do not exist? No: if I convinced myself of something then I certainly existed. But

there is a deceiver of supreme power and cunning who is deliberately and constantly deceiving me. In that case I too undoubtedly exist, if he is deceiving me; and let him deceive me as much as he can, he will never bring it about that I am nothing so long as I think that I am something. So after considering everything very thoroughly, I must finally conclude that this proposition, *I am, I exist*, is necessarily true whenever it is put forward by me or conceived in my mind. (2:16–17; AT 7:25)

The retrospective passage in the Fourth Meditation strongly suggests that in the famous passage in the Second Meditation the meditator is discovering that his existence is a condition of his doubting.

I must say that I do not think the *Discourse* has the same character. But I do not find this surprising, since in the *Discourse* many aspects of the *Meditations* strategies are missing.[3] The *Search for Truth*, though, quite clearly suggests the dependence strategy.[4] Here are two passages that leap off the page:

Eudoxus: Just give me your attention and I shall conduct you further than you think. For from this universal doubt, as from a fixed and immovable point, I propose to derive the knowledge of God, of yourself, and of everything in the universe. (2:409; AT 10:515)

Eudoxus: . . . if you simply know how to make proper use of your own

[3] In the *Discourse* Descartes seems torn between using a distinctive method of doubt in Part Four and representing himself as rebuilding the structure of knowledge by using the four rules sketched in Part Two. Röd (1987) raises good questions about this.

[4] Scholars are uncertain how to date the *Search for Truth*. I cannot pretend to settle the matter, but I am inclined to agree with Charles Adam that Descartes wrote it after writing the *Discourse* and before writing the *Meditations*. (See AT 10:531–32.) The *Discourse* sketches some of the same arguments but without the clear, constructive use of the method of doubt that we see in both the *Search* and the *Meditations*. As I will argue in the next chapter, the *cogito* reasoning of the *Meditations* represents an advance over the parallel reasoning in the *Search*, and I think that in writing the *Search*, Descartes must have realized that the work would be much too long and tedious if all three voices were allowed to speak about everything. I speculate that he then hit upon the happy idea of returning to the first-person-singular narrative form of the *Discourse*, while stripping the 'I' of his autobiographical trappings and allowing the "Polyander" voice to carry the narrative forward. This has the added virtue of making clear an idea that was half-submerged in the *Discourse*, that each of us inevitably must erase deeply ingrained error before being able to put together a clear and correct understanding of reality.

doubt, you can use it to deduce facts which are known with complete certainty. (2:415–16; AT 10:522)

Descartes is saying that he will somehow derive his knowledge from his doubt, by making "proper use" of it. Of course, these passages raise questions, and I will look at them more closely in the next two chapters. Here my purpose is simply to present evidence that Descartes has in mind a particular, unified, and constructive strategy for using the First Meditation doubt to establish various claims as absolutely certain, and that this strategy has something to do with uncovering what his use of the method of doubt implies or depends upon.

I want to concede at once, however, that Descartes does not reflect a great deal upon this strategy or treat it as being itself a topic of philosophical interest, nor does he advert to it everywhere we might expect, or want, him to. While I am confident that he used this strategy self-consciously, and that its availability was part of what led him to work out the method of doubt in the *Meditations*, I do not think he was struck by the same aspects of the strategy that would strike us, or that he registered the same potential difficulties that we do.

THREE TYPES OF DEPENDENCE ARGUMENT

Before I launch into detailed readings of parts of the Second and Third Meditations, I want to draw some distinctions concerning the ways in which a claim could be indubitable relative to some set of considerations. First, one broad way in which a claim could be indubitable relative to some set of considerations is if those considerations simply failed to bear upon the subject matter of the claim. For example, the dream argument, Descartes says, fails to call his mathematical beliefs into doubt, for "whether I am awake or asleep, two and three added together are five, and a square has no more than four sides" (2:14; AT 7:20). But the indubitability of a claim need not lie in its being beyond the scope of application of some set of skeptical considerations. Rather, the claim may be indubitable relative to some set of considerations because in some way its truth makes doubt based upon those considerations possible. This is the notion of indubitability that will concern me from here on in.

Now let me describe three somewhat different ways in which a claim might have this second sort of indubitability, though I hasten to say that Descartes himself does not draw these distinctions. These will involve three different ways of specifying something essential to raising doubt about a particular belief. In terms of the schema for the dependence strategy that I gave earlier, what follows are three versions of the first step: to raise a doubt whether (B), one must grant that (A) is true.

First, recall that the skeptical considerations Descartes offers in the First Meditation share a general structure: the lunacy argument, the dream argument, the deceiving God argument, and the "fate or chance" argument all have two main features:

1. The argument offers an account of how a certain sort of belief arises in me, an account on which such beliefs are false;

2. I cannot tell whether this is the correct account of my holding that sort of belief or not.

I have been calling considerations that have these two features, "skeptical scenarios." If the only way to doubt a claim is to construct a skeptical scenario about it, then one way in which such a claim might be indubitable is by being a claim whose truth is presupposed by the possibility that any skeptical scenario is correct. All skeptical scenarios will be powerless against such a claim, because either it is not possible that any scenario is correct, in which case no scenario can generate any reason for someone's doubting anything, or it is possible that some scenario is correct, in which case the claim in question is true and the scenario cannot provide any reason for someone's doubting that claim. I will be arguing that for Descartes this is one of the ways in which "I exist" is indubitable, and one of the ways in which a number of carefully worded reports about myself are indubitable—for example, "It seems to me that I am seeing a piece of paper."

Second, for someone to engage in the enterprise of methodic doubt described in the First Meditation, it is not enough that there simply *be* a relevant and possibly correct skeptical scenario about some set of beliefs. The meditator must also, for example, *consider* the scenario, *recognize* that he cannot tell whether it is correct, and on that basis *entertain doubt* about what he had believed. And surely he must also be able to *attribute to himself* those states of considering, recognizing, and so on. So the truth

105

of some claims is presupposed by someone's actually using a skeptical scenario to doubt a class of beliefs. Thus if the only way to doubt the truth of such a claim is to use a skeptical scenario, no one can rationally doubt whether such a claim is true. Someone actually using the method of doubt must do more than just doubt, of course: he must, for example, desire to achieve absolute certainty, and it may be that he must do additional things at different stages of his method-guided inquiry. I will be arguing that Descartes exploits a broad range of activities in identifying a number of claims that are indubitable. I will be interpreting him as offering arguments of this type for the indubitability of several sorts of claim: "I exist"; a number of self-reports; and the claim that I have an idea of a being of infinite perfection.

Finally, in order to raise doubts by using the method of doubt, the meditator must also accept and make use of rules or principles that regulate his stepwise progress through his inquiry. These rules or principles are conditions of his use of the method of doubt in roughly this sense: he must accept them in order to conduct the sort of inquiry he is conducting. Because he must accept them in order to conduct the sort of inquiry he is conducting, he cannot coherently both conduct the inquiry and refuse to accept—suspend judgment about—these principles. Principles of logical inference are good examples of such conditions. The meditator cannot coherently doubt whether p and "If p, then q" entail q; I will argue that for Descartes the principle of sufficient reason has a similar status.[5]

In one or another of these ways, Descartes will be arguing that there are propositions whose truth he cannot coherently doubt. He can thus pronounce himself absolutely certain about these propositions. When he wrote in 1638 that the "Pyrrhonists reached no certain conclusion from their doubts" (3:99; AT 2:38), he did not mean that they failed to use skeptical considerations to see whether any beliefs would be left standing after skeptical reflection. Rather, he meant that they did not realize "how one can make use of such doubts" (3:99; AT 2:39; trans. altered); they did not ask themselves what would have to be true, or what they would have to assent to, if they were to raise the sorts of considerations they said they were raising, and to use them as they claimed to be using them.

---

[5] Strictly speaking, using the method of doubt does not require the *truth* of these principles; it requires the meditator's *acceptance* of their truth or correctness. To stretch the

In Part One of this book, I emphasized a shared structure among the grounds for doubt that Descartes adduces, and I contrasted this structure with the sorts of skeptical considerations that the Pyrrhonists and Academics adduced. This suggests a critical question about Descartes's constructive procedure here at the outset: shouldn't he show that the truth of his favored propositions are conditions of *any* way of raising doubt? After all, it would be devastating if someone came up with some other way of raising doubt that did not have the truth of the favored propositions as its condition.

Recall, though, that Descartes is raising doubts aimed at classes of beliefs that are otherwise entirely in order when measured against our ordinary standards of belief. Short of entertaining the skeptical scenarios—the slight, exaggerated doubts—there is just no way for a person of common sense to doubt whether a hand is before him, or the sum of two and three is five. About *these* beliefs we have no grounds for doubt of any other type. They are not vulnerable to other sorts of objections: "You didn't see it yourself; you're taking it on someone else's say-so"; "you saw it yourself but it was too far away for you to discern its shape"; "your proof concerns a very complicated problem."

This is how I believe Descartes sees the power of his method of doubt. There are beliefs that we can doubt only by raising the sorts of considerations Descartes raises in the First Meditation. That means that by showing that we cannot coherently doubt some of those beliefs even by raising those sorts of considerations, Descartes will have shown that we cannot rationally doubt those beliefs at all. From some of these absolutely certain beliefs, he argues, great things follow: that God exists and that all clear and distinct ideas are true.

One caveat: not every belief that the meditator assumes to be perfectly in order is in every respect perfectly in order. He will discover, for example, that "Here is a hand" is perfectly in order only when it is carefully detached from "Here is a warm thing," for the latter is a claim that does not meet the standard of clarity and distinctness. This is to say that the *Meditations* does not give us back the world as we first found it. But that is not going to disappoint the meditator.

---

general argument schema so that it covers this case, I have articulated it in terms of what I must grant.

❖ 7 ❖

Inner Conditions

> Archimedes used to demand just one firm and immovable point in order to shift the entire earth; so I too can hope for great things if I manage to find just one thing, however slight, that is certain and unshakeable. (2:16; AT 7:24)

BY THE END of the Second Meditation, Descartes has found his "certain and unshakeable" point in his knowledge of his own mind. Famously, he first recognizes that "this proposition, *I am, I exist*, is necessarily true whenever it is put forward by me or conceived in my mind" (2:17; AT 7:25). He then goes on to form a new conception of himself and to reach absolute certainty about many of his states.

Descartes makes each of these advances by using the method of doubt. As Eudoxus says to Polyander in *The Search for Truth*, "[I]f you simply know how to make proper use of your own doubt, you can use it to deduce facts which are known with complete certainty" (2:415–16; AT 10:522). What I want to do in this chapter is to explain *how* Descartes uses his doubt in reaching the conclusions of the Second Meditation. I will be arguing that we need to distinguish among several ways he uses doubt, but that the dominant and indispensable use is the one I described in the previous chapter: to discover conditions that make the First Meditation doubt possible.

In giving this reading of key passages in the Second Meditation, I mean to be picking out only one strand among many that Descartes is weaving together. In highly economical fashion he is at once pursuing the strategy of doubt, with its attendant reform of commonsense thinking, *and* challenging the preoccupations and assumptions of the scholastic reader, *and* showing by example what clear and distinct ideas are. Nor is he concerned only with his ideas about himself. In the piece-of-wax passage he is concerned with his conception of material things as well, and this plays an important, if elusive, role in his development of a reformed idea of the material world.

Still, I think that the reading I will give identifies one important strand in the Second Meditation and serves to explain and elaborate the strategy Descartes is pursuing in using the method of doubt. In this chapter, I will take up three blocks of the text of the Second Meditation:

Block one: the passage that includes the *"cogito"* argument (2:16–17; AT 7:23–25)—misnamed, as I shall argue.[1]

Block two: the passage in which Descartes pares down his former conception of himself (2:17–19; AT 7:25–28).

Block three: the passage in which he amplifies this new conception of himself (2:19; AT 7:28–29).

I will be arguing that Descartes makes a distinctive use of his doubt in each of these passages, and that each use is, or relies upon, a dependence argument. One benefit of the reading I will be offering is that we will be able to see an argumentative structure organizing these three blocks, where there may otherwise appear to be puzzling repetition.

THE COGITO FIRST READING

I have two reasons for saying that the *cogito* passage is misnamed. The first is the fact, noted by many readers, that nowhere in the Second Meditation does Descartes actually enunciate the famous formula *"Cogito, ergo sum"*: "I think, therefore I am." By itself, this would not be especially significant. At roughly analogous places in the arguments of the *Discourse*

[1] I want here to acknowledge my debt to Ed Curley's work on the *cogito*. I read *Descartes against the Skeptics* in the late '70s, when it came out, but at the time I did not fully understand several of its interpretative claims. Still, they must have lodged somewhere in my mind, for although I have had the sense of working out all of the ideas in this book for myself, I find upon rereading Curley's book that I must have gotten from it at least the general idea that the certainty of "I exist" arises from its relation to methodic doubt and to the skeptical scenarios. I think in many respects my use of this idea is different from his, and beyond our points of contact we diverge greatly. But still, I clearly owe an important debt to Curley and want to acknowledge it gratefully here.

and the *Principles* he does say that "I think, therefore I am" is "the first principle of the philosophy I was seeking" (1:127; AT 6:32) and "the first and most certain [piece of knowledge] of all" (1:195; AT 8A:7); and in the Second Replies to the *Meditations* themselves (2:100; AT 7:140), he claims a special status for our grasp of the *cogito* formula.

But I have another reason for saying that the Second Meditation passage is misnamed. If we think of it as an elaborate way of saying, "I think, therefore I am," we will invite what I believe would be an important misreading. We will be inclined to say that for Descartes *certainty* about "I exist" is *derived from* certainty about "I think." More precisely, the mistaken view is this:

> *Cogito First reading*: Descartes is certain that the conclusion "I exist" is true only because (a) he infers the conclusion "I exist" from the premise "I think," and (b) he is certain that the premise "I think" is true.

I am calling this the Cogito First reading because on this view my certainty about "I exist" is conferred upon it by my prior certainty about "I think." I will be arguing for a different way of understanding how Descartes arrives at certainty about "I exist." But first let me lay out the support that Cogito First proponents might want to muster.

They would begin by insisting that Descartes thought "I exist" can be inferred from "I think." I agree, actually. Descartes *did* think this was a valid inference, and it is one that he himself sometimes made. Why exactly he thought it was a valid inference is not altogether clear. Perhaps he thought of it as an instance of the inference from $P(a)$ to $(\exists x)(x = a)$, an inference that is valid in many logical systems.[2] Or perhaps he thought of it as an inference from action to agent, or from property to substance.[3]

The Cogito First proponents will go on to say that if Descartes thought he could infer "I exist" from "I think," then surely the best way to explain his certainty about the conclusion of this inference is to say that he derives it from antecedent certainty about the truth of the premise. This would at any rate be sufficient to explain his certainty: if someone is certain that

---

[2] For example, see B. Williams 1978, 92–93; compare B. Williams 1967.

[3] See M. Wilson 1978, 64 ff.

p, and validly infers "*q*" from "*p*," then he is entitled to be certain that *q*. Valid inference is certainty-preserving.[4]

Of course, Descartes might nonetheless trace his certainty about "I exist" to some other source. But the Cogito First proponents will say it is perverse to look for some other source for certainty about "I exist": in the Fifth Replies Descartes himself *says* that certainty about "I exist" derives from certainty about "I think." Gassendi had complained about Descartes's use of the "elaborate pretense of deception" in arriving at certainty about "I exist": "I do not see that you needed all this apparatus, when on other grounds you were certain, and it was true, that you existed. You could have made the same inference from any one of your other actions, since it is known by the natural light that whatever acts exists" (2:180; AT 7:259). Here is Descartes's reply:

> [Y]ou are far from the truth, since I am not wholly certain of any of my actions, with the sole exception of thought (in using the word 'certain' I am referring to metaphysical certainty, which is the sole issue at this point). I may not, for example, make the inference 'I am walking, therefore I exist,' except in so far as the awareness of walking is a thought. The inference is certain only if applied to this awareness, and not to the movement of the body which sometimes—in the case of dreams—is not occurring at all, despite the fact that I seem to myself to be walking. Hence from the fact that I think I am walking I can very well infer the existence of a mind which has this thought, but not the existence of a body that walks. (2:244; AT 7:352)

Here Descartes does say straight out that he can be certain about "I think I am walking," and that this is why he can be certain of "the existence of a mind which has this thought."

Finally, the Cogito First proponents might want to highlight a point that surfaces in the reply to Gassendi. They might want to say that their reading of Descartes's argument is deeply true to his thought, since one of the most distinctive, fundamental, and influential aspects of his philosophy is his conception of his mental states as those whose occurrence, form, and content are known to him incorrigibly and therefore with cer-

---

[4] If the inference is short enough, at any rate. See Kitcher 1984, 40–48.

tainty.[5] From this the Cogito First proponents will conclude that nothing could be more natural for Descartes than to appeal to the transparency of the mental in order to conclude with certainty that he exists.

Despite all that can be said in favor of the Cogito First reading, I do not think it is the best interpretation of the famous passage in the Second Meditation. (I will thus stop calling the passage the *cogito* passage and will refer to it instead as the "I exist" passage.) The most casual reading of this passage reveals a large difficulty for the Cogito First reading: nowhere in it does Descartes argue that he can be certain he thinks. In fact, nowhere in that passage does he even *say* he can be certain he thinks.[6] He does not say anything like this for another three paragraphs, and as we will see, even there the claim he makes is narrower than the one the Cogito First reading attributes to him. In fact, I will argue, he makes and argues for the claim that he can be certain he thinks, in the relevant broad sense, only in the third block of the Second Meditation, long after he has claimed indubitability for "I exist."

Even the *Discourse* and the *Principles* contain hints that Descartes's certainty about "I exist" is not derivative from certainty about "I think." In the *Discourse*, right before "observing" that the "I exist" reasoning is certain, Descartes says, "I noticed that while I was trying thus to think everything false, it was necessary that I, who was thinking this, was something" (1:127; AT 6:32). The article of the *Principles* that contains the "I exist" reasoning is headed, "It is not possible for us to doubt that we exist while we are doubting; and this is the first thing we come to know when we are philosophizing in an orderly way" (1:194; AT 8A:6–7). And in the preface to the French edition of the *Principles* Descartes says that "someone who wishes to doubt everything cannot, for all that, doubt that he exists while he is doubting" (1:183–84; AT 9B:9). Although I think each of these passages contains reasoning that fits the Cogito First mold, Descartes also seems to suggest a different idea, that my certainty about "I exist" arises somehow out of the relation between "I exist" and my engaging in methodic doubt.

---

[5] For an influential version of this view, see Rorty 1980, 52, 62, 97.

[6] Frankfurt (1970, esp. 110) underlines this point in his own critique of what I am calling the Cogito First reading.

I think that in the *Meditations*, Descartes is pursuing this second idea, and that the challenge is to articulate more precisely what he thinks the relation is between "I exist" and the doubt. I believe Descartes tried out one idea about this relation in the *Search for Truth*, only to discard it in favor of a more subtle idea in the Second Meditation. Let us look briefly at the cruder idea first.

It can come as a jolt to find Eudoxus boasting that "from this universal doubt, as from a fixed and immovable point, I propose to derive the knowledge of God, of yourself, and of everything in the universe" (2:409; AT 10:515). Isn't the fixed and immovable point supposed to be "I exist"? Its relocation in the *Search for Truth* is significant, I believe. It suggests a view we might call "Dubito First," a view according to which

> *Dubito First reading:* Descartes is certain that the conclusion "I exist" is true only because (a) he infers the conclusion "I exist" from the premise "I doubt," and (b) he is certain that the premise "I doubt" is true.

This would be one way of trying to specify the general idea that certainty about "I exist" depends upon the relation between "I exist" and methodic doubt.

Other passages in the *Search for Truth* bear out this reading. Eudoxus gets Polyander to work through radical grounds for doubt and then says:

> Now, you see that you can reasonably have doubts about everything that you know only by means of the senses. But can you ever have doubts about your doubt, and remain doubtful whether you are doubting or not? (2:409; AT 10:514)

A little later he continues:

> You cannot deny that you have such doubts; rather it is certain that you have them, so certain in fact that you cannot doubt your doubting. Therefore it is also true that you who are doubting exist; this is so true that you can no longer have any doubts about it. (2:409–10; AT 10:515)

Descartes does not explain *why* I cannot doubt whether I am doubting. Perhaps the point is that if I doubt whether p, then I am making it to be the case that p, where p is "I doubt." That wouldn't make doubting whether I am doubting impossible, but it would show that it would be peculiarly unreasonable to doubt whether I am doubting. Or perhaps the point is one that is supposed to hold of any sort of conscious state I might be in: I can be certain I am in that kind of conscious state whenever I am in that kind of state. So "When I am doubting, I cannot doubt that I am doubting" would be just like "When I am fearing, I cannot doubt that I am fearing" or "When I am judging, I cannot doubt that I am judging."[7] Either of these ideas might be what Descartes has in mind, or neither; the text gives us no help in understanding his precise intentions.[8]

In the Second Meditation Descartes simply does not say that I cannot doubt that I am doubting; there are no passages parallel in this respect to the two from the *Search for Truth* that I have just quoted. Whatever the relation in the Second Meditation may be between methodic doubt and my certainty that I exist, it is not a Dubito First relation. Descartes is *not* saying that he is certain about "I exist" because he is certain about "I doubt." But then what *is* the relation between "I exist" and methodic doubt in the Second Meditation, and how does seeing this relation make Descartes certain about "I exist"?

MY EXISTENCE AS A CONDITION OF MY DOUBT

The Second Meditation opens with a reminder of the maxim of methodic doubt: "Anything which admits of the slightest doubt I will set aside just as if I had found it to be wholly false; and I will proceed in this way until I recognize something certain" (2:16; AT 7:24). Descartes reminds himself of the tremendous range of kinds of things he is suspending judgment about, and treating as no better than false; and he wonders whether this

---

[7] I am using examples that are "kinds" of conscious states in the sense that Descartes brings out in the Third Meditation when he talks about the "forms" that thoughts can have (2:25–26; AT 7:37). Possibly these sentences should read, "When I seem to myself to be x-ing, I cannot doubt that I am x-ing." I don't think it matters for the line of thought I am pursuing here.

[8] Arnauld and Nicole suggest a hybrid of Cogito First and Dubito First: the soul "could doubt everything without being able to doubt whether it is thinking, since doubting is itself a thought" (1996, 237).

range includes absolutely everything. He fails in his first effort to find something immune to his doubts:

> I will suppose then, that everything I see is spurious. . . . I have no senses. Body, shape, extension, movement and place are chimeras. . . . [Yet is] there not a God, or whatever I may call him, who puts into me the thoughts I am now having? (2:16; AT 7:24)

Although this effort is unsuccessful, it is instructive: Descartes has sought something immune to his doubt by identifying what at first seems to him to be a *necessary condition* of his doubt, namely, a causal condition of his having the doubting thoughts he is having. The trouble is that it isn't really a necessary condition after all: "But why do I think this, since I myself may perhaps be the author of these thoughts?" (2:16; AT 7:24).

Now Descartes's attention shifts to himself. He does not try to argue that his own existence is immune to his doubt because he himself must exist as the *"author"* of his thoughts of "[b]ody, shape, extension, movement and place." In a moment he *will* argue that his existence is a necessary condition of methodic doubt, but not because he is causally responsible for his having thoughts about the things he is doubting. He is not yet in any position to settle the question what is causally responsible for the occurrence in him of the thoughts that he has. He will return to this question in the Third Meditation, of course, when he takes himself to have assembled the materials for a partial answer. (The full answer does not come until the Sixth Meditation.)

Nor does Descartes try a strategy that the form of his question might suggest. His question is this: in doubting whether sky, earth, body, or minds[9] exist, have I also doubted whether I exist (2:16; AT 7:25)? But he does not try to answer this question by determining first whether he is one of the sorts of things that belong to the dubitable realm of sky, earth, body, and mind. Rather, in a distinctive argumentative maneuver, Descartes *first* answers the question about his existence and *then* answers, or at any rate addresses, the question about what sort of thing he is. (Again, the full answer does not come until the Sixth Meditation.)

---

[9] This may seem strange: isn't the indubitable 'I' a mind? Well, at this stage of his inquiry, Descartes has no clear conception of mind. Indeed, shortly he will say he always imagined his soul was a wind or fire or ether (2:17, 18; AT 7:26, 27).

Descartes believes he can postpone the question about what kinds of states or characteristics he can attribute to himself because he believes he can show independently that his existence is a necessary condition of his doubting things of any kind at all. His existence is a *necessary condition of his doubting* whether sky, earth, body, or minds exist. "I exist" must be true if I am to doubt, and so one thing I cannot rationally doubt, as I doubt everything possible, is that "I exist" is true.

Descartes works through this point twice, with slightly different emphases. Here is the first version:

> I have convinced myself that there is absolutely nothing in the world, no sky, no earth, no minds, no bodies. Does it now follow that I too do not exist? No: if I convinced myself of something then I certainly existed. (2:16–17; AT 7:25)

The "convincing" is part of the effort of methodic doubt; it is the setting aside of claims by regarding them as no better than false, or by "pretending" (2:15; AT 7:22) that they are false. Descartes does assert the proposition "If I convince myself, then I exist"; I am not denying that he endorses a claim that licenses an inference from "I convince myself" to "I exist." Rather, what I want to stress is that his *certainty* that he exists is not licensed by *prior* certainty that he is convincing himself of something. (Notice that he does not say he has absolute certainty that he is convincing himself of something.) His certainty about his existence is instead licensed by his seeing that his existence makes his doubting possible.[10] Here, Descartes is identifying his existence as a condition of his having carried out the intellectual activity he described in the First Meditation;[11] this is an instance of the second sort of condition for doubt that I described in chapter 6.

Let me spell out this "I exist" reasoning by using the dependence argument schema that I introduced in chapter 6. In the first step, we focus upon a particular essential aspect of the First Meditation doubt:

---

[10] The duc de Luynes's French translation has Descartes saying, "[I]f I convinced myself of something *or thought anything* then I certainly existed" (2:17; AT 9:19; trans. altered and emphasis added). This gloss gets ahead of the story, though. I will say more about this presently.

[11] Here is one place where my interpretation differs from Curley's.

1. If I use a consideration to doubt whether I exist, I must grant that I am doubting something.

Notice that here the nature of the skeptical consideration I am using doesn't matter; the point is that if I reflect upon that consideration as part of the complex activity of doubting, then I must grant that I am doubting something. The second step in the dependence argument spells out the dependence of the doubt upon the truth of the claim I am trying to doubt:

2. If I am doubting something, then I exist.

This licenses an inference, and it is crucial to Descartes's reasoning, but my certainty about the then-clause does not flow from any prior certainty about the if-clause. Rather, I am certain about "I exist" because I see that (1) and (2) together imply this:

3. If I use a consideration to doubt whether I exist, then I must grant that "I exist" is true.

By seeing that this if-then proposition is true, I see that I cannot entertain rational doubt about "I exist." Thus "I exist" is indubitable, which is to say that I can be absolutely certain that "I exist" is true.

Descartes next works through the same general point with a different aspect of First Meditation doubt in mind:

> But there is a deceiver of supreme power and cunning who is deliberately and constantly deceiving me. In that case I too undoubtedly exist, if he is deceiving me. (2:17; AT 7:25)

Here again Descartes is identifying his existence as a condition that makes methodic doubt possible, but instead of tying his existence to an aspect of his activity of doubting or suspending judgment, he ties it to an aspect of what I have called a skeptical scenario. Recall that a skeptical scenario is a story about the meditator whose truth he cannot rule out. The story has these elements: the meditator has various beliefs, and he is caused to have those beliefs in such a way as to make them false. In the passage about being deceived, Descartes is tying his existence to a necessary feature of skeptical scenarios: they must describe someone who has been caused to have false beliefs. Thus the meditator cannot construct a coherent skeptical scenario about his own existence.[12] The scenario would have to represent him as existing, because it would have to represent him as having false beliefs, but it would also have to represent him as not existing, because it would have to represent his belief that he exists as false. But if the meditator recognizes that there is no coherent skeptical scenario about "I exist," then he will see that he cannot have a reason for doubting whether he exists. (In the Second Meditation passage, Descartes works with the deceiving God hypothesis, but the point holds for all of the skeptical scenarios of the First Meditation.) This, then, is an example of the first sort of condition for doubt that I identified in chapter 6.

Again, let me lay out the reasoning by using the dependence argument schema. In the first step, we zero in on an essential aspect of the First Meditation doubt:

> 1. If I have a reason to doubt whether I exist, I must grant that while it may be that I believe I exist because it is true, it may instead be that I am caused by a deceiving God to believe that I exist (and I cannot tell which account of my belief is true).

Here it *does* matter what sort of consideration will generate a doubt about the claim in question; indeed, it matters that only a consideration with the structure of a skeptical scenario could give me a reason to doubt this otherwise impeccable claim. In the next step, we see a condition on the aspect of the doubt that the first step identifies:

> 2. If either I believe that I exist because it is true, or I am caused by a deceiving God to believe that I exist, then at least it must be true that I exist.

Again, my certainty that "I exist" is true does not arise from prior certainty about something else; rather, it rests upon my recognition that (1) and (2) together entail this:

---

[12] This is the point that Curley makes (1978, chaps. 4 and 5).

3. If I have reason to doubt whether I exist, I must grant that I exist.

By recognizing this, I see that I cannot rationally doubt whether "I exist" is true; I can be absolutely certain that I exist.

In the last sentence of the paragraph I have been analyzing, Descartes says,

> So, everything having been weighed enough and more, finally this statement is established: I am, I exist, necessarily is true whenever it is put forward by me or conceived in my mind. (2:17; AT 7:25; trans. altered)

He is saying here that the reasoning he has just gone through "establishes" something; by this he presumably means that he has shown something to be indubitable. Somewhat puzzlingly, he says that what he has established is this: when he conceives "I exist," "I exist" must be true.[13] I believe the best way to unpack this is to read him as claiming that his certainty about "I exist" is connected with the proposition "If I am conceiving that I exist, then I am existing." But this concluding sentence is not spelling out the nature of this connection; that was the work of the reasoning he just went through. On my view of that reasoning, the nature of the connection is captured by the dependence strategy. The if-then claim yields certainty about "I exist" by serving as step (2) in the schema I have described.

An interesting sidelight: In his commentary on Descartes's *Principles*, Spinoza seems to interpret Descartes as arguing that he cannot doubt whether "I exist" is true because he cannot construct a coherent skeptical scenario about "I exist." Here is Spinoza's reading of Descartes:

> When we previously discussed the certainty and evidence of our existence, we saw that we inferred it from the fact that, wherever we turned our attention—whether we were considering our own nature or feigning some cunning deceiver as the author of our nature, or summoning up, outside us, any other reason for doubting whatever—we came upon no reason for doubting that did not by itself convince us of our existence.[14]

[13] For a quite different reading that is very sensitive to the wording of this sentence, see Frankfurt 1970, chap. 10.

[14] Spinoza 1985, 236; 1925, 1:147. See Doney 1971 for further analysis of Spinoza's representation of Descartes's antiskeptical strategy.

"I think"

Let me move on now to the second block of the Second Meditation that I want to examine. Because Descartes has given dependence arguments about "I exist," he believes he can establish certainty about "I exist" before squaring up to the question what sort of thing "I" refers to; he reaches certainty about "I exist" before he considers how to characterize this 'I'. But, of course, "I" doesn't refer to just *anything*: Descartes has a great deal in mind, however vaguely, when he puts "I exist" forward or conceives it in his mind. Should he take it that he has achieved certainty about the existence of a thing that answers in every respect to his prereflective conception of himself? No: "I must be on my guard against carelessly taking something else to be this 'I' [that necessarily exists], and so making a mistake in the very item of knowledge that I maintain is the most certain and evident of all" (2:17; AT 7:25). Then what *can* he say about the thing of whose existence he is certain?

He is now poised to continue his inquiry in a particular way that will turn out to be crucial to his development of the metaphysics of the mind. He says, "I will . . . go back and meditate on what I originally believed myself to be . . . [and] I will then subtract anything capable of being weakened, even minimally, by the arguments I have brought forward, so that what is left at the end may be precisely what is certain and unshakeable" (2:17; AT 7:25; trans. altered). He is certain "I exist" is true, and he has a rich but vague conception of what it is that "I" refers to. But, he thinks, it may be that his doubt presupposes his existence only insofar as he has some, but not others, of the characteristics he attributes to himself. Now he makes a large assumption. Finding himself equipped with certainty about his existence and equipped with his prereflective conception, he assumes it must be possible for him to refine his prereflective conception in a particular way. It must be possible for him to form from it a coherent conception that is (a) still a conception of what it is that "I" refers to, and yet (b) a conception that includes only what he can say with certainty about the referent of "I."

Descartes will use two special procedures to draw out from his prereflective conception the elements he wants to isolate and make explicit. First he will make a new kind of use of his doubt in order to pare down his conception of himself; that is what he will be doing in the second block (2:17–19; AT 7:25–28). Then he will offer new dependence arguments to craft a number of carefully worded self-ascriptions and to claim certainty for them. That will be the work of the third block (2:19; AT 7:28–29). In both phases of this operation he will be clarifying the rich but vague idea of himself with which he began, and by the end of this operation he will be able to assert with absolute certainty the truth of many propositions in addition to "I exist."

By describing Descartes's general procedure in this way, I am extending my opposition to the Cogito First reading. It requires us to see the second and third blocks as making a great fuss about something Descartes has already established in the first block. For if his certainty that he exists is derivative from prior certainty that he thinks, then he already has his answer to the question what he can safely say about himself: he thinks.[15] He would also surely be wrong to say that he has been "ignorant until now" of what it means to say he is a thing that thinks (2:18; AT 7:27). I will be explaining the sense in which Descartes doesn't yet know that he thinks: he hasn't yet clarified the conception of thinking that is required if "I think" is to be a proposition to which he can assent with absolute certainty.

Let me turn now to the arguments of the second block. Descartes's paring-down operation begins with his articulation of the vague idea of himself that he has. He remarks that up until now he has thought of himself as having a body and a soul. To his body he attributes "the whole mechanical structure of limbs" (2:17; AT 7:26); to his soul he attributes being nourished, moving, having sense perception, and thinking.[16] He thinks of a body as a thing perceivable by the senses that is shaped, located in space, impenetrable, and moveable by contact with other things. He finds it harder to say what he thinks his soul is: either he doesn't think about its nature at all, or he imagines it to be something "subtle, like a

---

[15] M. Wilson (1978, 72) acknowledges this awkwardness.

[16] Carriero (1986) very helpfully explains how this stage of reflection meshes with the concerns of a scholastic meditator. Even here, though, I think the meditator must also be understood as articulating ideas that, broadly speaking, prereflective people may have about themselves.

wind or fire or ether, which permeated my more solid parts" (2:17; AT 7:26; trans. altered).[17]

Having articulated this conception of himself, Descartes performs surgery on it, using the First Meditation grounds for doubt as his scalpel. He generates a series of propositions from his conception of himself, and about each of them he asks whether it implies something that he has called into doubt in the First Meditation. I will call this the First Meditation test. If the claim "I am P" fails the First Meditation test, then Descartes cuts P out of his former conception of himself, for it does not belong in the special conception he aims to produce. (I have been giving prominence to the dependence strategy so far in this chapter. Here I want to be clear that I am *not* claiming that the First Meditation test somehow constitutes a dependence argument. Later, though, I will explain a limited sense in which some claims in the second block do rely upon the dependence strategy.)

For example, in considering the belief "I am a thing that has limbs," Descartes is in effect asking, "Does this belief imply something that I have called into doubt?" This one does; he has called into doubt the existence of his body, and "I am a thing that has limbs" implies that his body exists. When he reaches this answer to his question, of course, he reminds himself that he must suspend judgment about "I am a thing that has limbs," but he now uses these grounds for doubt to do something new. He excludes "has limbs" from a special *conception* of himself that he is trying to construct. This is not—yet—a conception of all and only what actually *belongs* to him; rather, it is at this stage a conception of what he *need not doubt* belongs to him.

"I am a thing that has limbs" is an easy case. The slightly harder ones are those that concern the capabilities Descartes has conceived to belong to his soul, for it is not immediately obvious whether the First Meditation grounds for doubt touch the soul. But, he reflects, "I am a thing that is

---

[17] In an early notebook, Descartes had written, "Just as the imagination employs figures in order to conceive of bodies, so, in order to frame ideas of spiritual things, the intellect makes use of certain bodies which are perceived through the senses, such as wind and light. By this means we may philosophize in a more exalted way, and develop the knowledge to raise our minds to lofty heights" (1:4; AT 10:217). He then seems to suggest that a natural connection in our minds makes wind signify spirit (1:5; AT 10:218). Perhaps he is attributing some such thought to his meditator.

sensing" implies that I have sense organs and therefore that I have a body; in fact, as he points out, the dream argument calls "I am a thing that is sensing" into doubt directly, for "when asleep I have appeared to perceive through the senses many things which I afterwards realized I did not perceive through the senses at all" (2:18; AT 7:27). Nutrition and self-movement fare no better. So Descartes cuts nutrition, self-movement, and sense perception out of the conception that he is forming of the 'I'.

But there is one more attribute that Descartes had conceived to belong to his soul, and that is "thinking." It is important to recognize that here Descartes is using *"cogitare"* in a special and somewhat narrow sense: it is the exercise of "intelligence [*animus*], or intellect [*intellectus*], or reason [*ratio*]" (2:18; AT 7:27). As he conceives it here, "thinking" is no more involved in having sense perception, for example, than it is in being nourished or moving about. In just a few more paragraphs, Descartes will broaden the notion of thinking with which he will work, so that sense perception *will* be a kind of thinking; but he has not broadened it yet.[18]

Still, his conclusion about the narrower conception of thinking entails at least one departure from his original conception. At first he had considered thinking to be just another vital activity of the soul, like nourishment or moving about. He now considers thinking to be significantly unlike those other activities, because "I am a thing that reasons," as he understands it, implies nothing that he has called into doubt in the First Meditation. Thus thinking is the only item in his original conception of himself that survives the First Meditation test. So far it is the only aspect of the old conception that belongs in the new conception of himself that he is creating with the help of the doubt. Of course, this leaves unanswered the question how thinking is related, if at all, to the soul, as Descartes had understood that part of himself. I will turn to that question presently. Right now, though, I want to pause to underline three points about the outcome of this paring-down procedure.

First, Descartes does not offer any special reason in favor of saying that "I think" is indubitable. He simply makes the negative and limited claim that so far as he can see, "I think" does not imply anything he has called into doubt in the First Meditation. That is, thinking *as he has conceived of*

---

[18] Of course, there are places where Descartes telescopes these stages of his inquiry and correspondingly these notions of thinking. I will discuss several of those places presently.

it does not evidently imply the existence of anything he has called into doubt. At this point Descartes does not even try to rationalize this conception of reasoning; he does not try to say why he thinks of reasoning as something that does not require a body.

Second, it is a mistake, I believe, to read this passage as making claims about the *essence* of the mind.[19] Descartes does say that "thought . . . is inseparable from me" (2:18; AT 7:27). But his point is not that thought is a characteristic without which I cannot exist. As to that he is quite tentative: "perhaps it could happen that were I totally to cease from thinking, I should totally cease to exist" (2:18; AT 7:27; trans. altered). Rather, his point is that if he separates from his conception of himself everything that fails the First Meditation test, then thinking will not be separated from himself as he works to conceive of himself in this special way.

Third, notice that only at this point has Descartes discovered that "I think" in some way resists doubt. On the Cogito First reading, he is being disingenuous when he says, "Thinking? *Here* [*hîc*] I discover" that thinking cannot be removed by doubt (2:18; AT 7:27; trans. altered; emphasis added). But he means it: only at this point has he conducted the thought experiment that yields some sort of certainty about "I think." And remember: the experiment shows only that thinking in the narrow sense does not, as Descartes conceives it, imply the existence of anything he has called into doubt. He is not affirming the transparency of consciousness to itself; he is not, as Richard Rorty puts it, claiming that "the mind is naturally 'given' to itself" (1980, 97) or that it enjoys a special "closeness to the Inner Eye" (62). Presently Descartes will make broader and more positive claims about thinking, but as I will argue, he believes he can rest those claims upon a distinctive sort of argument that no more appeals to the transparency of consciousness than does his use of the First Meditation test.

There is one more paragraph in the Second Meditation that belongs to the paring-down phase, and although it has the air of an afterthought, it is of central importance: it contains the seeds of Cartesian dualism.

[19] Here I agree with Frankfurt (1970, 118 ff.), though I disagree with his understanding of what *has* gone on in this passage. In saying Descartes is not making a claim here about his essence, I am disagreeing with M. Wilson (1978, 72 ff.). But I would concede that at *some* point Descartes shifts from talking about what is indubitably mine to what belongs to my essence, and that it is difficult to say where and why that shift occurs.

Here for the first time Descartes directly considers his former vague thoughts about the constitution or stuff of his soul, that it is "some thin vapour which permeates the limbs—a wind, fire, air, breath" (2:18; AT 7:27). In his former conception, it was a "subtle" thing like this that he "imagined" (2:17; AT 7:26; trans. altered) to be what carries out the activities of nourishment, sense perception, moving about, and reasoning. He has now found that the activity of reasoning survives the paring-down operation; perhaps, then, he must also count as a survivor the vaporous stuff he had imagined to be what carries out intellectual activity.

Descartes gives several reasons for resisting this suggestion. First, however subtle this stuff may be—however elusive to sight and touch—it is still the kind of stuff he called into doubt in the First Meditation.[20] Second, no amount of fine-tuning will help to salvage what he "imagines" his soul-stuff to be, for, he claims, "imagining is simply contemplating the shape or image of a corporeal thing" (2:19; AT 7:28). So whatever he imagines himself to be, he will inevitably be considering himself to be a type of thing that he has called into doubt in the First Meditation. He must, then, exclude any such imagined stuff from his conception of himself.

In the most difficult part of this paragraph, Descartes takes up a third point. He worries that he may be excluding elements from his conception of himself that are *correct*. For example, his ability to doubt whether anything extended exists does not rule out the possibility that he is in fact something extended—a vapor, perhaps. Descartes does not directly confront the claim that he is extended. Rather, he makes a point about the *conception* of himself that he is forming:

> It is most certain that the conception [*notitiam*] of this [the 'I' that I know], obtained in this way by cutting [dubitable elements out],[21] does not depend upon things I do not yet know [*novi*] to exist. (2:18–19; AT 7:27–28; trans. altered)

Suppose for a moment that the soul is a vapor. What point would Descartes be making about the conception of himself that keeps intellectual

---

[20] He does not spell out why; presumably the point is that even a wind has "extension, movement and place" (2:16; AT 7:24).

[21] Descartes's word is *"praecise."* This is an important term; it occurs four times in the second and third blocks (2:17, 18 (twice), 19; AT 7:25, 27 (twice), 29). See also 2:20; AT 7:30.

activity in but cuts vapors out? I think the point is supposed to be that even if his soul is in fact a vapor, and his intellectual activity emanates from this vapor, there is nevertheless no *inconceivability* in his soul's *not* being a vapor, or in his intellectual activity's emanating from something that is *not* extended.

But how has Descartes established that? This was Arnauld's central question about Descartes's argument for the distinction between the mind and the body. The exchange between these two philosophers on this subject is frustrating to read; each presents the other with a moving target.[22] But I think it is fair to say that Descartes has a two-part response to Arnauld's central challenge. First, he agrees that he is not, in the Second Meditation, able to say that thought can exist apart from extension. For until he knows that God exists and is not a deceiver, the method of doubt forbids him to assume that all his clear and distinct ideas of himself are true. And so from the fact that he can conceive of himself clearly and distinctly as thinking but not extended, he cannot infer that he really could exist as a thinking but unextended thing (see 2:159; AT 7:226).

To see the second part of Descartes's response, we must focus on the move that he understands Arnauld to have questioned. It is the move from the claim that

I have *an* idea of myself as thinking and nonextended,

to the claim that

I have an *internally coherent or consistent* idea of myself as thinking and nonextended.

In places Descartes simply begs the question, by claiming to observe that his idea of himself is clear and distinct (e.g., 2:158; AT 7:225). But he also says something that, though perplexing, is not patently question-begging. He says that in conceiving of himself as thinking but not extended, he is conceiving of himself as a "substance" (2:245; AT 7:355) or a "complete thing" (2:157; AT 7:223), that is, "as 'an entity in its own right [*ens per se*] which is different from everything else'" (2:156; AT 7:221; he is quoting

---

[22] And I should note that in the Fourth Objections and Replies, both Descartes and Arnauld blur the distinction between thought narrowly and broadly construed. So in one way they, and I, are getting ahead of the story.

his own words from the First Replies). This is what assures him that his idea of himself as thinking but not extended is coherent: he has not cut out anything that he must attribute to himself in order to be conceiving of himself as an entity in its own right.

Of course, the natural question to ask next is why Descartes is confident that his special conception of himself *is* a conception of an entity (thing, substance). It is easy to feel, reading the Fourth Replies, that he is slipping back into question begging. For he seems to be implying that he is confident that this conception is a conception of an entity because he sees clearly and distinctly that it is. But before we settle for this reading, notice that Descartes makes a point of saying that he has defended this conception *in the Second Meditation.*[23] Frustratingly, he doesn't say what it is about the Second Meditation that constitutes his defense of the claim that the idea of himself as thinking but nonextended is the idea of an entity. But perhaps we can make something of the fact that Descartes never objects to *Arnauld's* way of locating the issue in the Second Meditation. And here is what Arnauld said Descartes's argument is:

> I can doubt whether I have a body, and even whether there are any bodies at all in the world. Yet for all that, I may not doubt that I am or exist, so long as I am doubting or thinking.
>
> Therefore I who am doubting and thinking am not a body. For, in that case, in having doubts about my body I should be having doubts about myself. (2:139; AT 7:198)

It is a little odd that Descartes never disputes this account of his reasoning, since Arnauld seems to impute to him a fallacious argument. Arnauld seems to say that Descartes is reasoning in this way:

1. Bodies can be doubted by me to exist.
2. So if I were a body, I could be doubted by me to exist.
3. But I cannot be doubted by me to exist.
4. So I am not a body.

To see that this argument is fallacious, compare it to this one:

1. This masked man is not known by me.
2. So if my father is this masked man, my father is not known by me.

---

[23] 2:157 (AT 7:223); 2:159 (AT 7:226); 2:160 (AT 7:229); also 2:245 (AT 7:355).

3. But my father is known by me.

4. So the masked man is not my father.[24]

While it is true that *a* and *b* are identical only if *a* has all of *b*'s properties and *b* all of *a*'s, there are conditions on what, for these purposes, counts as a property; and "is doubted by me to exist" or "is known by me" do not meet these conditions.

Some readers think that the fallacious argument is the argument Descartes is giving. If they are right, then that would explain why Descartes does not object to Arnauld's paraphrase. But I do not see any signs in the Second Meditation or the Fourth Replies that Descartes himself reasons this way, and if he doesn't, then he must think something else about Arnauld's formulation is apt.

I believe that what struck Descartes as right was Arnauld's assumption that there is a link between the "I exist" reasoning and the special conception of himself that Descartes is forming by using the First Meditation test. This link, I believe, is what Descartes has in mind when he reiterates that in the Second Meditation he showed that his conception of himself as thinking and nonextended is a conception of a thing. The link Descartes sees is this: he treats his first use of the method of doubt, in the "I exist" reasoning, as guaranteeing the success of a particular thought experiment.[25] He cannot doubt that "I exist" is true. *So* (he takes it) *he must be capable of forming a specific sort of conception of the entity that "I" refers to*, namely, a coherent and contentful conception of that entity that excludes everything that fails the First Meditation test. So he must be capable of forming a coherent conception of the entity, himself, that cuts out being a vapor, for example. It cannot be the case that his conception

---

[24] This fallacy was known to the Hellenistic philosophers. See *Philosophers for Sale*, where Lucian has Chrysippus recount the Veiled Argument (Long and Sedley 1987, 227), and see references by Diogenes Laertius to the Veiled Argument (Long and Sedley 1987, 221–22). M. Wilson says (1978, 190) that Descartes knew this fallacy; she refers the reader to AT 7:225. Although that page does not support her claim, I agree with her that Descartes must have known the fallacy.

[25] Here I am reading him as making a stronger claim than one Carriero attributes to him (1984, 181–83). And I am in agreement with what I take M. Wilson to mean when she remarks that the indubitability of "I exist" "has brought him to the conclusion that he is a *true and truly existing thing*" (1978, 187; she is alluding to 2:18; AT 7:27).

of himself *must* include being vapor, even if his soul *is* a vapor, and even if this vapor somehow exudes intellectual activity. And the pared-down conception *must* be one by which he succeeds in thinking of himself as an entity in his own right.

At the risk of belaboring this point, let me now spell it out more explicitly, in stepwise fashion:

1. I cannot doubt that the entity "I" refers to exists.

2. So I must have a coherent and contentful representation of myself through which I represent myself as an entity whose existence I cannot doubt. (Call this, "representation X.")

3. Representation X has content in virtue of its attributing characteristics (kinds of properties, activities, or states) to me.

4. This content serves to represent me as an entity whose existence I cannot doubt only if its attribution of characteristics to me passes the First Meditation test.

5. What I have meant in speaking of "myself" is this: an entity that is a solid body (B) plus a vaporous entity (V) that carries out the activities of nourishment, moving, sensing, and thinking (N, M, S, and T).

6. So the candidates for X's content are B, V, N, M, S, and T.

7. Neither B, V, N, M, or S, passes the First Meditation test; T does.

8. So T provides the content of representation X.

9. So I have a coherent representation of myself as an entity that is T and not B, V, N, M, or S.

My aim in laying this argument out is not to defend it, but simply to explain as clearly as I can why Descartes insists that he has a coherent idea of himself as a thing that thinks and is not extended. He *must* have such an idea, he is saying, or else the "I exist" reasoning would not have worked.[26]

---

[26] Here I am reading Descartes as raising and trying to answer the question whether or not cutting extended things out of his conception of himself results in a coherent conception, and I am representing his answer as relying upon an appeal to the success of the "I exist" reasoning. For further elucidation of several Cartesian notions of "cutting things out," see Murdoch 1993, Thomas 1995, and Rozemond 1998, 12–19. Murdoch connects this notion with the first block of the Second Meditation, but in a way quite different from mine.

So in a limited way, Descartes's possession of the pared-down conception is itself a condition of his doubt. Of course, the conception he achieves depends in part upon the prereflective conception with which he began. But any user of the method of doubt who begins with such a conception of himself must be capable of coherently conceiving himself to be something that thinks and is not extended. It must be possible for him to conceive of himself in this way if he can carry out the "I exist" reasoning, and that reasoning uncovers a condition that makes First Meditation doubt possible. Arnauld is right, then, to single out the "I exist" reasoning as making a crucial contribution to the self-conception Descartes claims to form in the Second Meditation. But Descartes is not offering a fallacious argument for the nonidentity of the mind and body. Rather, he is articulating a conception whose coherence is guaranteed by the "I exist" reasoning—or so he thinks.

Where does this leave the vaporous soul? In the Second Meditation Descartes is arguing that it is *conceivable* that what thinks is not a vapor and not a physical thing at all. For all that he has shown there, it may nonetheless be true that some important part of us is a vapor and has some important relation to thinking. But if part of us is a vapor, and is related to thinking, there is one sort of relation the Second Meditation will have ruled out (supposing for the moment that God is not a deceiver). The thinking could not be a *mode* of the vapor, to use a term Descartes will introduce presently.[27] The relation between thinking and a vapor, or any physical thing (say, a brain), could not be the relation of a mode to a substance. It could not be like the relation between being round and being a physical object. That is an example of modal relation: an instance of roundness can exist only by being the roundness of some existing extended object. Being round cannot be conceived apart from being extended, because being round is a way of being extended. In denying that intellectual activity is modally dependent upon anything physical, Descartes is for now leaving open several other relations that might hold between intellectual activity and a physical thing. It might be that a physical thing causes intellectual activity to occur. Or it might be that the thing

---

[27] See 2:24 (AT 7:34) and 1:211 ff. (AT 8A:29 ff.). Rozemond stresses this point as well (1993, 107), though she gives a different account of Descartes's defense of the claim that the relation of thought to extension is not modal.

that is intellectually active is also, as a matter of fact, a physical thing. Descartes concedes that he is not yet in a position to articulate and evaluate these apparent possibilities.[28] But what he thinks he *is* in a position to do is to form a coherent conception of the referent of "I" as thinking and nonextended.

So we have seen a second way in which Descartes uses his doubt, one that is shaped by the first. The first way Descartes uses his doubt in the Second Meditation is to discover that the truth of "I exist" is a condition of the possibility of doubt. The second is to use the doubt to purge his conception of himself—to clarify it, in one sense of "clarify." And Descartes sees his ability to succeed in this as guaranteed by the fact that he has used his doubt to achieve certainty that he exists. So although the arguments of the second block are not themselves dependence arguments, Descartes thinks their success is guaranteed by the fact that in the first block he used dependence arguments to establish certainty about his existence.

CAREFUL SELF-ATTRIBUTIONS AS CONDITIONS OF DOUBT

I turn now to the third block of the Second Meditation, in which Descartes uses his doubt to provide dependence arguments to *add more to* the pared-down conception of himself that he has formed so far. In doing this, he will also be paring something down: not his former conception of himself, but his former conceptions of the sorts of activities or states that he can attribute to himself. His arguments here are as philosophically consequential as any he offers, I believe, though they are highly compressed and often misunderstood.

Descartes begins by boldly listing all the new material that he will argue he can add to the conception of himself that he is forming:

> But what then am I? A thing that thinks. What is that? Certainly a thing that doubts, understands, affirms, denies, is willing, is unwilling—and that imagines and senses, too. (2:19; AT 7:28; trans. altered)

[28] What he lacks is not just the validation of clear and distinct ideas but any explicit consideration of the metaphysical categories of substance and cause, and with them, the

Many readers suppose that here Descartes is summarizing what he has just been saying in the previous two paragraphs. But as we have seen, he *hasn't* said that all of these sorts of states belong to him, and in the very next sentence he makes clear his sense that he has yet to argue that these states *do* belong to him: "These are many things, *if* they all belong to me" (2:19; AT 7:28; trans. altered; emphasis added). Descartes aims now to broaden his conception of himself, to include more in it than just reasoning or exercising intelligence or intellect. But he will not be relaxing his insistence that his conception be a conception of himself that includes only characteristics he can be certain he has. The strategy he used in the paring-down phase of his reflections has taken him as far as it can go. He needs a new strategy.

To see what this new argumentative strategy is, we need to tease apart two conclusions Descartes is trying to reach. One is the conclusion that he can be certain that such-and-such a state belongs to him. The other is that such-and-such a state is nothing distinct from "thinking." I want to start by focusing on arguments for the first sort of conclusion.

In arguing that he can be certain that everything on the new, longer list belongs to him, Descartes says, "Are not all these things equally true as the fact that I exist, even if I am asleep all the time, and even if he who created me is doing all he can to deceive me?" (2:19; AT 7:28–29; trans. altered). Although his argumentative strategy here is hardly evident, I think he is giving us a clue: he is comparing the way he is arguing here to the way he established "I exist." So take for example one of the self-reports he mentions: "I am now doubting almost everything." Suppose I am right in seeing Descartes as establishing "I exist" by using a dependence argument, and suppose that he means now to be saying that a similar sort of argument will establish "I am doubting almost everything." Then his argument here would be this: it is a condition of my engaging in methodic doubt that I should now doubt almost everything, and so one thing I cannot rationally doubt is that I am now doubting almost everything. In terms of the schema I introduced in chapter 6, his argument would have this form:

---

relevant notions of dependence and independence. Descartes does not broach these topics until the Third Meditation.

1. If I use the method of doubt to doubt whether "I am doubting almost everything" is true, I must grant that I am using the method of doubt.

2. If I am using the method of doubt, then I must be doubting almost everything.

3. If I am using the method of doubt to doubt whether "I am doubting almost everything" is true, then I must grant that I am doubting almost everything.

This argument would enable Descartes to achieve certainty about "I am doubting almost everything" by enabling him to see that he cannot rationally doubt whether it is true, because its truth is a condition of doubt. (It would be a condition of doubt in the second of the three senses I distinguished in chapter 6.)

There is a complication here, one that emerges more clearly for another of the self-reports Descartes mentions. Consider the self-report "I affirm that 'I exist' is true" (see 2:19; AT 7:28). Its truth is hardly a condition on the construction of a skeptical scenario or on using a skeptical scenario to doubt something. After all, in the First Meditation, Descartes was engaging in methodic doubt, but he was not, then, affirming that "I exist" is true.

What we need here is room to expand the notion of engaging in methodic doubt. To that notion belongs not just what goes on in the First Meditation, but also whatever it is that method-guided use of the doubt leads us to do. As Descartes's meditations progress, then, he can enrich his account of his engagement in methodic doubt and, correspondingly, his account of what makes this engagement possible. So at this stage he can affirm with certainty that he "is now doubting almost everything, . . . understands some things, . . . affirms that this one thing is true, denies everything else, desires to know more, is unwilling to be deceived" (2:19; AT 7:28). All of these are conditions on his using the skeptical scenarios of the First Meditation in order to doubt, where the doubt is guided by the intellectual motivations and goals that I described in Part One.

Notice that Descartes is giving a new kind of argument for attributing to himself states like doubting, understanding, affirming, and denying. His point here is not that these intellectual activities pass the First Meditation test: he is not making the weak claim that as he conceives them these activities do not require the existence of something he has called into doubt. Rather, he is arguing that he must regard these self-ascriptions as indubitable, and that they are indubitable because they make methodic doubt possible. Of course, once he achieves certainty about these self-ascriptions, he can be sure they pass the First Meditation test. However, he achieves absolute certainty about them not by somehow determining directly that they lie beyond the scope of the First Meditation doubt, but instead by seeing that they make the First Meditation doubt so much as possible.

Now let me turn to the passage in which Descartes most fully works out a dependence argument about a kind of self-report. This is the passage in which he shows how to apply this sort of argument to the very difficult case of sensation; as I said earlier, he must carefully pare down his notion of sensing in order to make this sort of argument work for reports on his sensory states. Here is the argument:

> [I]t is also the same 'I' who senses, or takes notice of bodily things as it were through the senses. For example, I am now seeing a light, hearing a noise, feeling heat. But I am asleep, so all this is false. Yet I certainly *seem* to see, to hear, to be warmed. This cannot be false; this is what in me is properly called 'sensing', and taken thus precisely, it is nothing other than thinking. (2:19; AT 7:29; trans. altered)

I think that here Descartes is trying to show that carefully worded self-reports about sensing are conditions of the possibility of engaging in methodic doubt. What are the conditions of my doubting whether I am seeing a light? Well, of course, the doubt Descartes deploys is not the doubt that might arise when there is little or nothing to suggest to me that I *am* seeing a light—when I am wide awake with my eyes open in a very dark room, for example. The doubt that interests him is the doubt that arises when my current experience prompts me to believe that I am seeing a light. If I am to doubt whether I am seeing a light in *these* circumstances, I must be having a particular sort of experience. What sort is that? If Descartes answers, "Seeing a light," then he cannot have used the skeptical scenarios to doubt whether there is something luminous before him, because if someone sees a light, then he is using his eyes to detect the presence of a luminous object. That, at any rate, is how Descartes has been understanding what it is to see something. But clearly he thinks that this is much too quick a way with the skeptical arguments of the First Meditation: he does not think he can answer the question whether he is, say, dreaming by simply identifying his present experience as the experience of using his eyes to behold something luminous. Faced with this difficulty, he hits upon the idea of identifying his experience as that of seeming to see a light, or as the experience as of seeing a light.

Once he has taken this step, Descartes is able to argue that he can be *certain* he seems to see a light, because he can appeal to a dependence argument to bring out the way in which the correctness of this self-ascription is a condition of his doubt. Then by seeing this, he will be able to recognize that in his present circumstances, he cannot rationally doubt whether he seems to see a light. Here is Descartes's reasoning in this dependence argument, as I understand it:

1. If I have a reason to doubt whether I am seeing a light in the present circumstances, then I must grant that while it may be that my present experience is caused by a light, it may instead be that it is caused by whatever causes dreams (and I cannot tell which account is correct).

2. If either my present experience is caused by a light or it is caused by whatever causes dreams, then at least it must be true that I am having this experience: the experience as of seeing a light.

3. If I have a reason to doubt whether I am seeing a light in the present circumstances, then at least it must be true that I am having the experience as of seeing a light.

By reflecting on (3), I come to see that, as things are, I can be absolutely certain that I seem to see a light.

This short passage about sense perception is a philosophically significant one, I think, and I want to develop several points about it. First, the dependence argument implicit in it is not quite the same as the arguments Descartes used earlier in the third block. Those arguments concerned conditions on his *using* the skeptical scenarios of the First Meditation in order to pursue the project of methodic doubt. The argument about sensing, however, concerns conditions on the possible truth of the skeptical scenarios. "I seem to see a light," for example, must be true if skeptical

135

scenarios about what I see are to be possibly true—or so I take Descartes to be arguing. In the third block, then, he is moving freely between the first and second of the three sorts of dependence arguments that I distinguished in chapter 6; he is not appealing to a single consideration in claiming certainty about all of the states he is now attributing to himself.

Second, in giving this reading of this passage, I mean to be attributing to Descartes concerns and emphases that are a little different from the ones that are usually attributed to him.[29] His claim that he is certain about self-reports like "I am doubting" and "I seem to see a light" is usually thought to rest directly upon the doctrine of the transparency of consciousness to itself. According to this understanding of Descartes, he is saying these claims are certain because they report on states of the self of whose presence and nature the self must be conscious. Bernard Williams, for example, explains the "basis" of Descartes's "certainty" about these states by saying that he "takes those operations of the mind to be immediately obvious to the thinker, and the thinker to have immediate access to them. . . . [H]e regards some propositions about such states as both incorrigible and evident, and the states as being necessarily present to consciousness."[30]

I agree that Descartes thinks the mind is conscious of its states simply by its having them as its states. In the Second Replies, for example, he defines "thought" and "idea" in this way:

> I use ["thought"] to include everything that is within us in such a way that
> we are immediately aware of it. Thus all the operations of the will, the
> intellect, the imagination and the senses are thoughts. . . . I understand

---

[29] Curley reaches conclusions similar to mine here, though on slightly different grounds (1978, 170–92).

[30] B. Williams 1978, 80. I must add that I am puzzled by Williams's detailed account of the incorrigible and evident character of these self-reports. He says they fit this schema: A believes p if and only if p is true (306). So, for example, Descartes would be claiming, "I believe I seem to see a light if and only if I seem to see a light." But until he has reached this point in his meditations, Descartes *hasn't* had the belief that he seems to see a light on many of the occasions upon which it has been true of him that he seems to see a light. He hasn't had the belief because he has been unable to wield the requisite conception, that of what is "properly called 'sensing'." Radner (1988) gives a very interesting broad account of consciousness in Descartes's philosophy, an account upon which neither incorrigibility nor evidence is necessary to consciousness.

["idea"] to mean the form of any given thought, immediate perception of
which makes me aware of the thought. (2:113; AT 7:160)

But I don't think that in the Second Meditation he means for this doctrine
to serve as his *ground* for certainty about his carefully worded self-reports.
He thinks instead that this certainty arises from the relation between the
self-reports and the possibility of methodic doubt. Having said this, I must
add that Descartes himself may be partly responsible for obscuring his
point. By saying that it cannot be *"false"* that he seems to see, he may
mislead the reader into thinking that he is arguing that his belief that he
seems to see is indubitable because it is incorrigible,[31] and then the reader
may assume that Descartes is appealing to the transparency of the mind
to itself in order to explain its incorrigible knowledge of its states. But
Descartes is not claiming incorrigibility for these self-reports; he is claiming
indubitability. When he speaks in this passage of what is or cannot be false,
he is simply using the conceit that treats what is dubitable as if it were
false, something he does in other places in the Second Meditation as well.

Third, if I am right about how to read this passage, then Descartes is
not trying to make a point about "seems" that some people attribute to
him. Robert Brandom, for example, says this:

Descartes was struck by the fact that the appearance/reality distinction
seems not to apply to appearances. . . . While I may legitimately be challenged by a doubter—"Perhaps the item is not *really* red; perhaps it only
seems red"—there is not room for the further doubt, "Perhaps the item does
not even *seem* red; perhaps it only *seems* to seem red." If it seems to seem
red, then it really does seem red. The *looks*, *seems*, or *appears* operations
collapse if we try to iterate them. (1997, 136–37)

Descartes is not resting his case on the way in which "seems" works.

Finally, however, I must add that I do have sympathy for readers who,
like Brandom and Williams, look in this passage for something Descartes
is not actually providing, for there is indeed something missing from his
argument. I think that in this passage Descartes is trying to reach *two*
conclusions with the dependence strategy, but that he can use it to reach
at most only one. To distinguish the two conclusions, let me begin by

---

[31] For a good example of this very common reading, see Hacker 1972, esp. 79.

noting that in the dependence argument about sensing, step (3) does not say something of the form "To raise a doubt whether (B), one must grant that (B) is true." This is because the doubt is to be raised about *seeing*, and what must be true if I am to doubt is something different: that I *seem to see*. On the face of it this vitiates Descartes's use of the dependence strategy here: dependence arguments are supposed to reveal that an effort to doubt a claim must somehow presuppose the truth of *that very claim*.

I think it is clear how Descartes would reply to this objection. He would reply that his use of the dependence strategy is not vitiated, because seeming to see is an *aspect of* seeing. It is the element in seeing whose self-attribution I cannot coherently doubt. And this is something I am supposed to discover *by* discovering that there is a way in which I cannot coherently doubt whether I am seeing. I discover that seeming to see is "what in me is properly called sensing" (2:19; AT 7:29; trans. altered) by finding that it is what I can be certain I am doing. The dependence strategy is supposed to allow me *both* to identify seeming to see as an aspect of seeing *and* to achieve certainty that I seem to see.

Notice, however, that in step (2) of the dependence argument about sensing, Descartes simply *asserts* that if my present experience is that of seeing, then I am seeming to see a light. It is not at all clear what entitles him to make this assertion. Step (2) presents us with two cases: I am really seeing a light, or I am dreaming I am seeing a light. We can understand why Descartes says that if I am dreaming I am seeing a light, then I seem to see a light: he is using the *ordinary* notion of merely seeming to see, one that is *contrastive with* the notion of seeing and therefore one that is just right for expressing the difference between dreaming and waking experience. But that does not help to explain his basis for saying that in the case where I am really seeing a light, I am also, or at least, seeming to see. I do not think Descartes recognized that this claim needs a basis. I think he assumed that he could use the dependence strategy *both* to identify an aspect of sensing, *and* to establish certainty about it.[32] But he can use the dependence strategy to establish certainty that he seems to see only if has some other basis for claiming that seeming to see is an aspect of seeing.

---

[32] For a provocative discussion of related issues, see McDowell 1986.

Let me now turn to the second strand of argument in this complex passage. Intertwined with his dependence arguments for a number of self-ascriptions is Descartes's insistence that each of the states he is ascribing to himself is nothing distinct from "thinking," or that each belongs to "the same 'I'" (2:19; AT 7:28).[33] At the beginning of the passage, he seems to be saying merely that whatever it is that carries out his reasoning or intellectual activity *also* wills, desires, imagines, and senses. But by the end, he is claiming that all of these states he ascribes to himself—intellectual ones like doubting, understanding, affirming, denying, but also the operations of imagining and sensing—are so many different ways of doing one thing: thinking. Seeming to see a light, for example, is "what in me is properly called sensing," and "taken thus precisely, [this] is nothing other than thinking" (2:19; AT 7:29; trans. altered). In a retrospective passage from the beginning of the Third Meditation, Descartes says a bit more about the relation between all of these self-ascribed states and "thinking":

> [A]s I have noted before, even though the objects of my sensory experience and imagination may have no existence outside me, nonetheless the modes of thinking which I refer to as cases of sensory perception and imagination, in so far as they are simply modes of thinking, do exist within me—of that I am certain. (2:24; AT 7:34–35)

The self-ascribed states are all *"modes of thinking"*; just as it is inconceivable that a thing having a round shape should fail to be extended, so too is it inconceivable that a thing that seems to see should fail to be "thinking."

So in the complex passage I have been analyzing, Descartes is at once paring down the conceptions of desiring, willing, imagining, and sensing, and offering us a greatly broadened notion of thinking. The conceptions of sensing (and so on) are pared down to order: the point is to find the aspect of his state that he can ascribe to himself with certainty. But what

[33] Carriero (1984, 185 ff.) is helpful in explaining how the concern with "the same 'I'" might arise out of Descartes's implicit dialogue with an Aristotelian philosopher, who would have difficulties within his own philosophical system around the individuation of the 'I'.

is the broad notion of thinking that the meditator is invoking?[34] It is surely the notion of being conscious of something, or being aware of something. Descartes assumes that this notion of consciousness will emerge right away from the indubitable self-ascriptions that he has developed. Doubting, imagining, seeming to see: all of these are ways of being conscious. Descartes will tell us more about consciousness in the Third Meditation, and when he does we will find that there is considerably more structure to states of consciousness than is apparent in the Second Meditation (see, e.g., 2:25–26, 30; AT 7:37, 43–44). But in the Second Meditation it is enough to see that each of the states I can ascribe to myself indubitably is a way of my being conscious of something.

This, however, leaves unexplained the connection between this notion of consciousness and the narrow notion Descartes had earlier pulled out of his prereflective conception of himself. We may be strongly tempted to read a great deal into this connection. For example, we may want to see Descartes as supposing that all thoughts are representations that have a propositional character, so that all states of consciousness can have relations to one another that the mind can discover in operations of "intelligence, or intellect, or reason" (2:18; AT 7:27). Another reading, perhaps related to this one, would be to see Descartes as eventually concluding that the intellect is *purely* what the conscious mind is *essentially.*[35]

I would like, however, to be able to find a different account of the relation *in the Second Meditation* between the narrow and broad conceptions of thinking. At this early stage of his reflections, the meditator is in no position to appeal to the structure of thought, or to the nature of a mind distinct from the body, to explain the relation between intellect and consciousness. (Of course, Descartes the author may want to foreshadow ideas he will develop later. But he has to give his meditator a reason for thinking the portentous thought.)

Recall that in the second block of text, Descartes did not offer a rationale for conceiving of intellectual activity as activity that passes the First

[34] In the development of Descartes's own philosophical account of the mind, the ancestor of this broad notion of consciousness must be the notion of cognitive power, which, Descartes claimed in the *Rules*, is one and the same power whether acting "on its own [*sola*]" or in application to the common sense or the phantasia (1:42; AT 10:416).

[35] See Rozemond 1998, 59–60; compare the Sixth Meditation (2:54; AT 7:78–79).

Meditation test, nor did he offer any answer to the question what exactly counts as intellectual activity. So the boundaries of the category "intellectual activity" are not clear, and neither is my reason for saying I can be certain I am engaging in intellectual activity. I think it is useful to see the third block of text that I have been discussing as intended to remedy these deficiencies in the second block. The third block begins by revisiting "intellectual activity" and examining activities that might plausibly be included in this category: doubting, understanding, affirming, denying, willing, being unwilling. Having partly clarified his idea of himself, by forming the special conception of himself as only "thinking," Descartes is now in a position to notice and reflect upon the relation between "thinking" and carrying out the project of methodic doubt. What he discovers, though, is that what makes his self-ascription of these activities indubitable is not the fact that they are *intellectual*; it is rather the fact that they are the conscious states he must be in if his pursuit of methodic doubt is to be possible. Then he discovers that the *same* general sort of consideration applies more broadly, to the carefully pared-down imaginative and sensory states that he finds he can ascribe to himself indubitably. It is as if the term "thinking" is a placeholder for the states Descartes has at any point realized he can ascribe to himself indubitably. He chooses this particular term because he needs a term early on, in the second block, where it seems to him that his intellectual states are the ones he can ascribe to himself indubitably. He sticks with it because he finds he can so readily adapt it to cover the broader and more clearly defined category with which he emerges from the third block.

Although I believe this is the best way to see how the notion of "thinking" broadens in the Second Meditation, I do not think we can look outside the Second Meditation for much confirmation of this reading. This is because Descartes himself very often telescopes the sequence of discoveries that he lays out in the Second Meditation.[36] It is natural that

[36] I think it is also fair to say that Descartes did not himself clearly see how to lay out this sequence until he sat down and wrote the *Meditations*, where for the first time he engaged closely with the question how an inquirer could follow a chain of reflection that would lead from the general metaphysical outlook of common sense to the corrected Cartesian outlook. Since he himself had the Cartesian outlook before he wrote the *Meditations*, we should not be surprised to find the "telescoped" view surfacing

he should do so; after all, he himself holds the fully clarified view that the meditator must arrive at one strenuous step at a time. But this means that he sometimes obscures what are actually very interesting features of the argumentative course he is taking in the *Meditations*.

I believe that one place in which he unhelpfully telescopes the sequence of discoveries is in his reply to Gassendi, in the passage that seems to lend support to the Cogito First interpretation. In answering Gassendi, Descartes distinguishes between walking and the "awareness of walking" that I have when "I seem to myself to be walking" or "think I am walking" (2:244; AT 7:352). That is, he appeals to the sort of distinction he drew at the end of the *third* block of the Second Meditation, several eventful pages after the "I exist" passage that Gassendi had asked about. This appeal thus takes for granted all the hard work the meditator did in the second and third blocks. Recall that in the second block, the meditator excluded "movement" (*incedere*: to walk around) from the conception of himself that he proposed to develop (2:18; AT 7:27), and that he did not yet see any way to decompose his walking around into seeming to walk and traveling through space. That decomposition required the dependence arguments in the third block, the arguments that enabled the meditator to identify "precisely" "what in me is properly called sensing" (2:19; AT 7:29; trans. altered).

Of course, once those dependence arguments in the third block go through, the meditator is in a position to claim certainty about its seeming to him that he is walking. And then because the inference from "I think" to "I exist" is valid, his certainty about "I think" constitutes an entitlement to certainty about "I exist."[37]

But this route to certainty about "I exist" rests upon concepts and distinctions that Descartes did not have available to him early in the Second Meditation. In his exasperation with Gassendi, and in his eagerness to underline the difference between two ways of taking "I am walking,"

---

even in the *Meditations*, albeit more briefly than it did in earlier writings. Compare, for example, Descartes's reply to Gassendi with his letter of 1638 to Reneri for Pollot (3:98; AT 2:37–38).

[37] Perhaps this is a point Descartes means to be making at the end of the Second Meditation where he says, for example, that "when I see, or (now I do not distinguish this) think I see, it is simply not possible that I who am thinking am not then something" (2:22; AT 7:33; trans. altered).

Descartes conflates the dependence argument for the indubitability of "I exist" with a quite different argument that treats the indubitability of self-ascription of various thoughts as somehow already established.

In a way, there is nothing wrong with this: Descartes does, after all, have arguments in favor of treating "I think I am walking" as indubitable. But he is obscuring the special character of his argumentation in the Second Meditation, and he is blurring his own careful delineation of the meditator's steps toward a clear conception of himself. Perhaps this should not surprise us greatly: Descartes himself was far more eager to articulate the *results* he thought this inquiry had led to, than he was to dwell upon the method that guided it. His interests in what he was doing may in this respect be different from ours.

❖ 8 ❖

Outer Conditions

I<small>N THE</small> Second Meditation, Descartes discovered that his own existence is a condition of his engaging in inquiry guided by the method of doubt, and he used the doubts of the First Meditation to discover new ways to describe his nature and his states. In the Third Meditation, he goes on to argue that, ultimately, the existence of God as his creator is a condition of his engaging in inquiry guided by the method of doubt. This enables him to judge with complete certainty that God created him, and thus that everything he understands clearly and distinctly to be true, is true.

The existence of God, then, is an outer condition of Descartes's doubt. Of course, God is not outer in the sense of occupying a space that is somehow outside the doubter: God does not occupy any space at all. Rather, God is outer in the sense that he is something distinct from Descartes and his states. In most of this chapter I will be concerned with the argumentative steps that lead Descartes from doubt to God, but at the end I will look briefly at the character of the argument that leads Descartes to absolute certainty that extended things exist. Like God, extended things are "outer" objects in the sense that they are distinct from the meditator and his own states; unlike God, they occupy space.

Descartes's argument in the Third Meditation for God's existence is a sort of cosmological argument, moving from a contingent premise about what exists to the conclusion that this could not exist unless it were caused to exist by God. Descartes actually gives two somewhat distinct cosmological arguments in the Third Meditation, the first inquiring into the origin of my idea of God, and the second into the origin of me. But *my* idea of God cannot exist without me, and the second argument turns on the point that I must have an idea of God. So both arguments have much the same (compound) contingent premise: I exist and have an idea of God. Both arguments are powered by principles concerning causality; it is those principles that, when applied to the contingent premise, yield the conclusion that God exists. The second argument has a more complex structure and draws upon ideas about perfections and time that the first argument forgoes. But the second argument cannot forgo the causal premises of the first, which at bottom are simply this: *ex nihil, nihil fit*; from nothing, nothing comes. So with no further apologies, I will focus my attention on the first argument and leave the complexities of the second argument alone.[1]

The contingent premise and the causal principle do not yield the conclusion Descartes wants in any obvious way. Consider:

1. I have an idea of God.
2. From nothing, nothing comes.
3. So, God exists.

We would certainly ridicule an argument that proceeded in apparent parallel:

1. I have an idea of Athene.
2. From nothing, nothing comes.
3. So, Athene exists.

Not surprisingly, Descartes thinks there is something special about the idea of God that sets it apart from an idea like the idea of Athene. He also thinks it is crucial to see how to tailor the causal principle for effects that are ideas in someone's mind.

In what follows I will look more closely at what Descartes says about his idea of God and about the causal principle, and I will argue that we can see Descartes as treating both these premises as conditions of doubt. I must confess that although I think Descartes's way of identifying *inner* conditions of doubt in the Second Meditation is of intrinsic philosophical interest, I cannot say the same for his effort to show that God's existence is also a condition of doubt. What I think is interesting about the Third Meditation argument is what it reveals about Descartes's conception of the method of doubt: how it is supposed to work, and what it is supposed to yield.

---

[1] Although Stephen Menn (1998, 293 ff.) contrasts the conclusions of these arguments—one, he thinks, concerns God's existence as Nous and the other God's existence as Creator—he, too, sees no deep differences between the arguments.

The Idea of God

Descartes's contingent premise is compound: "I exist and have an idea of God." I have already traced the source of his certainty that "I exist" is true: it arises from his recognition that his existence is a condition of his doubt. But what about his certainty that he has an idea of God? And exactly what belongs to that idea?

Descartes says that his idea of God is the idea of "a substance that is infinite, . . . independent, supremely intelligent, supremely powerful, and which created both myself and everything else (if anything else there be) that exists" (2:31; AT 7:45). It is the idea of a "supremely perfect and infinite being" (2:31; AT 7:46), and "whatever I clearly and distinctly perceive as being real and true, and implying any perfection, is wholly contained in it" (2:32; AT 7:46). To meet his goal of making progress using the method of doubt, he must be able to say that he is absolutely certain that he has precisely this idea. To meet the goal of making the cosmological argument work, he must be able to say that this idea is one that he could not have constructed simply from the materials that he presents to himself in self-reflection, for otherwise he would himself be an adequate cause of his having the idea.

Let me begin with what he needs in order to meet the goal of certainty. I think many readers would agree with Bernard Williams, who says that for Descartes, in "knowing *that he has the idea of God*" Descartes has "a certainty of the psychological, immediate sort."[2] Although Williams does not elaborate, I take him to mean that Descartes is certain he has the idea of God in the same way in which he is certain that he seems to see a light or seems to hear a noise. And Descartes has already explained his certainty about ascribing those states to himself in the Second Meditation. Now, Williams himself claims that in the Second Meditation Descartes presented these self-ascriptions as incorrigible and evident, that is, as claims that the meditator believes are true if and only if they are true (1978, 79 ff., 306). I have argued that Descartes's point was, rather, that these self-ascriptions are absolutely certain: the meditator finds that he cannot coherently raise doubts, in the relevant circumstances, about whether they are correct. For my present purposes, it is not especially

[2] B. Williams 1978, 87; see also 146: this proposition "requires no proof."

important which of the accounts of the self-ascriptions in the Second Meditation is correct. The point I want to argue for here is that Descartes's ascription to himself of the idea of God does not work in the same way as the Second Meditation self-ascriptions do, on either of these accounts of them.

In crediting himself with the idea of God, Descartes is not, or is not simply, reporting upon a psychological state of his. Of course, when he thinks about God, he is in a particular state, and his argument for God's existence depends upon this fact about himself. But it depends equally upon the state's being one in which Descartes entertains a concept that can correctly be described in a particular way, as one that he could not have put together from the materials that reflection upon himself can provide. He is not using "immediate access" to the "psychological" to establish with certainty that when he thinks about God, he is entertaining a concept with this feature.

Instead, he uses a dependence argument to try to establish both that he can be certain he has a concept of God and that it has the character he needs it to have.[3] Here is what he says:

> It is true that I have the idea of substance in me in virtue of the fact that I am a substance; but this would not account for my having the idea of an infinite substance, when I am finite. . . . And I must not think that, just as my conceptions of rest and darkness are arrived at by negating movement and light, so my perception of the infinite is arrived at not by means of a true idea but merely by negating the finite. On the contrary, I clearly understand that there is more reality in an infinite substance than in a finite one, and hence that my perception of the infinite, that is God, is in some way prior to my perception of the finite, that is myself. For how could I understand that I doubted or desired—that is, lacked something—and that I was not wholly perfect, unless there were in me some idea of a more perfect being which enabled me to recognize my own defects by comparison? (2:31; AT 7:45–46)

Someone who uses the method of doubt must be able to think of himself as doubting, as desiring to know more, and as limited in knowledge and

---

[3] Menn sees parallels between Descartes's procedure here and Augustine's procedure in *Confessions* 7.17.23 (1998, 138 ff. and 281 ff.).

power. I think it is no coincidence that here in the Third Meditation Descartes mentions just these self-ascriptions,[4] and I think he is arguing that a condition of his being able to attribute these states to himself is that he have a concept of God that he could not have derived from self-reflection.

To unpack the argument, let me begin by considering just the line of thought that Descartes mentions in the retrospective passage from the Fourth Meditation that I quoted in chapter 6: "insofar as I consider the fact that I have doubts, or that I am a thing that is incomplete and dependent, there arises in me a clear and distinct idea of a being who is independent and complete, that is, an idea of God" (2:37; AT 7:53; trans. altered). Let me spell out just that much in terms of the dependence strategy:

1. If I raise a doubt whether I have an idea of God, I must grant that I doubt.
2. But if I grant (recognize) that I doubt, then I have an idea of God.
3. So if I raise a doubt whether I have an idea of God, I must grant that I have an idea of God.

Step (1) is simple and unexceptionable, but step (2) is complicated. Descartes apparently thinks it sums up these substeps:

2a. If I can recognize that I doubt, then I can recognize that I am limited (incomplete, lacking, defective).
2b. If I can recognize that I am limited, then I can deny that the concept of absolute perfection applies to myself.
2c. If I can deny that the concept of absolute perfection applies to myself, then I have the idea of absolute perfection.

Step (2a) draws upon the idea that to doubt is to be limited in knowledge. Step (2c) presumably rests on the plausible claim that to have the concept of something's not being P, I must also have the concept of something's

---

[4] Descartes makes the connection explicit in the *Discourse*: "reflecting upon the fact that I was doubting and that consequently my being was not wholly perfect . . . I decided to inquire into the source of my ability to think of something more perfect than I was" (1:127–28; AT 6:33).

being P.[5] So if (2b) is true, then by reflecting on the argument from (1) to (3) I will find that I cannot coherently doubt whether I have the idea of absolute perfection, because my having that idea is a condition of my doubt.

Step (2b), however, raises a question Descartes must answer: why does his recognition that he doubts entail that he can deny the concept of absolute perfection of himself? Why must he be thinking, even implicitly, that he is not God-like?[6] After all, there appears to be a different way in which he could think he is limited: he could simply recognize that he has *less* of something he might have had *more* of. For example, he has absolute certainty that he exists, but not that he has a body. He would have more knowledge if he knew both that he exists and that he has a body. It is not clear why being able to think in *this* way about himself would entail his having the concept or idea of absolute perfection, or more generally why he could not recognize his limitations simply by using the concept of having various virtues to greater and lesser degrees.

This might seem to be a minor problem for Descartes's argument, for even if he conceded the difficulty, he could still argue as follows:

2a. If I can recognize that I doubt, then I can recognize that I am limited.

2d. If I can recognize that I am limited, then I can deny that the concept of "more knowledgeable than this" applies to myself.

2e. If I can deny that the concept of "more knowledgeable than this" applies to myself, then I have the idea of being more knowledgeable than this.

And although (2e) does not attribute the idea of God to me, we might think that the sort of idea it does attribute to me is the only sort of idea

---

[5] As I understand him, Kenny argues that to the extent that this is what Descartes is saying, he is defeating his own purposes (1968, 136). I sympathize with this criticism but want to locate the problem more precisely.

[6] I think this is the question Bernard Williams is raising when he asks whether Descartes is taking for granted that "his own striving after knowledge is correctly to be seen as an aspiration to God's state of perfect knowledge, and an aspiration which is one in the right direction, as it were, and which represents the higher aspects of his nature" (1978, 146). Beyssade's discussion of the idea of aspiration is suggestive in this connection (1992, 180–82).

we need to have in order to construct the idea of God. This is what Gassendi thought; he argued as follows:

> [A]lthough every supreme perfection is normally attributed to God, it seems that such perfections are all taken from things which we commonly admire in ourselves, such as longevity, power, knowledge, goodness, blessedness, and so on. By amplifying these things as much as we can, we assert that God is eternal, omnipotent, omniscient, supremely good, supremely blessed and so on. (2:200; AT 7:286–87)

Descartes does not deny that we have the power of amplifying in our thoughts the things we "admire in ourselves"; indeed, in his reply to Hobbes he insists on it: "Now everyone surely perceives that there are things he understands. Hence everyone has the form or idea of understanding; and by indefinitely extending this he can form the [an?] idea of God's understanding" (2:132; AT 7:188).

Steps (2d) and (2e) do not, however, supply what Descartes needs. The concept of a being more knowledgeable, benevolent, and powerful than he finds himself to be will not serve his argumentative purposes, even if it is the concept of a being whose virtues are extended indefinitely beyond those he finds in himself. The reason why such a concept will not do is that Descartes needs to show that the concept he can be certain he has is one that he could not have constructed from the materials he finds in self-reflection. Otherwise the cosmological argument will not work, because then he himself will be an adequate cause of his idea of God.

Descartes is well aware that he must show that the idea of God he can be certain he has is also one of which he could not be the adequate cause. But how exactly does he think he can show this? In the Third Meditation passage I have quoted, he gives the impression that he thinks the dependence argument itself establishes that the idea of God is "in some way prior" to his recognition of his own limited virtues (2:31; AT 7:45). He must not think that his "perception of the infinite is arrived at not by means of a true idea but merely by negating the finite" (2:31; AT 7:45), as Gassendi would have it; the *reason* for this presumably comes in the sentence beginning, "For. . . ." But what that sentence gives us is just claims (2b) and (2c) themselves: "how could I understand that I doubted or desired—that is, lacked something—and that I was not wholly perfect, unless there were in me some idea of a more perfect being?" (2:31; AT

7:45–46). This cannot give us a reason for preferring (2b) and (2c) over (2d) and (2e).

Burman reports that Descartes commented on this passage by saying: "Explicitly we are able to recognize our own imperfection before we recognize the perfection of God. This is because we are able to direct our attention to ourselves before we direct our attention to God. Thus we can infer our own finitude before we arrive at his infinitude. Despite this, however, the knowledge of God and his perfection must implicitly always come before the knowledge of ourselves and our imperfections" (3:338; AT 5:153). But this is not really to the point. What Descartes needs to establish is not that his idea of God is implicit in his explicit recognition of his imperfections, but that the implicit idea is one that could not be accounted for by (2d), (2e), and a Gassendi-style derivation.

In his reply to Gassendi, Descartes says that "the idea of God is not gradually formed by us when we amplify the perfections of his creatures; it is formed all at once and in its entirety as soon as our mind reaches an infinite being which is incapable of any amplification" (2:256; AT 7:371). This suggests that the reply to Hobbes is at best incomplete: we can indefinitely extend our virtues only so far. But it also suggests that the reply to Hobbes is out-and-out misleading: extending our virtues in our thought is not really *relevant* to the formation of an idea of God, for without the idea of infinitude, which we cannot obtain by amplification, what we have is not an idea of God.[7]

So what belongs to the concept of infinitude? Descartes tells Gassendi that "it suffices for the possession of a true and complete idea of the infinite in its entirety if we understand that it is a thing which is bounded by no limits" (2:254; AT 7:368). But this just makes the original question more pointed: this seems tailor-made for precisely the view Descartes opposes, the view that "my perception of the infinite is arrived at not by means of a true idea but merely by negating the finite" (2:31; AT 7:45).

In the Third Meditation passage, though, Descartes may be trying to make a somewhat different appeal to what is special about the idea of infinitude. He says he clearly understands "that there is more reality in an infinite substance than in a finite one." In a similar vein, he told Bur-

---

[7] So I agree with Margaret Wilson that Descartes must think that our power of amplifying cannot give rise to our idea of God, despite what he says to Hobbes (1999, 120).

man, after the remark I quoted earlier, that "knowledge of God and his perfection must implicitly always come before the knowledge of ourselves and our imperfections. For in reality the infinite perfection of God is prior to our imperfection, since our imperfection is a defect and negation of the perfection of God. And every defect and negation presupposes that of which it falls short and which it negates" (3:338; AT 5:153). And in a 1641 letter to "Hyperaspistes," a supporter of Gassendi, he writes:

> It is quite true that we do not understand the infinite by the negation of limitation; and one cannot infer that, because limitation involves the negation of infinity, the negation of limitation involves knowledge of the infinite. What makes the infinite different from the finite is something real and positive; but the limitation which makes the finite different from the infinite is non-being or the negation of being. That which is not cannot bring us to the knowledge of that which is; on the contrary, the negation of a thing has to be perceived on the basis of knowledge of the thing itself. (3:192; AT 3:426–27)

But all of this is disappointing as way of filling in the argument in the Third Meditation. Descartes needs to explain how and why the dependence argument establishes that his concept of God cannot be constructed out of his recognition of his limited nature, but what he provides in these passages is an abstract and contentious metaphysical doctrine about the nature of being and infinitude. And if this is how he wants to fill in the Third Meditation argument, then he will be detaching the argument for the apriority of the concept of God from the dependence argument that was supposed to give him certainty that he possessed such a concept. He will instead be denying that the concept of God is constructed out of our recognition of our limitation by asserting that the concept of an infinite being could not be just the concept of a being whose virtues are unlimited. But then we would have no way to understand how he could have hoped to show he can be certain he really has such a concept of infinite being.

I suspect that Descartes assumed that the dependence argument established the apriority of the concept of God, but that he sensed some of the difficulties I have been tracing. There is, after all, something very odd about the crucial passage in the Third Meditation. Here it is again:

> And I must not think that, just as my conceptions of rest and darkness are arrived at by negating movement and light, so my perception of the infinite

is arrived at not by means of a true idea but merely by negating the finite. On the contrary, I clearly understand that there is more reality in an infinite substance than in a finite one, and hence [*proinde*] that my perception of the infinite, that is God, is in some way prior to my perception of the finite, that is myself. For [*enim*] how could I understand that I doubted or desired— that is, lacked something—and that I was not wholly perfect, unless there were in me some idea of a more perfect being which enabled me to recognize my own defects by comparison? (2:31; AT 7:45–46)

Notice that Descartes first represents the apriority claim as a consequence of the metaphysical claim about reality and infinitude, and then represents it as a consequence of the move from recognition of limitation to possession of the concept of God. This is an uneasy arrangement of grounds and consequents, and I suspect it reflects some uneasiness in Descartes's own mind about exactly what he can establish here by using the dependence strategy.

Still, I think the dependence argument about the concept of God is interesting for the methodological ambitions it reveals. It suggests that Descartes is extending into the Third Meditation his effort to "use" his doubt by uncovering its conditions, and it suggests that he thinks he will be able to go on to conclude with certainty that God's existence is a condition of his use of his doubt. I am struck by the way in which Norman Kemp Smith describes the importance of the argument about the concept of God: "The centre of gravity of Descartes' philosophy thus shifts away from the self to that which in thought is disclosed to the self as other than the self, and as preconditioning the self, and (what in this connection is specially significant) as preconditioning the self's awareness even of its own nature" (1966, 301). I read Kemp Smith's language here as colored by his studies of Kant's philosophy—a coloration that is becoming, if I am right about the general character of Descartes's argumentation.

Causal Principles

Suppose that Descartes has achieved certainty about having a concept of God that he could not have derived from reflection upon himself. The other ingredient his cosmological argument requires is a causal principle according to which his possession of the idea of God requires God himself as its cause. The specific principle to which he appeals is this: the cause of an idea must have as much formal reality as the idea has of objective reality. Very few readers of the *Meditations* have found this principle plausible; in fact, the first question in the First Objections is this: "[W]hat sort of cause does an idea need?" (2:66; AT 7:92). I do not aim here to make this principle plausible; instead, I want to explore Descartes's grounds for holding it to be true, and to speculate about why he thought, not only that it is true, but also that he could be absolutely certain it is true.[8]

For Descartes, the principle about the causes of ideas is supposed to be a special application of a far more general causal principle. Unfortunately, in the Third Meditation he introduces the general principle in a misleading fashion. He says:

> Now it is manifest by the natural light that there must be at least as much <reality> in the efficient and total cause as in the effect of that cause. For where, I ask, could the effect get its reality from, if not from the cause? And how could the cause give it to the effect unless it possessed it? It follows from this both that something cannot arise from nothing, and also that what is more perfect—that is, contains in itself more reality—cannot arise from what is less perfect. (2:28; AT 7:40–41)

This way of putting it suggests that the general principle mainly concerns degrees of "reality," whatever those might be, and that this is a more basic principle than the *ex nihilo* principle, the principle that something cannot come from nothing.[9]

In fact, however, Descartes thinks that *every* aspect of what comes about in an effect must somehow preexist in its cause. That is his general causal principle; it is a principle specifying a necessary condition on something's being the cause of a particular effect. It is sometimes called an adequacy principle, because it says what would make something adequate to cause a specified effect. Descartes also says that the *ex nihilo* principle elucidates why this general adequacy principle holds; the *ex*

[8] For a useful survey of the questions about causation that occupied seventeenth- and eighteenth-century philosophers and scientists, see Clatterbaugh 1999, esp. chaps. 1–3.

[9] What he implies here is that the *ex nihilo* principle is a special case of the general causal principle he is introducing, presumably because "something" has some degree of reality and "nothing" has zero degrees of reality.

nihilo principle is one of the most basic ideas about causality to which he appeals. Both points emerge in the Second Replies:

> The fact that 'there is nothing in the effect which was not previously present in the cause, either in a similar or in a higher form' is a primary notion which is as clear as any that we have; it is just the same as the common notion 'Nothing comes from nothing.' For if we admit that there is something in the effect that was not previously present in the cause, we shall also have to admit that this something was produced by nothing. And the reason why nothing cannot be the cause of a thing is simply that such a cause would not contain the same features as are found in the effect. (2:97; AT 7:135)

Although this is clearer than the passage in the Third Meditation, much remains obscure. Indeed, I believe that what we see here is an uneasy mingling of two rather different ways of thinking about the source of the general principle about the adequacy of causes to effects. When Descartes appeals, as he does here, to the *ex nihilo* principle, he rests his general adequacy principle simply upon the idea that the cause provides the components of the effect. But as we will see, he also slides from this basis to a different one: the idea that the cause provides a sufficient reason for the occurrence of the effect.

When Descartes says that "if we admit that there is something in the effect that was not previously present in the cause, we shall also have to admit that this something was produced by nothing," we might naturally take him to be appealing to a basic thought about how new things come to be. For example, if a sandbar is formed in a river, then each of its component grains of sand must have existed elsewhere in the river before the sandbar was formed. More generally, a thing that comes into existence must have parts that are describable in such a way that each part, so described, existed before the effect came into existence.

Now, Descartes applies his general principle about causal adequacy to a very broad range of cases: not just to the material parts composing an effect, but also to quantities of motion,[10] to the representational aspects

---

[10] I believe that this is implied in the arguments of *Principles*, pt. 2, arts. 36 and 37 (1:240–41; AT 8A:61–63).

of ideas,[11] to God insofar as he is understood as his own effect,[12] to the world, understood as a creature of God, and to "degrees of reality," as the Third Meditation tells us. In all of these cases, Descartes insists that if something were in the effect that was not contained in the cause, then that something would be "produced from nothing." Can we find any way to extend the basic thought about component materials to this broad range of cases?

Although a quantity of motion is not a "something," we can perhaps see the appeal of saying that if a cue ball moving at two miles per hour were to hit an object ball and set it into motion at three miles per hour, then there would be a quantity of motion—one mile per hour—that came from nothing. Part of the reason we can see the appeal of saying this may lie in our assumption that the cue ball loses a quantity of motion that is at least as great as the quantity of motion that the object ball gains: the cue ball gives away—loses or donates—to the object ball "what comes about in the effect," and it cannot give what it does not have.

We cannot help ourselves to a similar thought in the full range of cases, however. God does not lose anything in being the cause of his own being or in creating finite substances; nor do the causes of the representational aspects of ideas give something up to the ideas; nor do causes lose the degrees of reality that come to be in their effects.[13] Descartes's application of his general adequacy principle outstrips the intuitive appeal of the basic thought that may at first seem to provide all of its intellectual motivation.

But that basic thought is not, I think, the only motivating thought that lies behind Descartes's general adequacy principle.[14] I think Descartes is also saying that if we admitted that something could be "produced by nothing," we would be allowing that something could come about without having been produced, or caused, by anything. Then the "primary" and "clear" notion Descartes would be invoking in the Second Replies

[11] That is what he is doing in the Third Meditation when he gives an adequacy principle for the objective reality of ideas.

[12] E.g., 2:78–80 (AT 7:108–11); 2:164–71 (AT 7:235–45).

[13] For a broader exploration of these different sorts of case, see Frankel 1986.

[14] Certainly Descartes would not endorse any version of this idea that depended upon an Aristotelian distinction among material, formal, final, and efficient causes. See Broughton 1977 and 1986.

would be the idea that everything must have been produced or caused by something, or must have a cause or reason why it exists. If this reading is correct, then at least part of the basic source for Descartes's general causal adequacy principle is a principle of sufficient reason.[15]

This reading gains support from several quarters. First, it helps to explain something that might otherwise be perplexing. The cosmological argument may strike post-Humean readers as requiring the premise that everything that exists has a cause of its existence. If we read the general adequacy principle as saying *only* what a thing must be like to be the cause of such-and-such a thing, then Descartes will have quite surprisingly left out an important premise of his argument: he will not have said that everything must *have* a cause. But if we see a principle of sufficient reason as part of Descartes's basic intellectual motivation for holding the general causal principle, then we can see why he would not have thought there was any need to offer a separate premise saying that everything has a cause.

Second, by seeing the general adequacy principle as fueled by a principle of sufficient reason, we can explain a puzzling remark that Descartes makes in the Second Replies. In the arguments "in geometrical fashion" that he gives there, he says: "Concerning every existing thing it is possible to ask what is the cause of its existence. This question may even be asked concerning God, not because he needs any cause in order to exist, but because the immensity of his nature is the cause or reason why he needs no cause in order to exist" (2:116; AT 7:164–65). Here Descartes says explicitly that we have given the "cause" (in one sense) of something when we have given the "reason" for its existence, even if (in another sense) the thing has no cause.[16]

We might now wonder whether we should interpret Descartes as resting the general adequacy principle *only* on a sort of principle of sufficient reason, and as making no appeal to the idea about the preexistence of an effect's components. I think this would be a mistake. The general ade-

[15] Delahunty reads the *ex nihilo* principle as *mainly* motivated by a principle of sufficient reason (1997, 89), and then reads the adequacy principle as drawing upon an additional principle: "If x is Φ because of y, then y is at least as Φ as x is" (90).

[16] Elsewhere Descartes explains that while we might not want to say that God has an *efficient* cause of his existence, he is nonetheless correctly regarded as the *cause* of his own existence. See 2:79–80 (AT 7:109–11) and 2:164–71 (AT 7:235–45).

quacy principle does not say only that everything has a cause or reason sufficient to explain its existence. It states a condition on what could constitute the reason why the effect exists. One thing could not constitute the reason why another thing exists if it failed to contain at least what comes to characterize the other thing.[17]

I do not see any fully satisfying way to explain how Descartes thought of the basis for his general adequacy principle. Understood through the idea that a cause must contain the material components of its effects, Descartes's principle is plausible for only a small portion of the full range of cases to which he applies it. Understood through an underlying principle of sufficient reason, it is plausible for the full range of cases but detached from the particular requirement of adequacy that Descartes means to be imposing. I think that as readers, we must simply say to ourselves that Descartes understood his general causal principle both as requiring that there should be a sufficient reason for the existence of everything that exists, and as requiring that causes must contain what comes about in their effects, and that he thought that both these requirements were made "clear" through the idea that something cannot come from nothing.

In the Third Meditation, Descartes wants to apply the general adequacy principle to a doubly special kind of case. First, he is interested in "degrees of reality" (rather than, say, quantities of motion), and consequently he articulates this more specific version of the causal principle:

A cause must have at least as much reality as its effect has.[18]

Second, he is interested in cases where the effects are ideas in someone's mind, and so he argues at length for this principle:

The cause of an idea must have at least as much formal reality as the idea has of objective reality.

---

[17] In the Second Replies Descartes gives as axioms not just the one I have quoted, but another stating the *ex nihilo* principle and yet another stating that the reality of an effect must be "present either formally or eminently in its first and adequate cause" (2:116; AT 7:165). For an interesting account of how the general principle of sufficient reason is connected to the requirement that the cause contain what comes to characterize its effect, see Frankel 1986.

[18] For a somewhat different way of understanding how degrees of reality come into play, see Clatterbaugh 1980.

I think that each of these special principles is even less plausible than the general principle, but again, my aim here is not to defend these principles but to explain what they say and why Descartes thought they were true.

By speaking of degrees of reality, Descartes does not, of course, mean to imply that tables and chairs can hover somewhere between existing and not existing. He comes closest to explaining what he *does* mean in the Third Replies. Hobbes had asked, "Does reality admit of more and less?" (2:130; AT 7:185), and Descartes answered:

> I have . . . made it quite clear how reality admits of more and less. A substance is more of a thing than a mode; if there are real qualities or incomplete substances, they are things to a greater extent than modes, but to a lesser extent than complete substances; and, finally, if there is an infinite and independent substance, it is more of a thing than a finite and dependent substance. All this is completely self-evident. (2:130; AT 7:185)

What he apparently has in mind is a hierarchy of dependence and independence. A mode, like the shape of a chair, depends for its existence upon the existence of an extended thing; an extended thing depends for its existence on something different from itself; and an "infinite and independent substance" depends upon nothing else for its existence. So a mode of a finite substance has a double dependence (on its substance and on what its substance depends on), and a finite substance has a single dependence, on something else. Infinite substance has no dependence on anything different from itself. As Descartes's mention of "real qualities or incomplete substances" suggests, there may be additional slots in this scheme, but the basic idea is that degrees of "reality" are measures of metaphysical dependence.[19]

The causal principle about degrees of reality, then, says that something with less independence cannot bring into existence something with more independence. Again, Descartes's ostensible basis for thinking that this is true is that otherwise we would be allowing that some component increment of independence could come from nothing. And again, I do not

---

[19] For a stimulating discussion of the notions of independence that might be involved, see Loeb 1981, 78–100. For discussion of the question whether some ideas have less objective reality than the degree of objective reality that an idea of a mode has, see M. Wilson 1978, 110 ff.

think we can muster much sympathy for the perspective from which this would look intuitively right: metaphysical independence is not a component "something" of the sort that "cannot come from nothing." We can try instead to understand Descartes as invoking a principle of sufficient reason, but then we are left with no definite line of thought that could lead us from the general adequacy principle to this specific one about degrees of reality.

The adequacy principle that Descartes uses in his cosmological argument for God's existence is more specific still: it is a principle about the causes of ideas, and it is supposed to flow from the principle about degrees of reality. The principle Descartes gives us concerns the causes of the "objective reality" of ideas. The notion of objective reality in Descartes's philosophy is a difficult one, and I do not propose to elucidate it here. What we need to see is that for Descartes, all my ideas have the same (lowish) degree of "formal" reality: all equally are modes of a finite substance, namely, me. But my ideas may differ from one another in their degrees of "objective" reality, which depend upon what the ideas are ideas *of*. An idea of a mode has less objective reality than an idea of a finite substance, and the idea of a finite substance has less objective reality than the idea of an infinite substance. The adequacy principle Descartes wants to use says that the cause of an idea must have at least as much formal reality as the idea has of objective reality. Rather than worry about the comparability of two scales of reality, formal and objective, I think it is best to think of this principle as a quicker way of saying all these things: that the idea of a mode must be caused by something with at least as much formal reality as a mode; that an idea of a finite substance must be caused by something with at least as much formal reality as a finite substance; and that an idea of an infinite substance must be caused by something with at least as much formal reality as an infinite substance.[20]

---

[20] Bernard Williams attributes a weaker claim to Descartes, the claim that "if there are two ideas I(a) and I(b), having as objects respectively A and B; and if A has (as a type of thing) more reality than B; then I(a) needs proportionately more reality in its cause than I(b) does" (1978, 140). But Williams agrees that Descartes does *state* the stronger claim that I am attributing to him. He is reluctant to attribute the stronger claim to Descartes because it has, he argues, the absurd consequence that Descartes's idea of God possesses as much reality as God does (141). But he also concedes that without the stronger claim, the cosmological argument will fall short of its intended conclusion (141).

Descartes thinks that if the principle failed to hold in any of these cases, then an increment of (objective) reality would have popped into existence, in some sense or other.

Descartes tries to motivate this principle by using an analogy:

> [I]f someone possesses in his intellect the idea of a machine of a highly intricate design, it is perfectly fair to ask what is the cause of this idea. . . . [I]n order for the idea of the machine to contain such and such objective intricacy, it must derive it from some cause. . . . Perhaps the cause was a real machine of this design which was seen on some previous occasion, thus producing an idea resembling the original. Or the cause might be an extensive knowledge of mechanics in the intellect of the person concerned, or perhaps a very subtle intelligence which enabled him to invent the idea without any previous knowledge. But notice that all the intricacy which is to be found merely objectively in the idea must necessarily be found . . . in its cause, whatever this turns out to be. And the same must apply to the objective reality in the idea of God. (2:75–76; AT 7:103–4)

The analogy suggests that *some* principle about the causes of ideas is true: it suggests that there are conditions on what will count as an adequate explanation of how it is possible for a person to have such-and-such an idea. But I confess I think the analogy does little to illuminate or motivate the *specific* principle Descartes is invoking, or its connection with the general adequacy principle.

Let us put such reservations aside, though, and summarize the cosmological argument as Descartes saw it. He regarded its causal principle about ideas as a principle that flows from the general adequacy principle, simply expressing in a particular sort of causal case what the general principle says generally about everything. The causal principle about ideas says that the cause of an idea with infinite objective reality must itself have infinitely much formal reality. The contingent premise of the cosmological argument says that I have an idea of an infinite and altogether independent thing. So by applying the causal principle about ideas to the contingent premise, I straightaway reach the conclusion that an infinite substance, that is, God, exists.[21]

---

[21] I think there are large questions to be raised about moving from the conclusion that a substance with infinite formal reality exists to the conclusion that a supremely intelligent, powerful, and good substance exists. But I do not want to pursue them here.

We can see, then, why Descartes would have distinguished sharply between his cosmological argument and the seemingly parallel argument about Athene. My idea of Athene does not have infinite objective reality. Its degree of objective reality is the same, in fact, as the degree of objective reality that my idea of myself has, even though I attribute greater perfections to Athene than I do to myself. For she is, as I conceive of her, a being who depends for her existence on something else: the forehead of Zeus. By applying the causal principle to my idea of her, I can conclude only that there must exist some finite or infinite substance that caused my idea of her to exist. But I do not need to look far for something able to fill this causal bill: I myself am a finite substance. So I cannot argue for the existence of something outside myself by considering the possible causes of my idea of Athene.

I have been arguing that Descartes saw the adequacy principles he invokes as so many ways of making the fundamental point that something cannot come from nothing, either through the basic thought that the components of effects must preexist in their causes, or through the basic thought that everything must have a sufficient cause or reason for its existence. This helps to explain why he thought these principles are "manifest by the natural light" (2:28; AT 7:40) and "as clear as any that we have" (2:97; AT 7:135). But it does not explain why he treated these principles as indubitable. Why would he think these principles cannot be doubted, when he is prepared to doubt whether two plus three equals five? This is a question I must address if I am to fill out the general interpretation I am giving of what the method of doubt is, for as I read Descartes, he aims first to uncover conditions that make his doubt possible, then to argue from some of these conditions to the existence of God, and finally to conclude that his creation by God guarantees the truth of his clear and distinct ideas. That is how, on my view, he uses his doubt to establish certainty about the principles of First Philosophy. So the premises of the cosmological argument must be claims that Descartes takes to be conditions making his doubt possible. We have already seen the reasons he has for ascribing this special status to the subpremise that he exists, and to the premise that he has an idea of God. Now we must ask why he would think the causal principles have the same special status.

I must say right away that Descartes says nothing that directly ascribes this special status to the causal principles, and he says nothing that clearly explains why he would. But I think we can find a way to understand why he would assume that the causal principles do have this status, and I think we can see indirect evidence that he himself did make this assumption. I think we can even understand why he did not explicitly discuss the indubitability of the causal principles. I turn now to a defense of these claims.

Let me begin by saying a little about logical principles, like the rule of modus ponens or the principle of noncontradiction. Descartes thinks that such principles are "eternal truths" with a metaphysical status like that of mathematical truths (see, e.g., 3:235; AT 4:118–19), but in the *Meditations* he shows no signs of calling such principles into doubt alongside the truths of mathematics. Rather, he treats them as though they are exempt from doubt, and he uses them confidently at every step of his inquiry.

Despite giving them this special treatment, he does not offer any explicit rationale for doing so. It is easy to see what his rationale would be, though: a meditator cannot carry forward any sort of rational inquiry without accepting that, say, p and "If p, then q" together exclude the falsity of q. The rational character of an inquiry means that someone conducting it must accept basic logical principles such as this. Thus if the meditator is using the method of doubt as a method for rational inquiry, it is a condition of his using the method that he accept these logical principles. Acceptance of these principles is not a condition peculiar to the method of doubt, but we may still correctly say that accepting these principles is a condition on using the method of doubt. And precisely because acceptance of these principles is so obviously constitutive of Descartes's inquiry, we should not be surprised to find that he sees no need to rehearse this point.

I believe that for Descartes the role of the causal principles is broadly analogous to that of logical principles.[22] Of course, right away this reading faces a problem: it is true, and obviously true, that someone using the method of doubt must accept, say, the principle of noncontradiction, but

[22] This general reading receives some support from the Second Replies, where Descartes invites readers "to ponder on those self-evident propositions that they will find within themselves, such as 'The same thing cannot both be and not be at the same time', and 'Nothingness cannot be the efficient cause of anything', and so on" (2:115; AT 7:162–63). The support is fairly limited, though; nothing in the passage explains why an invitation to ponder, say, "Two plus three equals five" would not be equally apt.

no one is obliged to accept the principle that the cause of an idea contains at least as much formal reality as the idea has of objective reality. As I argued earlier in this chapter, however, Descartes thinks this implausible-sounding principle is a consequence of a general adequacy principle whose basis can be illuminated by appeal to the *ex nihilo* principle that something cannot come from nothing. And for Descartes, one of the basic thoughts the *ex nihilo* principle expresses is that everything must have a cause or reason.[23]

So why might Descartes assume that the principle of sufficient reason has a special relation to the method of doubt? Some readers may feel that we can answer this question plausibly by pointing to the way in which "explanatory rationalism" pervades seventeenth-century philosophy.[24] The idea might be that it is irrational to countenance brute facts, facts conceded to have no cause or reason for their being as they are, and so if the method of doubt guides a rational inquiry, then the inquirer must accept the principle of sufficient reason.

Perhaps in the end this is the best thing to say about the special status of the principle of sufficient reason, but this is not the line of thought I want to develop. I am not going to argue that for Descartes the special status of the principle of sufficient reason is, like that of logical principles, derived from the nature of rational inquiry. I am reluctant to claim that Descartes saw *all* rational inquiry as demanding acceptance of the principle of sufficient reason; for example, it is not clear how for Descartes inquiry in mathematics would demand acceptance of this principle.[25]

What I will argue is that the special status of the principle of sufficient reason flows from something special about the sort of rational inquiry

[23] In what follows I will be concerned with the status of this principle by itself, rather than in conjunction with the idea that the *ex nihilo* principle states a condition on what can constitute a cause or reason. The line of thought I want to pursue is easiest to see in relation just to the principle of sufficient reason; the difficulty of extending this line of thought to the idea to which Descartes weds it is, I think, not an objection to the interpretation I am offering but rather an objection to the wedding.

[24] The term is Jonathan Bennett's (1984, 29–32).

[25] For a fascinating account of the idea of a "cause" in seventeenth-century philosophy of mathematics, see Mancosu 1996, esp. chap. 1. It may even be that, if the claim is suitably qualified, Descartes would agree that the possibility of mathematical inquiry requires acceptance of some sort of principle of sufficient reason.

that is guided by the method of doubt. Interestingly enough, Spinoza also interprets Descartes as connecting the principle of sufficient reason to what is distinctive about the method of doubt. In chapter 7 I mentioned that in his commentary on Descartes's *Principles*, Spinoza reads Descartes as claiming certainty for "I exist" by arguing that "I exist" is a condition of the possible truth of any skeptical scenario. A few pages after identifying that dependence argument, Spinoza says:

> I shall admit . . . only those things that each of us observes in himself, insofar as he is thinking. E.g., that he wills this and that, that he has ideas of a certain sort, that one idea contains in itself more reality and perfection than another, that the idea which contains objectively the being and perfection of substance is far more perfect than the one which contains only the objective perfection of some accident, and finally that the idea of a supremely perfect being is the most perfect of all. . . . Next we shall also say that those [propositions] agree with this principle which cannot be called into doubt unless at the same time this unshakable foundation of ours should be put in doubt. E.g., if someone should wish to doubt whether something comes from nothing, he will at the same time be able to doubt whether we exist when we think. For if I can affirm something of nothing . . . I shall be able at the same time, with the same right, to affirm thought of nothing, and to say that I am nothing when I think. But since I cannot do that, it will also be impossible for me to think that something may come from nothing. (1985, 242–43; 1925, 1:153–54)

The passage is complex, and in places it points in directions I do not think Descartes actually went. But what interests me about it is Spinoza's general conviction that for Descartes the principle of sufficient reason has a special status that is to be elucidated by reference to the requirements that the method of doubt imposes upon inquiry.

Let me now develop this general thought, though in a way that differs from Spinoza's in its particulars. Recall that the meditator's aim in using the method of doubt is to establish truths. The meditator will regard himself as having established the truth of a proposition if, and only if, he finds that there is not even a slight reason for doubting whether it is true. He quickly puts to one side all the propositions for which he finds a reason for doubt of some standard type: for example, that the tower is too far away for him to see its shape clearly. A subclass of what he has believed remains: that here is his hand, that two plus three equals five. The meditator at first thinks he cannot come up with any reasons for doubting these propositions, but he finds that there is, after all, one way to doubt them. He can construct skeptical scenarios about them, that is, explanatory accounts of how certain sorts of belief arise in him that are accounts upon which such beliefs are false. (To be a skeptical scenario, an account must also be such that the meditator cannot tell whether it is correct, but this feature is not important for our present purposes.)

Exactly how would ruling out such skeptical scenarios establish the truth of beliefs like "Here is a hand" and "Two plus three equals five"? In chapter 3 I focused upon the rationality of believing what cannot be doubted, even in this way, *over* what can be doubted, albeit only in this way. Now I am raising a different question about Descartes's inquiry. He clearly thought that if we find some proposition to be indubitable after using the First Meditation skeptical strategies, we are entitled to regard that proposition as true. For Descartes, indubitability establishes truth. The question I am raising is this: what is the meditator committed to in virtue of holding that indubitability establishes truth?

In chapter 5, I argued that for the meditator, there is a core of common-sense beliefs that are innocent until proven guilty: we are right to accept them as true unless they can be maligned by a reason for doubt. Now I want to suggest that we can describe the meditator's initial position as one in which he takes it that

> a. He holds these beliefs *because* (as he can clearly see) they are true.[26]

Backing up this understanding of his position are the general beliefs that he holds about the trustworthiness of his senses in the favorable circumstances he is considering (and, in the case of his simple mathematical beliefs, the transparency of the propositions he believes to be true). But as part of his use of the method of doubt, he constructs and considers skeptical scenarios, in which he articulates far-fetched reasons or causes

---

[26] Here I am leaving out all the important complications that arise from the displacement of obscure and confused ideas by clear and distinct ones, and the way in which Descartes restricts the scope of "believes because true" to ideas that are clear and distinct or are properly related to clear and distinct ideas.

for his holding these beliefs in a world in which they are false. (His brain is addled; he is the creature of a deceiving God; and so on.) So he considers this sort of possibility:

b. He holds these beliefs *because* [far-fetched cause].

And if (b) is right, then the beliefs are false. But for the class of beliefs he is considering, these skeptical scenarios with their far-fetched causes are the only reasons for doubt that there are. Suppose that somehow, for some beliefs, the meditator can deny (b). He thinks he would be entitled to move from the denial of (b) to the affirmation of

a. He holds these beliefs because they are true.

That is a way of spelling out the claim that the meditator thinks indubitability establishes truth.

Now, imagine a meditator who does not accept the principle of sufficient reason. Suppose he thinks that it is possible that some of the things that are the case, are the case inexplicably. He will then be unable to rule out the possibility that it is a brute fact about him that his beliefs are false; he will be unable to rule out this possibility:

c. He *inexplicably* believes five is the sum of two and three (and the like) in a world in which such propositions are false.

If he cannot rule out such a possibility, then although he has ruled out any reasons for doubting whether these propositions are false, he will still not be able to regard himself as having established that these propositions are true.

The actual meditator does not find himself in this predicament. He moves straight *from* ruling out reasons or causes for his believing these things falsely *to* regarding himself as believing these things because they are true.[27] Ruling out reasons for doubt counts as establishing truth *for*

[27] I suspect that this is at least part of the point he is making in the Second Replies, when he writes: "as soon as we think that we correctly perceive something, we are spontaneously convinced that it is true. Now if this conviction is so firm that it is impossible for us ever to have any reason for doubting what we are convinced of, then there are no further questions for us to ask: we have everything that we could rationally [*cum ratione*] want. What is it to us that someone may make out that the perception whose truth we are so firmly convinced of may appear false to God or an angel, so that it is, absolutely

someone who accepts the principle of sufficient reason. So someone using the method of doubt must accept the principle of sufficient reason in order to be able to use the method constructively, to establish truths.[28] Acceptance of the principle of sufficient reason is thus a condition of using doubt in the third of the three senses I distinguished in chapter 6.[29] In terms of the schema for dependence arguments, Descartes would be relying upon this line of thought:

1. If I raise a doubt whether everything has a reason for its existence, then I am engaged in using doubt to establish truth.

2. But if I am engaged in using doubt to establish truth, then I must grant that everything has a reason for its existence.

3. So if I raise a doubt whether everything has a reason for its existence, then I must grant that everything has a reason for its existence.

Reflection on this argument would show the meditator that he cannot coherently doubt whether the principle of sufficient reason is true; he would thus be able to be absolutely certain about it.

Notice that I am not claiming that the meditator must *succeed* in establishing truths if he is to use the method of doubt.[30] For example, he might fail to establish truths by failing to dispose of the skeptical scenarios. What I am claiming is that for the meditator to use the method of doubt, he must meet whatever conditions there may be on leaving open the general *possibility* of his establishing truths. The rational space within which he is meditating must not close off the possibility of success.

---

speaking, false? Why should this alleged 'absolute falsity' bother us, since we neither believe in it nor have even the smallest suspicion of it?" (2:103; AT 7:144–45 trans. altered).

[28] On the face of it, this is too strong: someone could accept a restricted principle and still make the move from (b) to (a). (One such principle might be that there must be a sufficient reason why I believe truly and why I believe falsely.) Of course, Descartes would not have thought it possible to conceive clearly and distinctly that *some but not all* of the things that are the case require a reason or cause. Only the unrestricted principle captures a clear and distinct idea about explanation; I think this is enough to explain why it is the unrestricted principle to which Descartes gives a special status.

[29] So I am disagreeing here with the line of thought I pursued in Broughton 1984.

[30] I mean to be distinguishing my interpretative strategy here from that of Bernard Williams, who seems to me to slide from (a) treating the possibility of a successful outcome of use of the method as a condition of its being used, to (b) treating the success of using the method as a condition of its being used (1978, 62 and 200–202).

Someone might want to object to this reading by saying that if this is what Descartes thought, he would have said so. After all, he devoted several pages of the Third Meditation to the causal principles without once giving any such argument as this.

I am not claiming that Descartes explicitly thought through the status of the principle of sufficient reason in just this way. But neither am I merely claiming that we can produce a rational reconstruction of Descartes's thought in terms of which *we* can try to defend a special status for the principle of sufficient reason. Rather, I believe that Descartes made assumptions about the principle of sufficient reason much like those he made about the various logical principles: he saw acceptance of all of these principles as constitutive of our ability to structure our thinking around norms of reason giving and truth seeking. These principles form a necessary background for this sort of thinking, and precisely because they form such a background, Descartes does not see a need to bring them to the fore and offer them an explicit defense.[31] My interpretative effort here is to articulate a description of the background position these principles occupy for Descartes and to do so in a way that will allow us to appreciate why he treated them as principles whose truth he could not doubt.

To all of this, an objector might reply, "Descartes does not ever even *mention* any of the logical principles the meditator uses, so we are free to imagine, if we like, that he ascribes a special status to them. But he devotes several pages to the causal principles, so if he thought they had this special status, he would surely have explained it." While it is true that in the Third Meditation Descartes makes various causal principles explicit, all his argumentative and expository energies are devoted to showing how the general adequacy principle is supposed to yield the implausible-sounding specific principles that he needs to be able to use, the principles about degrees of reality and about the causes of ideas. He anticipated—correctly—that many readers would need to see these lines of thought worked out. As I understand Descartes, he left the indubitability of the basic principle of sufficient reason in the background, side by side with

---

[31] Of course, Descartes has a metaphysical theory about "eternal truths" that he explicitly applies even to logical principles (see 3:235; AT 4:118–19).

that of the logical principles.[32] What he thought he needed to make explicit was the controversial derivation from that basic principle of the claim that the cause of an idea must contain at least as high a degree of formal reality as the degree of objective reality that the idea has.[33]

THE PHYSICAL WORLD

I have been arguing in this chapter that for Descartes, the premises of the argument that God exists have a special status. He has already discovered that he cannot rationally doubt that he himself exists and has the many states—states of thought—that are conditions of his using the method of doubt. Now he claims he cannot doubt that he has an idea of God or that the principle of sufficient reason is true. But his possession of the idea of God entails that God exists, given the principle of sufficient reason and the consequences Descartes thinks it has. This means that he is entitled to absolute certainty about the existence not just of himself and his modes of thought, but also of God, the infinitely perfect creator of everything.[34]

[32] Perhaps it is worth noting that the meditator uses a principle of sufficient reason even *before* he devotes those several pages to the adequacy principles. He quietly but clearly relies upon a principle of sufficient reason in the Second Meditation—for example, in its third paragraph, where the meditator's line of thought relies upon the assumption that *something* is the cause of his thoughts (2:16; AT 7:24).

[33] Perhaps this helps to explain why Descartes does not bother to mention the causal principle when he summarizes his argument at the end of the Third Meditation (2:35; AT 7:51–52) and reviews it in the Fourth (2:37; AT 7:53).

[34] The ontological argument could not therefore play the same role in the meditator's inquiry, because the premise "That which we clearly and distinctly understand to belong to the true and immutable nature, or essence, or form of something, can truly be asserted of that thing" (2:83; AT 7:115) does not have the special status that the premises of the cosmological argument have. As far as I know, Descartes did not himself ever make this point when explaining why he gave the cosmological argument in the Third Meditation and the ontological argument later, in the Fifth. Instead, he suggests that it can be difficult for some people to "keep in mind all the elements which make up the [ontological] proof" (2:85; AT 7:120), especially people who do not already have a "clear mental vision" that is "free of preconceived opinions" (2:118; AT 7:167).

Because he is entitled to certainty about God, Descartes is also entitled to certainty that his clear and distinct ideas are true. As he says at the beginning of the Fourth Meditation, "[F]rom this contemplation of the true God, in whom all the treasures of wisdom and the sciences lie hidden, I think I can see a way forward to the knowledge of other things" (2:37; AT 7:53). The way forward lies in recognizing that with such a creator "I shall unquestionably reach the truth, if only I give sufficient attention to all the things which I perfectly understand, and separate these from all the other cases where my apprehension is more confused and obscure" (2:43; AT 7:62). In other words, Descartes can now replace the strong maxim of the First Meditation, which required him to withhold assent from what is not completely certain, with a new maxim for judgment: to "restrain my will so that it extends to what the intellect clearly and distinctly reveals, and no further" (2:43; AT 7:62).

What does the intellect reveal clearly and distinctly about the physical world? In the Second Meditation, Descartes begins the work of clarifying his ordinary conception of the world around him. As he reflects upon a piece of wax, he finds that his ordinary way of thinking about it depends upon his having a conception of it that he had never recognized before.[35] According to his ordinary conception,

    1. The piece of wax is a body that has sensible qualities (for example, color and shape).

He had also vaguely thought this:

    2. My conception of this body is just a compound of my sensings of its qualities.

But upon reflection he finds that this cannot be right: the compound of sensings can change while the conception of the wax as a body does not. So, he sees, this must be true:

---

[35] This is one way in which the piece-of-wax passage is like the passage in the Third Meditation in which the meditator finds that his ordinary thought of himself as doubting depends upon his having another conception, that of God. The two passages are alike in another way: in both, the underlying conception that is made explicit turns out to be one that cannot be derived from sense experience. Descartes's argumentative strategy does not, however, require him to claim that he can be *certain* he has the idea of body as

3. My conception of this body has content that is different from my sensings of its qualities.

But what precisely (*"praecise"*) is this conceptual content (2:20; AT 7:30)? Descartes's work on his conceptions of himself and of his states has given him practice in cutting out conceptual content with precision, and now, by putting aside the sensory contents of his conception of the wax, he can recognize[36] this:

4. My conception of this body is the conception of something that is extended and can undergo innumerably many changes in size and shape.

By ridding himself of the vague, false thought in (2), and by explicitly recognizing (4), he achieves greater clarity and distinctness in his thoughts about the physical world.

In the Fifth Meditation, Descartes connects this conception of body with the conception of "'continuous' quantity" (2:44; AT 7:63) that underwrites mathematics. He needs only the divine guarantee that clear and distinct ideas are true in order to assent to the propositions of mathematics and in order to be certain that bodies, understood as extended things, *can* exist (2:50; AT 7:71). In order to argue that they *do* exist, however, he needs to enlist the help of additional clear and distinct ideas: the ideas of God's perfection, of the principle of sufficient reason, of the existence of his sense perceptions, and of his natural inclination to think those perceptions are caused by physical things (2:55; AT 7:79–80). From all these ideas he concludes that bodies exist and cause his sensations. By observing various complex restraints, he can also make further judgments about the physical world, and these, he argues, are enough to show that the dream scenario is not a reason for doubting what his sense perceptions tell him (2:59–62; AT 7:86–90). But that does not mean he can assent to all of his prereflective beliefs. His new maxim directs him to give up many of his former beliefs about the objects of his senses: for example, he is to withhold assent from the claim that "when a body is

---

continuous quantity: the piece-of-wax passage does not contain a dependence argument. For a related interpretation of the wax passage, see Schmitter 2000.

[36] Bernard Williams argues persuasively that there is no intervening argumentation that takes the meditator from (3) to (4) (1978, 222).

white or green, the selfsame whiteness or greenness which I perceive through my senses is present in the body" (2:56–57; AT 7:82).

Descartes can make all of these "treasures of wisdom and the sciences" his own by using the new maxim of clear and distinct ideas. His absolute certainty that he will judge correctly by using the new maxim is itself a consequence of his use of the First Meditation maxim, because "Clear and distinct ideas are true" is entailed by propositions that are absolutely certain, and the absolute certainty of those propositions arises from the ways in which they make the use of the method of doubt possible.

Can we say, then, that for Descartes the truth of "A physical world exists" is itself a condition of his use of the method of doubt? I think the answer to this question is no. To argue that a physical world exists, the meditator needs to have sensations, and he needs to have an inclination to think that their cause is physical things. Descartes gives us no reason for thinking that it is a condition of his using the method of doubt that the meditator have sensations, or that he be inclined to believe that they are caused by physical things. The most we can straightforwardly say is that *if* the meditator has sensations and the inclination to believe, then by uncovering the conditions of his using the method of doubt, he can be absolutely certain that he has those sensations and that inclination, that there is a cause for his having them, and that God exists and is no deceiver. And then, based on his certainty about those claims, he will be entitled to absolute certainty that physical things exist.

I want to close this chapter by speculating about whether Descartes *could* have had reasons for connecting the method of doubt with his living an embodied life in a physical world. Can we really conceive of a being's having a use for the method of doubt *without* having sense perceptions and an inclination to trust them? Try imagining a being—an angel, perhaps—who does not have sense perceptions or any natural inclination to believe that it lives in a physical world. Let us grant that it could suspend judgment, recognize its own existence, desire to know more, and exercise many more of the cognitive abilities that we have. Descartes's dualism seems to commit him to the possibility of such a being. But could this being ever find itself in the initial position that, according to Descartes, makes using the method of doubt make sense? This is not clear: this being would somehow have to have undergone the sort of cognitive development that we do, a development that results in confused ideas. Otherwise it would have no need, even once in the course of its life, to demolish everything in order to achieve lasting results in the sciences.

Does this mean that the being would have to have sense experiences and an inclination to trust them? Well, perhaps there are other ways than ours in which beings can come to have ideas that are so confused that they need to demolish everything. Perhaps other limited beings suffer from pervasive confusion through having some nonsensory but receptive faculty. Descartes is silent about these matters.[37]

But if he would want to say that ours is the only way of coming to be as pervasively confused as we are, then there may be a connection after all between our being users of the method of doubt and our being embodied creatures with sensations and the inclination to trust them. And if there is such a connection, then perhaps we can say that for Descartes the existence of the physical world is an outer condition of methodic doubt. If so, we must surely add that the Cartesian road from doubt to world is a long and winding one indeed.

[37] He does say that "if an angel were in a human body, he would not have sensations as we do, but would simply perceive the motions which are caused by external objects" (3:206; AT 3:493). He also thinks that "the human mind separated from the body does not have sense-perception strictly so called; but it is not clear by natural reason alone whether angels are created like minds distinct from bodies, or like minds united to bodies" (3:380; AT 5:402). But he also says (in a passage I can't resist quoting at length), "Being perceivable by the senses . . . is [not] . . . an adequate description of [perceptible things]; for if it refers to our senses, then it does not apply to the smallest particles of matter; if it refers to other senses such as we might imagine God to construct, it might well apply also to angels and souls. For sensory nerves so fine that they could be moved by the smallest particles of matter are no more intelligible to me than a faculty enabling our mind to sense or perceive other minds directly" (3:372; AT 5:341).

❖ 9 ❖

Reflections

I AM ATTRIBUTING to Descartes a specific and unified way of using the doubts of the First Meditation to establish the principles of First Philosophy. This understanding of the method of doubt intersects with two large philosophical problems, one old and one not so old. The problem of the "Cartesian Circle" was first raised by Mersenne (2:89; AT 7:124–25) and Arnauld (2:150; AT 7:214) in their objections to the *Meditations*. More recent is the problem of characterizing and assessing "transcendental" arguments. I want to reflect on the method of doubt in connection with each of these, and then I will close by returning, as I have promised I would, to the relation between philosophical inquiry and the perspective of common sense.

THE CARTESIAN CIRCLE

Here is the apparent problem of circularity. In the First Meditation, Descartes presents the deceiving God scenario (or the fate-or-chance scenario) as a reason for doubting the truth of anything he grasps clearly and distinctly. Now, to be absolutely certain that his clear and distinct ideas are true, he must be absolutely certain that God exists and is not a deceiver. To be absolutely certain of that, he must be able to be absolutely certain of the premises from which he draws that conclusion. He grasps these premises clearly and distinctly, but to claim to be absolutely certain that they are therefore true, he must be absolutely certain that God exists and is not a deceiver. His circular bind, then, is that he can be absolutely certain about God only if he is already absolutely certain about clear and distinct ideas, and he can be absolutely certain about clear and distinct ideas only if he is already certain about God. Arnauld raises the difficulty in this general form;[1] Mersenne raises the narrower difficulty that Descartes claims to be certain that he is a thinking thing before he is in a position to achieve certainty about God's existence, and yet also claims that he cannot be certain of anything without being certain about God's existence.

If what I have said about the method of doubt is correct, then we have a good interpretative strategy for tackling this difficulty. Descartes would be offering dependence arguments for some of his clear and distinct ideas, and the dependence strategy would show how he can be absolutely certain that these ideas are true even before he achieves absolute certainty about God's existence and the truth of *all* his clear and distinct ideas. Let me explain this interpretative strategy in more detail.

I will begin by sketching out a familiar view of how the method of doubt manages to lead to knowledge:

The simple picture: The meditator raises the radical skeptical scenarios and carefully considers which of his beliefs can survive them. He does not see how to defend his sense-based beliefs or his clear and distinct ideas in mathematics, and so he suspends judgment about them. He finds, however, that he *can* defend the beliefs that he exists and that he thinks. But that is not all. He claims that he is somehow also able to add other bits of knowledge to the meager stock of "I exist" and "I think." Understood in a particular way, his beliefs about his own states constitute knowledge: "I seem to see a light," for example. Most such beliefs are, at this stage of the inquiry, dead ends; but one—"I have an idea of a benevolent God"—is not. For Descartes also somehow adds to his stock of knowledge the general adequacy principle about causes, and with it the subsidiary principle that says that the cause of an idea must have at least as much formal reality as the idea has of objective reality. He puts these causal principles together with his knowledge of his own existence and of his possession of the idea of God, and infers that a benevolent God exists. And then straightaway he can also claim to know that all his clear and distinct ideas are true, since a benevolent God would not have made him so that he clearly understood to be true what actually was false. From this point on, further inquiry can be safely guided by the rule "Accept only what I clearly and distinctly perceive to be true."

---

[1] Bourdin may be raising the general difficulty, too, though his fulminations do not make this clear (2:359–60; AT 7:528–29).

At this point in the inquiry, this rule is effective. Descartes has already formed various ideas that he can identify as clear and distinct, and his general doubt-induced detachment from his senses allows him to start teasing apart what was obscure and what was clear in his former beliefs. This means that if he heavily qualifies some of his former beliefs, he can stop suspending judgment about them. From here on in, the hard intellectual work comes with the effort to find the right ways to qualify his ideas, that is, to make them clear and distinct.

According to this simple picture, Descartes achieves certainty that all of his clear and distinct ideas are true by achieving certainty that God exists and is not a deceiver, and he achieves certainty about God's existence by achieving certainty about propositions which, taken together, constitute an argument for the conclusion that God exists. I think most readers find that the simple picture gives a highly natural reading of the first four Meditations, and I think there are many texts that invite such a reading.

One especially compelling text comes at the beginning of the Second Meditation, where Descartes introduces the "I exist" reasoning by saying:

> Anything which admits of the slightest doubt I will set aside just as if I had found it to be wholly false; and I will proceed in this way until I recognize something certain, or if nothing else, until I at least recognize for certain that there is no certainty. Archimedes used to demand just one firm and immovable point in order to shift the entire earth; so I too can hope for great things if I manage to find one thing, however slight, that is certain and unshakeable. (2:16; AT 7:24)

The reader naturally expects that Descartes's subsequent achievement of the "great things" he hopes for will *rest upon* the certainty he first achieves about himself, and this is how the simple picture depicts the subsequent course of the argument.

Someone might object[2] that the Archimedes metaphor suggests a strategy at odds with the simple picture: doesn't it suggest that certainty about *one* thing" will lead to certainty about everything else? And wouldn't that one thing be "I exist"? Yet that is only one part of one premise in the argument for God's existence.

[2] I am grateful to Ed McCann for pressing me to consider this objection.

Descartes actually goes on to treat all his discoveries about himself as his Archimedean point: not just "I exist," but all that "I think" comprises too. For example, at the beginning of the Third Meditation, he rehearses his knowledge of himself: he is "a thing that doubts, affirms, denies, understands a few things, is ignorant of many things, is willing, is unwilling, and also which imagines and senses" (2:24; AT 7:34; trans. altered). He sums this up by saying, "I am certain that I am a thinking thing," and then refers to *that* as his "first item of knowledge [*prima cognitione*]" (2:24; AT 7:35). In chapter 7, I gave a reading of the Second Meditation that would explain why Descartes would be equally certain of "I exist," I doubt," "I sense," and so on, and in chapter 8 I explained why Descartes thought that he could not have recognized that he doubted unless he had an idea of God. As for the causal principles, even Archimedes needed a lever as well as a fixed point to move the earth. The causal principles are Descartes's argumentative lever, and if they are to work they must be as solid and firm as his other premises. While Descartes does not explicitly say why he thinks the causal principles are indubitable, in chapter 8 I tried to explain why he would take it that they are.

The Third and Fourth Meditations strongly suggest a reading that accords with the simple picture. Descartes says that the *first* great thing he produces from knowledge of himself is knowledge that God exists and is not a deceiver, and that *because* he has knowledge of God, he can achieve knowledge of a *second* great thing, namely, the truth of all of his clear and distinct ideas. As he puts it in the Fourth Meditation:

> [F]rom this contemplation of the true God, in whom all the treasures of wisdom and the sciences lie hidden, I think I can see a way forward to the knowledge of other things. To begin with, I recognize that it is impossible that God should ever deceive me. . . . And since God does not wish to deceive me, he surely did not give me the kind of faculty which would ever enable me to go wrong while using it correctly. (2:37; AT 7:53–54)

So the simple picture seems a natural way to depict the trajectory of the first four Meditations as Descartes uses the method of doubt to achieve certainty that all of his clear and distinct ideas are true.

But reflective readers are bound to be troubled by a basic philosophical objection to Descartes's procedure as the simple picture depicts it. Early in his inquiry, before he knows that God exists and is not a deceiver,

Descartes cannot claim to know something *simply* because he has a clear and distinct idea of it. For all he knows, he has been created by a deceiving God so that he perceives clearly and distinctly to be true propositions that actually are false. The method of doubt thus requires him to suspend judgment about things he perceives clearly and distinctly; he must, for example, suspend judgment about whether "Two plus three equals five" is true. So consider Descartes's claims to know that he thinks and that he exists, that he has an idea of God, and that the causal principles are true. On the simple picture, Descartes is claiming that somehow he can know each of those things before he knows that God exists and is not a deceiver. But at that same stage of his inquiry, he must suspend judgment about "Two plus three equals five"! It seems outrageous that he should claim knowledge of his privileged few clear and distinct ideas when he cannot even claim to know something as simple as the sum of two and three. It is hard to see how Descartes could have a principled reason for insisting that the deceiving God argument requires him to suspend judgment about "Two plus three equals five" but not about "Causes must be adequate to their effects." Without such a principled account, Descartes seems to be obtuse, or even intellectually dishonest, in his claim for success in using the method of doubt. He seems simply to be ignoring his maxim about suspense of judgment (or ignoring the deceiving God argument) whenever he finds it convenient.

Reflecting on this difficulty, some readers have tried to interpret Descartes as treating all clear and distinct ideas alike at this stage of his inquiry, and thus as obviating any need to justify treating some but not all of them as absolutely certain. There are two general ways to give such a reading. One is to suppose that Descartes assumes that all, or a great many, of his clear and distinct ideas are absolutely certain just because they are clear and distinct. In *Logic or the Art of Thinking*, Arnauld and Nicole write in a way that is suggestive of a crude version of this strategy. They claim that "some things are so simple and evident—such as: 'I think, therefore I am'; 'the whole is greater than its part'—that it is impossible to doubt seriously whether they are in themselves the way we conceive them to be. The reason is that we could not doubt them without thinking of them, and we could not think of them without believing them to be true, and consequently we could not doubt them" (1996, 248). Although they are not talking about the problem of the Cartesian Circle, Arnauld and Nicole are painting a picture of clear and distinct perception that could be naturally extended to an attempt to solve the circularity problem. All simple clear and distinct ideas are absolutely indubitable, or absolutely certain; and from some of those we can obtain a proof that God exists and therefore that all clear and distinct ideas, no matter how complex, are also absolutely certain.

There are at least two problems with this attempt to solve the problem of circularity. First, we are still left with no explanation for why Descartes is willing to call into doubt the truth of "Two plus three equals five." This idea is as simple as can be, and so on this reading it would have to be one of the favored ideas of which Descartes can be absolutely certain, even before he banishes the skeptical scenarios. But Descartes does not say he cannot doubt whether two plus three equals five; he says he can (2:14; AT 7:21). Perhaps even more seriously, the notion of absolute certainty that Arnauld and Nicole describe is something like a notion of a compulsion to believe: we cannot doubt these ideas because whenever we think of them, we cannot help believing that they are true. But, of course, the absolute certainty Descartes seeks is the discovery that the skeptical scenarios do not impugn his claims to knowledge, and the power of the deceiving God scenario does not flicker on and off, impugning "Two plus three equals five" when I don't entertain a clear and distinct idea of the sum, and then not impugning it when I do. If we keep to the forefront the relevant notion of absolute certainty, then Descartes cannot claim absolute certainty about all of his clear and distinct ideas—not even about all of his simple clear and distinct ideas—before he can be certain that God exists and is not a deceiver.

Another possibility is to suppose that Descartes thinks *none* of his clear and distinct ideas is absolutely certain before he reaches the conclusion that God exists. This is a reading that a fair number of readers have developed. Rather than conclude that Descartes is obtuse or dishonest or arguing in a circle, these readers reject the simple picture of how the method of doubt is supposed to lead to knowledge. Taking their cue from some suggestive texts (to which I will turn presently), they *complicate* the simple picture. They hold that Descartes intends us *not* to be absolutely certain about "I exist," "I think," "I see a light," "I have an idea of God," and "Something cannot come from nothing" until the end of the argument that God exists and is not a deceiver. That is, at an early stage of the inquiry, Descartes is in some way withholding assent from "I exist" as well as from "Two plus three equals five."

Proponents of this more complicated picture face a difficulty of their own, however, for they will need to explain how doubt can yield knowledge of God's existence and the truth of clear and distinct ideas, if not in the simple way I have sketched out. Interpreters of Descartes have been especially clever and imaginative in providing such explanations, and I will briefly return to that enterprise later.[3]

As I have just been suggesting, basic questions about the simple picture turn upon how we understand the method of doubt. I believe that by understanding the method of doubt in the way I have been proposing, we will see that Descartes has a good rationale for treating some but not all of his clear and distinct ideas as absolutely certain in the early stages of his inquiry. On the reading I am proposing, each of the premises for the argument that God exists and is not a deceiver is among the clear and distinct ideas that have a special status: they are all claims that are conditions of using First Meditation doubt. This means that the meditator can be absolutely certain they are true even before he has ruled out the skeptical scenarios. Once the meditator sees that these absolutely indubitable claims together imply that God exists and is not a deceiver, he is in a position to be absolutely certain that God exists and is not a deceiver, for God's existence is a condition of his doubt too. And by achieving absolute certainty that God exists, the meditator can also achieve absolute certainty that *all* of his clear and distinct ideas are true.

Early in his inquiry, then, Descartes will take himself to have shown that *some* ideas are indubitably true insofar as their truth is a condition of even the most radical of grounds for doubting anything. Among those favored ideas are "I exist," "I am doubting," "I desire to know more," "I seem to see a light," "I have an idea of God," and "Something cannot come from nothing." But mathematical ideas are *not* among the favored few, despite their clarity and distinctness; not even the idea that two plus three equals five is indubitable. So using the method of doubt provides a

---

[3] The secondary literature on the Cartesian Circle is huge, and I do not mean to be suggesting that the contrast between "simple" and "complicated" interpretations neatly and perspicuously categorizes every interesting view in the literature. For a different way of categorizing interpretations, and for a useful list of references to some of the recent literature, see Newman and Nelson 1999.

rationale for treating some clear and distinct ideas, but not all, as absolutely certain in the early stages of the inquiry. Of course, once Descartes sees that some of the favored ideas imply that God is no deceiver and that all his clear and distinct ideas are true, he can be absolutely certain that "Two plus three equals five" is true, along with any other clear and distinct ideas he finds he has.

Does the defense of the simple picture that I have offered constitute a knockdown argument in its favor? If I am right about how the method of doubt is supposed to work in the *Meditations*, then I think this much is safe to say. First, Descartes has in mind a specific *way* in which using the method of doubt can yield absolute certainty even before the skeptical scenarios are vanquished. He uses this strategy to reach absolute certainty about some, but not all, of his clear and distinct ideas before he reaches the conclusion that God exists and is not a deceiver, and the premises in his argument to that conclusion are among the clear and distinct ideas he is absolutely certain are true. Thus I think that in the first four Meditations, the case for the simple picture is overwhelmingly strong.

There is one passage in the first four Meditations that might seem to suggest a complicated picture. Near the beginning of the Third Meditation Descartes says that if he does not know that God exists and is not a deceiver, "it seems that I can never be quite certain about *anything* else" (2:25; AT 7:36; emphasis added). But notice first that Descartes expresses only tentatively the thought that at this stage of his inquiry he cannot be certain of anything: he says this *seems* to him (*videor*) to be true. Second, the sentence appears in a passage of great dialectic complexity. Descartes has reflected on the "I exist" reasoning and noticed its clarity and distinctness. That makes him wonder whether he is already in a position to say that *all* clear and distinct ideas are true. He certainly cannot see, as he considers any particular clear and distinct idea, how it could be false, or how he can withhold his assent from it.[4] Then again, as he reminds himself, he has not yet eliminated the deceiving God scenario, and that

---

[4] Though, as Marleen Rozemond has helpfully pointed out to me, even here, where Descartes is dramatizing the assent-compelling character of clear and distinct ideas, he represents "Two plus three equals five" as being a bit less persuasive than "I exist." In a phrase that Cottingham et al. do not translate, he says that "perhaps even [*forte etiam*]" the proposition "Two plus three equals five" compels assent (AT 7:36; see 2:25). That is,

scenario applies to clear and distinct ideas. It is at *that* point that he says it seems he cannot be certain of anything.

Well, it is *hard* for him to see why some clear and distinct ideas cannot be doubted, while others—equally clear, distinct, and compelling—can be. The sentence in question is an expression of this difficulty, I think. It is not a dismissal of the "I exist" reasoning as merely psychologically compelling. That reasoning still provides an Archimedean point—an absolutely indubitable truth—from which inquiry can proceed.

So the case for the simple picture that rests simply upon the first four Meditations is compelling, I think. But if we enlarge our view to take in the Fifth Meditation and the replies to Mersenne (2:100–105; AT 7:140–46) and Arnauld (2:171; AT 7:245–46), then I think some readers will want to say that it is not at all clear that the simple picture is the right one. For in one way or another, Descartes seems to be saying that there is certainty and there is *certainty,* or that there is knowledge and there is *knowledge.* There is the certainty we may have as we grasp an argument and its conclusion in one sweep of thought, and the certainty we may have when no subsequent considerations can get us to retract our assent to the conclusion, even when we do not recall the argument that leads to it (e.g., 2:48–49; AT 7:69–71). There is knowledge that is awareness of primary notions, and knowledge that isn't (2:100; AT 7:140–41). Perhaps there is a relevant difference between cognition (*cognitio*) and knowledge (*scientia*).[5]

The *point* of these distinctions is very obscure, I think, but because Descartes draws them in the course of replying to the charge of circularity, some readers have taken them to be evidence in favor of a complicated picture of how the method of doubt is supposed to yield its fruits. Let me briefly examine two interpretations of this type.

Alan Gewirth (1941) argues that in these passages Descartes is illustrating the difference between a kind of certainty we can have whenever we have a clear and distinct idea, and the metaphysical certainty about the truth of clear and distinct ideas that can come only with the defeat of the

---

even here, he indicates a distinction between "I exist" and "Two plus three equals five" with respect to their indubitability.

[5] John Carriero (unpublished) develops a reading upon which Descartes is making significant use of such a distinction; so does Ernest Sosa (1997).

deceiving God scenario. Before we are metaphysically certain that all our clear and distinct ideas are true, we are metaphysically certain of none of them, though psychologically certain of all of them as we entertain them clearly and distinctly. For Gewirth, this psychological certainty is not mere dogmatic compulsion; rather, it has a normative component to it, for clear and distinct ideas are as it were entirely in order internally, and we need only knock out the deceiving God scenario in order to be metaphysically certain that they are true. Gewirth sees Descartes as trading on the built-in normativity of clear and distinct ideas by insisting that any skeptical scenario be one whose possible truth I can *clearly and distinctly* understand. Gewirth then reads the Third Meditation as containing this sequence of discoveries: first, Descartes finds that he cannot clearly and distinctly understand his creator to be a deceiver; second, that allows him to rule out the deceiving God scenario as a ground for doubt; third, this leaves him with no reason to doubt the truth of his clear and distinct ideas; and fourth, that in turn allows him to claim absolute certainty for all of his clear and distinct ideas, and in particular his clear and distinct idea that his creator is no deceiver.

Bernard Williams gives a rather different "complicated" reading of Descartes (1978, chaps. 2 and 7). He takes it that in the Fifth Meditation and the replies to Mersenne and Arnauld, Descartes is distinguishing between time-bound certainty, which we may enjoy in having any of our clear and distinct ideas even before we answer the deceiving God doubt, and the acceptance as ongoing beliefs of the matters that we grasp clearly and distinctly, an acceptance that allows us to treat the proof that God exists and is no deceiver as a decisive answer to the deceiving God doubt. Again the normative character of clarity and distinctness is important: for Williams, it motivates Descartes to adopt the acceptance rule "Accept as on-going beliefs just those propositions which are at any time clearly and distinctly perceived to be true" (1978, 203), and that in turn leads him to adopt as ongoing the belief that God exists and is not a deceiver. Finally, from the fact that God exists and is not a deceiver, it follows that our clear and distinct ideas are true, and thus that the acceptance rule Descartes has adopted is sound.

These complicated pictures have two troubling features, however. The first is that they attribute to the meditator the view that he cannot be absolutely certain whether he exists until he knows that God exists and is not a deceiver. This would require the meditator somehow to be taking back what he said in the Second Meditation when he reasoned:

> But there is a deceiver of supreme power and cunning who is deliberately and constantly deceiving me. In that case I too undoubtedly exist, if he is deceiving me; and let him deceive me as much as he can, he will never bring it about that I am nothing so long as I think that I am something. (2:17; AT 7:25)

Not only is there no sign that Descartes meant for the meditator to take this reasoning back; he explicitly denied that that was his intention. Mersenne objected that "you are not yet certain of the existence of God, and you say that you are not certain of anything, and cannot know anything clearly and distinctly until you have achieved clear and certain knowledge of the existence of God. It follows from this that you do not yet clearly and distinctly know that you are a thinking thing" (2:89; AT 7:124–25). Descartes replied,

> [W]hen I said that we can know nothing for certain until we are aware that God exists, I expressly declared that I was speaking only of knowledge of those conclusions which can be recalled when we are no longer attending to the arguments by means of which we deduced them. . . . When someone says 'I am thinking, therefore I am, or I exist', he does not deduce existence from thought by means of a syllogism, but recognizes it as something self-evident by a simple intuition of the mind. (2:100; AT 7:140)

While there is much in this reply to puzzle us, we must not miss its main point, which is to say that we *can* be certain of *some* things before achieving certainty that God exists and is no deceiver, and that "I exist" is one such thing.[6]

Second, these complicated pictures of the method of doubt depict Descartes as achieving metaphysical, or ongoing, certainty that God exists and is not a deceiver *by first* achieving metaphysical or ongoing certainty that his clear and distinct ideas are true. Both of these versions of a complicated picture *reverse* the order of Descartes's discoveries in the Third

---

[6] Presumably Descartes is here saying that "I think" is another. Notice that Descartes is here telescoping the discoveries the meditator made in the Second Meditation, much as he did in his reply to Gassendi.

and Fourth Meditations. As Descartes takes pains to explain, his absolute certainty that all of his clear and distinct ideas are true *rests upon* his absolute certainty that God exists and is not a deceiver. I think that an interpretation that reverses this order must have gone wrong somewhere. Thus I cannot agree with Gewirth, who has Descartes *first* achieving metaphysical certainty that all his clear and distinct ideas are true and *then* achieving metaphysical certainty that God exists; nor can I agree with Williams, who has Descartes *first* adopting as his acceptance rule "Accept as on-going beliefs just those propositions which are at any time clearly and distinctly perceived to be true," and *then* accepting as ongoing the belief that God exists.

None of this is to say, however, exactly what we are to make of the passages in the Fifth Meditation and the Second and Fourth Replies that fuel the complicated picture. So all I want to insist upon here is this: our reading of those passages must respect the simple picture of the first four Meditations, whether by rendering them compatible with the simple picture, or by attributing to Descartes two incompatible accounts of the way in which doubt is supposed to yield knowledge. In other words, I think that there is a compelling case for seeing the simple picture as describing at least one way, and perhaps the only way, in which Descartes thought the method of doubt produces knowledge.

Transcendental Arguments

Now I want to take a closer look at the relation between Descartes's arguments and a type of contemporary argument called "transcendental." Let me begin by saying something about what makes arguments "transcendental" and how such arguments have been used.[7] Here are the starting points and conclusions of several transcendental arguments:

[7] I am deeply indebted to Daniel Warren for all the ways in which he has greatly clarified my thinking about transcendental arguments. I should say that I think it is a good question whether the sort of argument that concerns me here is the sort offered by Kant, either in the Transcendental Deduction or in the Refutation of Idealism. For helpful discussion of this question, see Förster 1989. Nor is it clear whether this sort of argument shares crucial features with arguments given by Hegel, Fichte, and others. Paul Franks (1999) considers this question in a way I have found illuminating.

1A. I can attribute sense-datum experiences to myself.

1B. I have experience of objects. (See Strawson 1966, 85–111.)

2A. We identify things using a single spatiotemporal framework.

2B. We can make reidentifications that assert the continued existence of objects unperceived. (See Strawson 1996, 14–58.)

3A. I know how things seem to me to be.

3B. I can have knowledge of objective particulars. (See Hacker 1972.)

4A. We can attribute beliefs to people.

4B. Those beliefs are largely true. (See Davidson 1986.)

5A. I can report that I am in pain, using "pain" with its established meaning.

5B. My judgments about whether others are in pain, when based on the behavior of others, are largely true. (See Shoemaker 1963, chaps. 5 and 6.)

6A. "There are extended objects" is intelligible.

6B. "There are extended objects" is knowable. (See Stroud 1968.)

A transcendental argument has as its starting point a claim that concerns people's experiences or their cognitive states or capacities. The argument then aims to show that the truth of some other statement is a necessary condition of the starting point. In each case, the intervening argumentation from (A) to (B) will be a way of trying to show that "If (A), then (B)" is true.

This does not yet delimit the class of transcendental arguments, though. Consider this argument:

A. Cortez saw the Pacific Ocean.
B. The Pacific Ocean existed.

The starting point, (A), concerns someone's experience; the conclusion states a necessary condition of the truth of (A); and argumentation could be provided to show why "If (A), then (B)" is true. But this isn't a transcendental argument. The reason is that if I gave an adequate justification for claiming that (A) is true, I would have to cite (B) as part of my warrant for asserting (A). ("There was Cortez; there was the Pacific Ocean; and Cortez was facing it with his eyes wide open"—or something like that.) In transcendental arguments, the A-claims are independent of the B-claims, in this sense: (B) need not be part of the warrant for asserting (A).[8]

Of course, there are many nontranscendental arguments of which that much is true. For example, consider:

A. Unsupported objects fall to the ground.
B. The Earth's mass exerts a gravitational pull.

Statement (B) need not be part of the warrant for asserting (A): my warrant for believing (A) might simply be what I have observed to happen when the things around me have their supports removed. But, of course, this is not a transcendental argument, because the truth of (B) is not a necessary condition of the truth of (A).

Transcendental arguments, then, have *both* of these features:

1. The truth of (B), the conclusion, is a necessary condition of the truth of (A), the starting point.
2. The warrant for (A) need not include (B).

It may be that there are further features transcendental arguments have, and I will return to this possibility later. For now, though, I will be concerned only with these two core features.

As I have just characterized them, transcendental arguments could usefully contribute to various philosophical projects, for example, criticizing certain forms of empiricism, or arguing that thought and language must have a social dimension. The best-known project for which philosophers have used transcendental arguments, though, is that of confounding the skeptic who in some way grants the truth of the A-claims but professes to doubt the truth of the B-claims (or to deny their truth, if they express a claim to knowledge). If the transcendental argument works, then the skeptic cannot consistently doubt the B-claims so long as he grants that the A-claims are true.

But even a completely sound and valid transcendental argument may have little antiskeptical force if it is easy for the skeptic to wiggle out of his bind by saying he will keep doubting the B-claims and stop granting

---

[8] Daniel Warren has been especially helpful in clarifying this feature of transcendental arguments.

the A-claims. One way to tighten the grip of the argument on the skeptic, then, would be to show that success in doubting the B-claims would *depend* in some way upon granting the A-claims.[9] So one good antiskeptical strategy for a transcendental arguer to pursue is to show that the skeptic could doubt the B-claim *only if* he granted the truth of the A-claim. Then the transcendental argument from (A) to (B) would show that once the skeptic has granted the A-claim, he must concede the truth of the B-claim. Overall, then, the skeptic would see that he could doubt the B-claim only if he granted the B-claim, and so he would see that he cannot rationally doubt the B-claim.

This general antiskeptical strategy should look familiar: it is the dependence strategy that I introduced in chapter 6, the one whose aim is to show that the raising of doubt about (B) is dependent upon the truth of (B). What we are now considering is the idea of embedding a transcendental argument within a dependence argument in order to block a skeptical response to the transcendental argument. Again, here is how it would work schematically:

1. If I raise a doubt whether (B), I must grant that (A) is true.
2. But if (A), then (B). (This is the embedded transcendental argument.)
3. So if I raise a doubt whether (B), I must grant that (B) is true.

By following this argument, the skeptic will see that he cannot rationally doubt whether (B) is true.

To illustrate, let us imagine how the dependence strategy would work with the sixth argument I sketched, from the premise that "There are extended objects" is intelligible to the conclusion that "There are extended objects" is knowable. For the skeptic to doubt whether there are extended objects, he must be able to make intelligible at minimum what it is whose truth he is doubting. Then the transcendental argument from (6A) to (6B) will show that the skeptic cannot rationally doubt "There are extended objects" and thus will show that it is knowable after all.

But the dependence strategy may be a very demanding one to carry out, for it requires clarifying both what is involved in doubting the B-

---

[9] Of course, the skeptic's readiness to grant the A-claims may have had its source in some set of considerations that are not intimately connected with his doubting (B), and if the skeptic is willing to rethink those considerations, then the antiskeptical transcendental

claims and what motivates the skeptic's readiness to grant the A-claims. For example, consider the third argument, from the premise that I know how things seem to me to be, to the conclusion that I can have knowledge of objective particulars. (This is how Peter Hacker represents the starting point and conclusion of a paradigm transcendental argument.) Let us imagine how a skeptic might try to wiggle out of accepting the conclusion, and what would be required if we tried (as Hacker did not) to use the dependence strategy to pin him. So imagine a skeptic who responds to Hacker's argument by saying that his reasons for denying the conclusion, together with the transcendental argument itself, show that he was wrong to have granted the premise. That is, he responds to the transcendental argument by saying that he doesn't have knowledge of how things seem to him to be. If we want to reply to this by using the dependence strategy, we must show that the skeptic's doubting the conclusion about knowledge of objective particulars somehow *depends upon* his ability to know how things seem to him to be. But it is not at all clear how such an argument would go. Consider the skeptical position as Hacker describes it:

> Descartes' sceptical challenger succeeds in throwing doubt upon all cognitive claims concerning objective particulars. But with respect to the contents of Descartes' own mind, his challenge is impotent. For the mind knows with certainty the "thoughts" which occur to it. . . . [O]ur knowledge of how things seem to us to be does not rest on evidence. . . . The problem which the sceptic now poses is—how can one justifiably infer, from statements about one's "thoughts," statements about objective particulars? . . . There is no entailment relation between statements about thoughts of objects and statements about objects. And the arguments from illusion or from dreaming bear witness to the possibility of the truth of the former and falsity of the latter. (1972, 79)

Hacker is saying that the skeptic's motivation for granting that he knows how things seem to him is his "Cartesian doctrine of thoughts" (79), and that his reasons for doubting claims about objective particulars are arguments from illusion or dreaming that show we could have all the thoughts we do even if the statements we make about objects were false.

---

arguer will need to find some other way to keep the skeptic from wiggling out of his bind.

But the arguments from illusion and dreaming do not (at least as Hacker represents them) depend upon the claim that I *know* the truth of statements about how things seem to me to be. So unless we can come up with some fresh considerations, the skeptic will still have his wiggle room: as things stand, he can doubt claims about objective particulars and give up his "Cartesian doctrine of thoughts."

Even the argument from (6A) to (6B)—from the intelligibility to the knowability of the claim that extended things exist—may not make the dependence strategy as easy to execute as at first it seems. The appeal of using this argument within a dependence argument lies in the appeal of the idea that to doubt whether *p* is true, one must grant that *p* is intelligible. But the skeptic may reply that the transcendental arguer is mistaken if he thinks that we must grant that *p* is intelligible in order to doubt whether *p* is true. The discovery that an apparently intelligible claim is not, after all, intelligible, itself constitutes the discovery that we do not know what we thought we knew—or so the skeptic might claim, citing perhaps the illustrious precedent of Hume's reflections on our ideas about necessary connection and about bodies (1978, 168, 226–31). Perhaps the transcendental arguer can find a way to continue pursuing the dependence strategy in his antiskeptical use of the argument from the intelligibility to the knowability of the claim that extended things exist; perhaps not. Very deep and central questions about human knowledge are at the heart of this debate between the skeptic and the transcendental arguer, and it seems to me that at this point the questions concern not the distinctive character of transcendental arguments but rather the nature of knowledge, meaning, doubt, and reason giving.

So let me now turn back to the arguments that I think Descartes is giving in the *Meditations*. I have been arguing in Part Two of this book that Descartes is using the dependence strategy, just as many transcendental arguers do, or are thought to do. But I also believe that for Descartes the embedded arguments need not be transcendental, because the nature of the warrant for the A-claims is not important to the line of thought I believe he is pursuing.[10] To explain this claim, let me use as

---

[10] Arguably the transcendental character of the embedded argument is *never* important to the antiskeptical success of the dependence strategy. I think that when a transcendental argument is embedded within a dependence argument, all of the antiskeptical work is

examples several of Descartes's arguments as I have interpreted them in chapters 7 and 8:

1. If I have a reason to doubt whether (B) I exist, I must grant that (A) while it may be that I believe I exist because it is true, it may instead be that I am caused by a deceiving God to believe that I exist (and I cannot tell which account of my belief is true).

2. If (A) either I believe that I exist because it is true, or I am caused by a deceiving God to believe that I exist, then at least it must be true that (B) I exist.

3. So if I have reason to doubt whether (B) I exist, I must grant that (B) I exist.

1. If I raise a doubt whether (B) I have an idea of God, I must grant that (A) I recognize that I doubt.

2. If (A) that I recognize that I doubt, then (B) I have an idea of God.

3. So if I raise a doubt whether (B) I have an idea of God, I must grant that (B) I have an idea of God.

1. If I raise a doubt whether (B) everything has a reason for its existence, then (A) I am engaged in using doubt to establish truth.

2. If (A) I am engaged in using doubt to establish truth, then I must grant that (B) everything has a reason for its existence.

3. So if I raise a doubt whether (B) everything has a reason for its existence, I must grant that (B) everything has a reason for its existence.

Now, are the if-then claims in the various second steps transcendental arguments? In each case the truth of the B-claim is clearly supposed to be a necessary condition of the A-claim. But is the warrant for the A-claim supposed to be independent of the B-claim? I believe that for Des-

---

done by one of the two features of transcendental arguments that I have sketched. The transcendental argument must show that the truth of (B) is a *necessary condition* of (A), or else the dogged skeptic cannot be charged with incoherence. But the independence from (B) of the warrant for (A) is not important, so long as the strategist adequately connects the *truth* of (A) with the possibility of offering a reason of such-and-such a sort for doubting whether (B) is true. The *warrant* one would need to offer for (A) on its own does not seem important for the antiskeptical success of the dependence strategy. This suggests that whenever arguments are embedded within a dependence argument, it is not important whether they are transcendental or not.

cartes, the nature of the warrant for the A-claims is unimportant. Here are the A-claims:

A. While it may be that I believe I exist because it is true, it may instead be that I am caused by a deceiving God to believe that I exist (and I cannot tell which account of my belief is true).

A. I recognize that I doubt.

A. I am engaged in using doubt to establish truth.

My *warrant* for these claims is unimportant for the method of doubt: what is important is that they are the middle link in a chain connecting my having a reason for doubting (B) to my granting the truth of the various B-claims. It is by seeing this chain that I see I cannot coherently doubt that (B) is true.

Some readers may now want to see my having a reason for doubting (B) as itself being the starting point of an antiskeptical transcendental argument. Schematically, we would be seeing Descartes's arguments in this way:

7A. I raise a doubt about *p*.

. . . .

7B. I must grant that *p* is true.

Certainly part of the structure of Descartes's thinking requires the truth of the conditional "If (7A), then (7B)." And it may be that this argument meets both of the two conditions on transcendental arguments that I sketched earlier, that is, that the truth of (7B) depends upon the truth of (7A) and that the warrant for (7A) need not include (7B).

I do not think, however, that this captures the structure of Descartes's arguments. Recall Hacker's description of the antiskeptical power of transcendental arguments: that power depends upon the skeptic's having to grant, when it comes to (A), that "his challenge is impotent" because "the mind knows with certainty" the truth of (A). If we think of the argument from (7A) to (7B) as an antiskeptical transcendental argument, then we will need to see its power as depending upon the meditator's being able to claim with *certainty* that he is raising doubt about *p*. But it is a mistake to see the method of doubt this way, I believe. The antiskeptical force of Descartes's arguments does not arise from a starting point about which he has certainty. The meditator does not need to start out by claiming he is *certain* he is raising doubts. Rather, Descartes's arguments get their antiskeptical force by showing the meditator that there are some propositions he cannot rationally doubt, because the possibility of doubting them depends upon granting their truth.[11]

This is a generalized version of a claim I stressed in chapter 7 when I argued against the Cogito First interpretation of the "I exist" reasoning. In general, I think it is important *not* to see Descartes as in some way carrying out an antiskeptical strategy that depends upon the meditator's *starting* with certainty about a "Cartesian doctrine of thoughts," to use Hacker's phrase. The meditator doesn't start with certainty about anything, not even with certainty about his doubting. His ambition is to *achieve* certainty by *using* doubt, and I think that laying out the dependence strategy helps to clarify this ambition. Of course, by the end of the Second Meditation the meditator has embraced the "Cartesian doctrine of thoughts," but for him that is the *outcome* of his use of doubt, not its basis. Descartes is as it were beginning further back than we might suppose, but not because he thinks there are other *certainties* behind the "Cartesian doctrine of thoughts."

Let me return now to the question whether Descartes is giving transcendental arguments, either just from the A-claims to the B-claims in the second step of a dependence argument, or in the manner I have just been discussing, where the A-claim is that I am raising doubt. I have said that for Descartes, the warrant for his starting point is not important, so that it is not important to his antiskeptical strategy whether his arguments are transcendental or not. Still, we might wonder whether they are. If they are, the meditator's warrant for the A-claims would have to be independent of the corresponding B-claims. So consider an example: is the meditator's warrant for saying that he doubts independent of his having an idea of God? Surely it is. His actually doubting would give him warrant for saying, "I am doubting." I think the same is true for the other dependence arguments in the *Meditations* (though I must say this is not entirely clear in the case of the principle of sufficient reason).

---

[11] As I suggested in n. 10, I am inclined to say the same about the antiskeptical force of any transcendental argument that is embedded in a dependence strategy.

So should we say that Descartes's arguments are transcendental? If there were no more to being a transcendental argument than meeting the two conditions I have sketched, then my answer would be "Yes, though that does not explain how Descartes thought they get their anti-skeptical force." But I think Descartes's arguments are missing at least one feature that is prominent in contemporary transcendental arguments. If the contemporary arguments succeed, they show that we are entitled to the claims with which the arguments both begin and end. We have experience of objects as well as the ability to attribute sense-datum experiences to ourselves; we can have knowledge of objective particulars as well as knowledge of how things seem to us to be; "There are extended objects" is knowable as well as intelligible; and so on. At the end of the day, we are able to say that both the A-claims and the B-claims are true.

But at the end of his meditations, Descartes *jettisons* his A-claims. By using the dependence strategy, he establishes not just the B-claims but also the further claims that they entail. This means, for example, that he no longer accepts the A-claim that he cannot tell whether he has been created by a deceiving God to believe that he exists; now he knows that he has been created by a perfect being. Similarly, he no longer accepts the A-claim that he cannot tell whether his present experience is caused as dreams are caused. He *can* sometimes tell, when he sees things, that he is "completely free from error" (2:62; AT 7:90). He no longer doubts; he no longer uses doubt to establish truths. He needs to make use of the method of doubt only "once in the course of life" (2:12; AT 7:17).[12] From his vantage point at the end of his meditations, he can look back at himself as he was when he worked through the First Meditation and say: "I *thought* I had a reason to doubt whether a hand is here, or two plus three equals five, but I didn't. Of course, so long as I thought I had a reason for doubt, I was right to suspend judgment, given the rules of the game I was playing. But I was right to suspend judgment only because I then had a false belief, namely, that I had reasons for doubt. Now what I am in a position to see is that that belief *is* false: there are no skeptical scenarios that I can construct for 'Here is a hand' or 'Two plus three equals five.'"

---

[12] "*Semel in vitâ.*" The phrase also appears in three versions of Rule Eight of the *Rules* (1:30–31; AT 10:395–98), and in the first article of the *Principles* (1:193; AT 8A:5).

So Descartes's use of the method of doubt is in this respect very different from the use philosophers make of transcendental arguments. It is not a way of trying to get a lot from a little: it is a way of trying to get a lot from nothing.[13]

THE FATE OF COMMON SENSE

In Part One, I argued that Descartes takes seriously the commonsense idea that when we are awake and sane, and looking at things that are close enough and large enough to see clearly, we are in an excellent epistemic position. If someone is in such a position, he can very reasonably assent to such propositions as "Here is a hand." Descartes also takes seriously the commonsense idea that when we grasp something evident, like "Two plus three equals five," we are in an excellent epistemic position. Indeed, only the radical skeptical scenarios can raise a doubt about such claims as these, and the doubt they raise is slight, or hyperbolic. That is why I described beliefs like "Here is a hand" and "Two plus three equals five" as morally certain.

The question I now want to raise is this: does the meditator, at the end of his inquiry, find that these prereflective, commonsense ideas were altogether wrong? I think this is a hard question with a complicated answer.

In chapter 3, I claimed that the high strategy behind the method of doubt turns partly on the idea that whenever a moral certainty conflicts with an absolute certainty, we ought to assent to the proposition about which we are absolutely certain, and disbelieve the conflicting proposition in which we had reposed moral certainty. This is what gives the method of doubt the authority to demand that we change our minds.

But change them about what, exactly? By uncovering the conditions of his doubt, Descartes discovers that he can be absolutely certain about the truth of whatever he grasps clearly and distinctly, and he adopts a new maxim for assent, that he ought to believe only what he clearly and distinctly understands. I want now to see where this leaves him, first in

---

[13] Bourdin was right about that much: Descartes's method, he said, "struggles to derive something from nothing" (2:359; AT 7:528).

connection with his mathematical beliefs, and then in connection with his sense-based beliefs.

Adhering to his new maxim does not force upon him any changes in his mathematical beliefs: he need not revise his prereflective belief that two plus three equals five. But even in the mathematical arena, the meditator does not end up exactly where he started. One difference between his ending point and his initial position is, of course, that he is now really entitled to the absolute certainty that at first he thought he had. But that is not the only difference. First, by identifying and clarifying his idea of God as infinite, and by concluding with certainty that such a God exists, the meditator is in a position to understand what mathematical facts *are*. He begins to achieve this metaphysical understanding in the Fifth Meditation, though Descartes does not represent him as having yet made the amazing discovery that God freely created all of the eternal truths that there are (see, e.g., 2:291–92, 293–94; AT 7:431–33, 435–36). Second, the meditator is now in a position to do something he could not have done at the outset, and that is correctly to explain *why* his clear and distinct ideas in mathematics are worthy of his assent. In the First Meditation, he said that "Two plus three equals five" is an example of a "transparent" truth about "the simplest and most general things" (2:14; AT 7:20). By the end of his meditations, he understands that it is the clarity and distinctness of these ideas that makes them worthy of his assent, and that the clarity and distinctness of ideas makes them not just the best of the ideas he has, but as good as good can be. This is something he can see only after he has achieved absolute certainty about the nature of his creator.

Still, concerning mathematics, the meditator is not so much displacing as enriching his former beliefs. His particular beliefs about the subject matter of mathematics are unchanged. His philosophical beliefs about mathematics—about its metaphysics and epistemology—are new additions to his stock of beliefs, but they do not exactly displace former beliefs of his, because he did not begin with any substantive competing views about these matters.[14]

---

[14] There is room for disagreement here in two directions. One is that taken by Frankfurt (1970, chap. 7), who attributes to the meditator a sort of naive empiricism about mathematics. Another is to build upon the meditator's distinction between mathematical truths

Concerning sense perception, the relation between the meditator's starting and ending positions is more complicated. First, the meditator *does* need to change at least part of what he believed on the basis of sense perception. His prereflective belief that, say, his hand is before him is entangled in a web of beliefs that are not clear and distinct: that a warm thing is before him, that a beige thing is before him, and so on. The meditator's new maxim—assent only to what is clear and distinct—requires him to jettison these entangling beliefs about the particular things around him. I will return presently to the question where this leaves his beliefs about particular things.

Second, the meditator is, of course, also committed to changing at least some of the general beliefs he had had about the objects of his senses and about the way his sense perception gives him knowledge of these objects. He will no longer assent to the general belief that things have the colors we see, the warmth we feel, the savor we taste, and so on. He will assent only to the general belief that the objects of his senses are extended, have shapes, positions, and sizes, and can move. He will also revise his former opinion about how his senses give him knowledge of these objects. It's not that he began with an elaborate theory about this; nonetheless he must change what he had thought. He had thought his senses give him knowledge by somehow acquainting him with the very features the objects have. Now he realizes that his sense perception decomposes without remainder into motions in his own body that are caused by other bodies, plus his awareness of patterns of sensed qualities; and he sees that his awareness of these patterns generally corresponds to patterns of changing shapes and motions in the objects that caused the motions in his body.

Was there nonetheless something right about the meditator's initial commonsense perspective, something that he does not later need to retract but rather to understand better? I think so, but it is hard to identify just what it is. Let me begin with some general beliefs about sense experience.

In the Second Meditation, the meditator claims to discover that *all along* his perception of the piece of wax revealed to him the nature of the

---

and those of physics, astronomy, or medicine (2:14; AT 7:20); for example, Carriero (1997) sees here a moment in a distinctively scholastic train of thought.

wax as "extended, flexible and changeable" (2:20; AT 7:31). So to the extent that such a conception played a role in his initial perspective, his initial perspective had something right about it. It is difficult, however, to say exactly how this conception played a role in his initial perspective, since at least some aspects of the conception were not ones he could then have articulated. (For example, he could not at first have said that this conception involved the conception of "*countless* changes" [2:21; AT 7:31; emphasis added].)

In the Sixth Meditation, the meditator remarks that he has a "great propensity" to believe that his sense perceptions are sent to him by corporeal things (2:55; AT 7:79–80). I think he means that he has had this propensity all along, and not just toward the end of his meditations. Of course, there are changes in the way he is able to articulate the proposition he is inclined to assent to. By the Sixth Meditation, he means something different—clearer and more distinct—by "sense perceptions" and "corporeal things," and he sees more clearly that the relation between them is that of (efficient) causality. In addition to articulating "Bodies cause sensations" more clearly, though, the meditator is now able to do something else: he can understand *why* his belief is one that he is right to hold. It is right not just because he has a propensity to think it is right; brought by the method of doubt to embrace the new maxim, the meditator acknowledges that common sense does not *by itself* have the authority to rationalize this belief. What the meditator now can do, though, is to draw upon supporting philosophical claims: that God has given him his propensity to believe this, that God has not given him any way to correct it if it is wrong, and that God is no deceiver. Using these, he can explain why his propensity to believe that corporeal things cause his sensations is a trustworthy propensity.

Much the same philosophical reasoning enables him to understand why he is right to believe what he is "taught by nature": that he has a body to which he is united, that his internal sensations indicate its needs, that other bodies exist around his own body, that he should seek some of these and avoid others, and that "the bodies which are the source of . . . various sensory perceptions possess differences corresponding to them" (2:56; AT 7:81). Again, I think Descartes means to be saying that the meditator had had these general beliefs all along, though he needed to extract them from an entangling set of beliefs that are not clear and distinct. And again, what the meditator is now in a position to do is to give the correct account of why he is right to accept these teachings of nature. He understands the principles of First Philosophy that underwrite his acceptance of these general beliefs about sensation and its objects.

Let me return now to the meditator's initial certainty about particular sensible objects. He began his meditations thinking that many of the beliefs he had are ones "about which doubt is quite impossible . . . —for example, that I am here, sitting by the fire, wearing a winter dressing-gown, holding this piece of paper in my hands, and so on. Really, how could it be denied that these hands or this whole body are mine?" (2:12–13; AT 7:18, trans. altered). At the very end of the *Meditations*, Descartes has the meditator dismiss "any further fears about the falsity of what my senses tell me every day" (2:61; AT 7:89), for example, that a real man is before him. While he recognizes that he is "liable to make mistakes about particular things," he is often able to be "quite certain that when I encounter these things I am not asleep but awake" (2:62; AT 7:90), and he seems equally confident that he can tell when his body is in good working order.

It seems, then, that what the meditator discovers is that he was right to have thought that "doubt is quite impossible" about such judgments as "Here is a man" or "I am holding a piece of paper." Once again, it seems that what his meditations supply is a corrected understanding of why the prereflective beliefs were true.

While I think that this is how Descartes actually does *represent* the relation between the meditator's beginning and ending perspectives, I think he is not taking sufficiently into account the consequences of the various clarifications the meditator is supposed to make in judgments like "Here is a man" or "This is a piece of paper." If the meditator *really* clarifies "This is a piece of paper," he must somehow think of "this" as a collection of minute bits of *res extensa*, a collection that is distinct from contiguous stuff (air, flesh) only insofar as the bits that compose it tend to move together. But, of course, he would also have to think in the same way about this air, this flesh, this fabric, this *anything* extended, distinguishing each from the others only by thinking of their differing sizes, shapes, and motions.

There are good questions about whether this scientific conception of the world is coherent: for example, we might wonder whether the missing notion of force is really dispensable. There are also questions about whether we can really conceive of the sensible world using *any* conception according to which the world does not have in it the colors that we see, the textures that we feel, and so on. But there is still another question, and it is one intimately bound up with the fate of common sense. That is the question how, if at all, this scientific conception is connected with the map of the world that our ordinary concepts of things lay out for us. Our ordinary conceptions of things—of people, pieces of paper, dressing gowns—are at least in part constituted by the relations we think the things can have to one another: dressing gowns are worn by people; people can grasp pieces of paper, but dressing gowns can't; dressing gowns have pockets into which pieces of paper, but not people, can be stashed; and so on. It is entirely unclear how Descartes would construct the scientifically expressed analogues of these relations, or whether he would even think such constructions are possible. Yet without them, he cannot plausibly claim that the principles of First Philosophy underwrite the particular judgments with which we identify the things around us. To see this point from a slightly different perspective, consider this passage in a letter Descartes wrote to Regius:

> [W]e perceive that sensations such as pain are not pure thoughts of a mind distinct from a body, but confused perceptions of a mind really united to a body. For if an angel were in a human body, he would not have sensations as we do, but would simply perceive the motions which are caused by external objects, and in this way would differ from a real man. (3:206; AT 3:493)

An angel in a human body would have clear and distinct perceptions— of the motions in that human body that are caused by external objects. Even if we imagine that such a mind could rapidly draw inferences from what it knows about the motions in its human body to the distributions of motions in the neighborhood of its body, Descartes would still owe us an explanation of how, from these perceptions, such a mind could construct the concepts indispensable to *our* conception of the world around us. "Piece of paper," "dressing gown,"—how would an angel connect these concepts to the patterns of experiences his perceptions give him?

I think, then, that Descartes represents the meditator as clarifying the beliefs, both general and particular, that constituted his prereflective certainties, and as explaining why he is entitled to hold those beliefs, or at any rate to hold what is clear in them. I must confess that I am pessimistic about the fate of common sense if its authority must be underwritten by principles like those of First Philosophy. In the Third Meditation, the meditator says, looking back at the sense-based beliefs with which he began, "[I]f my judgment was true, it was not on the strength of my perception" (2:25; AT 7:35; trans. altered). Perhaps he is right that it is not enough simply to say that I can judge that a hand is before me "on the strength of my perception"; but if he is right, and that is not enough, I doubt whether First Philosophy can supply what is missing.

❖ References ❖

Annas, Julia, and Jonathan Barnes, eds. 1985. *The Modes of Scepticism*. Cambridge: Cambridge University Press.

Arnauld, Antoine, and Pierre Nicole. 1996. *Logic or the Art of Thinking*. Edited and translated by Jill Vance Buroker. Cambridge: Cambridge University Press.

Ayers, Michael. 1991. *Locke: Epistemology and Ontology*. London: Routledge.

Beck, Leslie John. 1952. *The Method of Descartes: A Study of the "Regulae."* Oxford: Oxford University Press.

Bennett, Jonathan. 1984. *A Study of Spinoza's "Ethics."* [Indianapolis, Ind.]: Hackett Publishing Company.

Beyssade, Jean-Marie. 1992. "The Idea of God and the Proofs of His Existence." In *The Cambridge Companion to Descartes*, edited by John Cottingham, 174–99. Cambridge: Cambridge University Press.

Brandom, Robert. 1997. "Study Guide." Afterword to *Empiricism and the Philosophy of Mind*, by Wilfred Sellars. Cambridge: Harvard University Press.

Broughton, Janet. 1977. "Aspects of Descartes's Conception of Causation." Ph.D. diss., Princeton University.

———. 1984. "Skepticism and the Cartesian Circle." *Canadian Journal of Philosophy* 14 (4): 593–615.

———. 1986. "Adequate Causes and Natural Change in Descartes's Philosophy." In *Human Nature and Natural Knowledge*, edited by Alan Donagan, Anthony N. Perovich, Jr., and Michael V. Wedin, 107–27. Dordrecht: D. Reidel.

———. 1999. "The Method of Doubt." In *The Rationalists: Critical Essays on Descartes, Spinoza, and Leibniz*, edited by Derk Pereboom, 1–18. Lanham, MD: Rowman & Littlefield.

———. Forthcoming. "Dreamers and Madmen." In *The History of Early Modern Philosophy: Essays in Honor of Margaret Wilson*, edited by Christia Mercer and Eileen O'Neill. Oxford: Blackwell.

Burnyeat, Myles. 1982. "Idealism and Greek Philosophy: What Descartes Saw and Berkeley Missed." *Philosophical Review* 91 (1): 3–40.

———. 1983. "Can the Skeptic Live His Skepticism?" In *The Skeptical Tradition*, edited by Myles Burnyeat, 117–48. Berkeley and Los Angeles: University of California Press.

———. 1997. "The Sceptic in His Place and Time." In *The Original Sceptics: A Controversy*, edited by Myles Burnyeat and Michael Frede, 92–126. Indianapolis, Ind.: Hackett.

Carriero, John. 1984. "Descartes and the Autonomy of the Human Understanding." Ph.D. diss., Harvard University.

———. 1986. "The Second Meditation and the Essence of the Mind." In *Essays on Descartes' "Meditations,"* edited by Amélie O. Rorty, 199–221. Berkeley and Los Angeles: University of California Press.

———. 1997. "The First Meditation." In *Descartes's "Meditations": Critical Essays,* edited by Vere Chappell, 1–31. Lanham, Md.: Rowman & Littlefield.

———. Unpublished. "*Cognitio, scientia* and the Cartesian Circle."

Cavell, Stanley. 1979. *The Claim of Reason.* Oxford: Clarendon Press; New York: Oxford University Press.

Cicero. 1951. *De natura deorum; Academica.* With a translation by H. Rackham. Loeb Classical Library.

Clarke, Desmond. 1982. *Descartes's Philosophy of Science.* University Park: Pennsylvania State University Press.

Clatterbaugh, Kenneth. 1980. "Descartes's Causal Likeness Principle." *Philosophical Review* 898 (3): 379–402.

———. 1999. *The Causation Debate in Modern Philosophy, 1637–1739.* New York: Routledge.

Curley, Edwin M. 1978. *Descartes against the Skeptics.* Cambridge: Harvard University Press.

———. 1986. "Analysis in the *Meditations*: The Quest for Clear and Distinct Ideas." In *Essays on Descartes' "Meditations,"* edited by Amélie O. Rorty, 153–76. Berkeley and Los Angeles: University of California Press.

Davidson, Donald. 1986. "A Coherence Theory of Truth and Knowledge." In *Truth and Interpretation: Perspectives on the Philosophy of Donald Davidson,* edited by Ernest LePore, 307–19. New York: Basil Blackwell.

Dear, Peter. 1998. "Method and the Study of Nature." In *The Cambridge History of Seventeenth-Century Philosophy,* edited by Daniel Garber and Michael Ayers, 1:147–77. Cambridge: Cambridge University Press.

Delahunty, Robert. 1997. "Descartes' Cosmological Argument." In *Descartes' "Meditations": Critical Essays,* edited by Vere Chappell, 87–102. Lanham, MD: Rowman & Littlefield.

Descartes, René. 1971. *Descartes: Philosophical Writings.* Edited and translated by Elizabeth Anscombe and Peter Geach. Indianapolis, Ind.: Bobbs-Merrill.

———. 1972. *The Philosophical Works of Descartes.* Edited and translated by Elizabeth Haldane and G.T.R. Ross. 2 vols. Cambridge: Cambridge University Press.

———. 1984. *The Philosophical Writings of Descartes.* Edited and translated by John Cottingham, Robert Stoothoff, Dugald Murdoch, and (vol. 3 only) Anthony Kenny. 3 vols. Cambridge: Cambridge University Press.

———. 1996. *Oeuvres de Descartes*. Edited by Charles Adam and Paul Tannery. 11 vols. Paris: Libraire Philosophique J. Vrin.

Doney, Willis. 1971. "Spinoza on Philosophical Skepticism." *Monist* 55 (4): 617–35.

Fine, Gail. 2000. "Descartes and Ancient Scepticism: Reheated Cabbage?" *Philosophical Review* 109 (2): 195–234.

Flage, Daniel, and Clarence A. Bonnen. 1999. *Descartes and Method: A Search for a Method in the "Meditations."* London: Routledge.

Fogelin, Robert. 1994. *Pyrrhonian Reflections on Knowledge and Justification*. New York: Oxford University Press.

Förster, Eckart. 1989. "How Are Transcendental Arguments Possible?" In *Reading Kant: New Perspectives on Transcendental Arguments and Critical Philosophy*, edited by Eva Schaper and Wilhelm Vossenkuhl. Oxford: Basil Blackwell.

Frankel, Lois. 1986. "Justifying Descartes's Causal Principle." *Journal of the History of Philosophy* 24 (3): 323–41.

Frankfurt, Harry. 1970. *Demons, Dreamers, and Madmen*. Indianapolis, Ind.: Bobbs-Merrill.

Franks, Paul. 1999. "Transcendental Arguments, Reason, and Scepticism: Contemporary Debates and the Origins of Post-Kantianism." In *Transcendental Arguments: Problems and Prospects*, edited by Robert Stern, 111–45. Oxford: Clarendon Press.

Frede, Michael. 1983. "Stoics and Skeptics on Clear and Distinct Impressions." In *The Skeptical Tradition*, edited by Myles Burnyeat, 65–93. Berkeley and Los Angeles: University of California Press.

———. 1997. "The Sceptic's Beliefs." In *The Original Sceptics: A Controversy*, edited by Myles Burnyeat and Michael Frede, 1–24. Indianapolis, Ind.: Hackett.

Garber, Daniel. 1986. "*Semel in vita*: The Scientific Background to Descartes' *Meditations*." In *Essays on Descartes' "Meditations,"* edited by Amélie O. Rorty, 81–116. Berkeley and Los Angeles: University of California Press.

———. 1992. *Descartes' Metaphysical Physics*. Chicago: University of Chicago Press.

Gaukroger, Stephen. 1989. *Cartesian Logic: An Essay on Descartes's Conception of Inference*. Oxford: Clarendon Press.

———. 1993. "Descartes: Methodology." In *The Renaissance and Seventeenth-Century Rationalism*, edited by G.H.R. Parkinson, 167–200. London and New York: Routledge.

———. 1995. *Descartes: An Intellectual Biography*. Oxford: Clarendon Press.

Gewirth, Alan. 1941. "The Cartesian Circle." *Philosophical Review* 50 (4): 368–95.

Gilbert, Neal. 1963. *Renaissance Concepts of Method*. New York: Columbia University Press.

REFERENCES

Gouhier, Henri. 1958. *Les premières pensées de Descartes*. Paris: Vrin.

Gueroult, Martial. 1968. *Descartes selon l'ordre des raison: l'ame et Dieu*. Paris: Aubier.

Hacker, Peter. 1972. "Are Transcendental Arguments a Version of Verificationism?" *American Philosophical Quarterly* 9 (1): 78–85.

Hatfield, Gary. 1986. "The Senses and the Fleshless Eye: The *Meditations* as Cognitive Exercises." In *Essays on Descartes' "Meditations,"* edited by Amélie O. Rorty, 45–79. Berkeley and Los Angeles: University of California Press.

———. 1993. "Reason, Nature, and God in Descartes." In *Essays on the Philosophy and Science of René Descartes*, edited by Stephen Voss, 259–87. Oxford: Oxford University Press.

Hume, David. 1975. *Enquiries concerning Human Understanding and concerning the Principles of Morals*. Edited by L. A. Selby-Bigge, with text revision and notes by P. H. Nidditch. Oxford: Clarendon Press.

———. 1978. *A Treatise of Human Nature*. Edited by L. A. Selby-Bigge, with text revision and notes by P. H. Nidditch. Oxford: Clarendon Press.

Kant, Immanuel. 1965. *Critique of Pure Reason*. Translated by Norman Kemp Smith. New York: St. Martin's Press.

Kemp Smith, Norman. 1966. *New Studies in the Philosophy of Descartes*. London: Macmillan.

Kenny, Anthony. 1968. *Descartes: A Study of His Philosophy*. New York: Random House.

Kirwan, Christopher. 1983. "Augustine against the Skeptics." In *The Skeptical Tradition*, edited by Myles Burnyeat, 205–23. Berkeley and Los Angeles: University of California Press.

Kitcher, Philip. 1984. *The Nature of Mathematical Knowledge*. Oxford: Oxford University Press.

Kosman, Aryeh. 1986. "The Naive Narrator: Meditation in Descartes' *Meditations*." In *Essays on Descartes' "Meditations,"* edited by Amélie O. Rorty, 21–43. Berkeley and Los Angeles: University of California Press.

Leibniz, Gottfried. 1875–1890. *Philosophischen Schriften von G. W. Leibniz*. Edited by C. I. Gerhardt. 7 vols. Berlin: Weidman.

Lewis, Clarence Irving. 1971. *An Analysis of Knowledge and Valuation*. LaSalle, Ill.: Open Court Press.

Loeb, Louis. 1981. *From Descartes to Hume: Continental Metaphysics and the Development of Modern Philosophy*. Ithaca: Cornell University Press.

Long, Anthony, and David Sedley. 1987. *The Hellenistic Philosophers*. Vol. 1. Cambridge: Cambridge University Press.

MacArthur, David. 1999. "Skeptical Reason and Inner Experience." Ph.D. diss., Harvard University.

206

Malebranche, Nicolas. 1997. *The Search after Truth*. Edited and translated by Thomas Lennon and Paul Olscamp. Cambridge: Cambridge University Press.

Mancosu, Paolo. 1996. *Philosophy of Mathematics and Mathematical Practice in the Seventeenth Century*. New York: Oxford University Press.

Markie, Peter. 1986. *Descartes's Gambit*. Ithaca: Cornell University Press.

McDowell, John. 1986. "Singular Thought and the Extent of Inner Space." In *Subject, Thought, and Context*, edited by Philip Pettit and John McDowell. Oxford: Clarendon Press.

McRae, Robert. 1972. "Innate Ideas." In *Cartesian Studies*, edited by R. J. Butler, 32–54. Oxford: Basil Blackwell.

Menn, Stephen. 1998. *Descartes and Augustine*. Cambridge: Cambridge University Press.

Moore, G. E. 1962. "Proof of an External World." In G. E. Moore, *Philosophical Papers*, 126–48. New York: Collier Books.

Murdoch, Dugald. 1993. "Exclusion and Abstraction in Descartes' Metaphysics." *Philosophical Quarterly* 43 (170): 38–57.

Nelson, Alan. 1995. "Micro-chaos and Idealization in Cartesian Physics." *Philosophical Studies* 77:377–91.

Newman, Lex, and Alan Nelson. 1999. "Circumventing Cartesian Circles." *Noûs* 33 (3): 370–404.

Plato. 1992. *Theaetetus*. Edited by Bernard Williams. Translated by M. J. Levett. With revisions by Myles Burnyeat. Indianapolis, Ind., and Cambridge: Hackett.

Popkin, Richard. 1968. *The History of Scepticism from Erasmus to Descartes*. New York: Harper & Row.

Radner, Daisie. 1988. "Thought and Consciousness in Descartes." *Journal of the History of Philosophy* 26 (3): 439–52.

Reid, Thomas. 1969. *Essays on the Intellectual Powers of Man*. Edited by Baruch Brody. Cambridge: MIT Press.

Röd, Wofgang. 1987. "L'explication rationnelle entre méthode et métaphysique." In *Le Discours et sa méthode*, edited by Nicolas Grimaldi and Jean-Luc Marion, 89–107. Paris: Presses Universitaires de France.

Rorty, Richard. 1971. "Verificationism and Transcendental Arguments." *Noûs* 5:3–14.

———. 1980. *Philosophy and the Mirror of Nature*. Princeton: Princeton University Press.

Rosenthal, David M. 1986. "Will and the Theory of Judgment." In *Essays on Descartes' "Meditations,"* edited by Amélie O. Rorty, 405–34. Berkeley and Los Angeles: University of California Press.

Rozemond, Marleen. 1993. "The Role of the Intellect in Descartes's Case for the Incorporeity of the Mind." In *Essays on the Philosophy and Science of René Descartes*, edited by Stephen Voss, 97–114. New York: Oxford University Press.

———. 1998. *Descartes's Dualism*. Cambridge: Harvard University Press.

Sanches, Francisco. 1988. *That Nothing Is Known*. Edited and translated by Elaine Limbrick and Douglas F. S. Thomson. Cambridge: Cambridge University Press.

Schmitt, Charles B. 1972. *Cicero Scepticus: A Study of the Influence of the "Academica" in the Renaissance*. The Hague: Martinus Nijhoff.

Schmitter, Amy. 2000. "The Wax and I: Perceptibility and Modality in the Second Meditation." *Archiv für Geschichte der Philosophie* 82 (2): 178–201.

Sextus Empiricus. 1993. *Outlines of Pyrrhonism*. With a translation by R. G. Bury. Loeb Classical Library.

———. 1997. *Against the Logicians*. With a translation by R. G. Bury. Loeb Classical Library.

Shoemaker, Sidney. 1963. *Self-Knowledge and Self-Identity*. Ithaca: Cornell University Press.

Sosa, Ernest. 1997. "How to Resolve the Pyrrhonian Problematic: A Lesson from Descartes." *Philosophical Studies* 85 (2–3): 229–49.

Spinoza, Baruch. 1925. *Spinoza Opera*. Edited by Carl Gebhardt. 4 vols. Heidelberg: Carl Winter.

———. 1985. *The Collected Works of Spinoza*. Vol. 1. Translated and edited by Edwin M. Curley. Princeton: Princeton University Press.

Strawson, Peter. 1996. *Individuals*. London: Methuen, 1959. Reprint, London: Routledge.

———. 1966. *The Bounds of Sense*. London: Methuen.

Stroud, Barry. 1968. "Transcendental Arguments." *Journal of Philosophy* 65:241–56.

———. 1984. *The Significance of Philosophical Scepticism*. Oxford: Clarendon Press.

Thomas, Bruce. 1995. "Abstraction and the Real Distinction between Mind and Body." *Canadian Journal of Philosophy* 25 (1): 83–102.

Walker, Ralph. 1983. "Gassendi and Skepticism." In *The Skeptical Tradition*, edited by Myles Burnyeat, 319–36. Berkeley and Los Angeles: University of California Press.

Williams, Bernard. 1967. "The Certainty of the Cogito." In *Descartes: A Collection of Critical Essays*, edited by Willis Doney, 88–107. Garden City, N.Y.: Doubleday.

———. 1978. *Descartes: The Project of Pure Enquiry*. Atlantic Highlands, N.J.: Humanities Press.

———. 1983. "Descartes's Use of Skepticism." In *The Skeptical Tradition*, edited by Myles Burnyeat, 337–52. Berkeley and Los Angeles: University of California Press.

Williams, Michael. 1986. "Descartes and the Metaphysics of Doubt." In *Essays on Descartes' "Meditations,"* edited by Amélie O. Rorty, 117–39. Berkeley and Los Angeles: University of California Press.

———. 1996. *Unnatural Doubts.* Princeton: Princeton University Press.

Wilson, Catherine. 1995. *The Invisible World: Early Modern Philosophy and the Invention of the Microscope.* Princeton: Princeton University Press.

Wilson, Margaret. 1978. *Descartes.* London: Routledge & Kegan Paul.

———. 1984. "Skepticism without Indubitability." *Journal of Philosophy* 81 (10): 537–44.

———. 1999. "Can I Be the Cause of My Idea of the World? (Descartes on the Infinite and Indefinite)." In Margaret Wilson, *Ideas and Mechanism*, 108–25. Princeton: Princeton University Press.

Winters, Barbara. 1981. "Sceptical Counterpossibilities." *Pacific Philosophical Quarterly* 62:30–38.

❖ Index ❖

Academica (Cicero), 13, 13n.13, 33n, 36n, 43n.2

Academic skepticism, 13, 13n.13; on common sense, 78, 81–82; as criticism of Stoic epistemology, 33–37, 49n.12, 68, 72–73, 81–82; on dreaming, 36–37, 40–41, 68, 75–76, 77–78, 81–82, 89; and suspense of judgment, 37, 60–61. *See also* ancient skepticism

Adam, Charles, 103n.4

Against the Logicians (Sextus Empiricus), 34n, 35n.4, 36nn, 39n.12, 72n

agnostics, 67, 67n. *See also* atheists

ancient skepticism: assent/judgment as focus of, 33–34, 60–61; vs. Cartesian dream argument, 68, 68nn.11–12, 75–76; Descartes's familiarity with, 33n; dream/lunacy arguments of, 66, 66n; rehashed in First Meditation, 42–43, 43n.1, 43n.4. *See also* Academic skepticism; Pyrrhonian skepticism

angels, 69n, 167–68n, 173–74, 174n, 201

Annas, Julia, 68n.12

Archimedes, 108, 177, 178

Arnauld, Antoine: on the Cartesian Circle, 175–76; *Logic*, 3n.4, 114n.8, 179–80; on mind/body dualism, 126, 126n, 127–28, 130

assent. *See* maxim for assent; suspense of judgment

atheists, 9, 10, 67, 67n

Augustine, Saint, 43n.1, 147n

Ayers, Michael, 44n.5

Barnes, Jonathan, 68n.12

Beyssde, Jean-Marie, 149n

body, conception of, 121–23, 171–72, 172n.36

Bourdin, Pierre, 176n, 196n

bracketing beliefs, 54–61, 55n

Brandom, Robert, 137

Burman, Frans, 14, 42, 151–52

Burnyeat, Myles, 39–40n.14, 43n.3, 90–92, 91nn

Carriero, John, 26, 27, 121n.16, 128n.25, 139n, 183n.5, 198n

Cartesian Circle, 175–86; Arnauld on, 175–76; and causal principles, 177–78; and certainty/indubitability about "I exist," 177–78, 180–81, 185; and clear and distinct ideas, 179–80, 181–84, 182n, 185–86; and the deceiving God argument, 179, 180, 181–86; Gewirth on, 183–84, 186; Mersenne on, 175, 176; Bernard Williams on, 184, 186

causal principles, 144–45, 153–70; adequacy principle, 2, 155–58, 157n.15, 160–62, 256n.11; and Aristotelian distinction among types of causes, 156n.14; and the Cartesian Circle, 177–78; a cause must have at least as much reality as its effect, 154, 158–60; the cause of an idea has at least as much formal reality as the idea has objective reality, 2, 154, 158–61, 160n, 170, 170n.33; certainty/indubitability of, 162–64; *ex nihilo* principle (something cannot come from nothing), 154–55, 154n.9, 156, 157n.15, 158n.17, 162, 164; vs. logical principles, 163–64, 163n. *See also* sufficient reason, principle of

Cavell, Stanley, 78n

certainty/indubitability, 99–100; absolute certainty, 97–98; of causal principles, 162–64; and conflict among certainties, 51; doubts ruled out by, 8; doubts vs., 48, 49, 49n; of the *ex nihilo* principle, 164; of "I exist," 105, 106, 112, 117, 123–24, 128n.25 (see also *cogito* passage); of mathematical claims, 104; moral certainty, 63, 78–79, 79n; moral

211